A Working Life

A.F. Lodge

Clink Street

London | New York

Published by Clink Street Publishing 2019

Copyright © 2019

First edition.

ISBN:
978-1-912850-50-1 paperback
978-1-912850-51-8 ebook

To Dawn, my much deserted wife, who through my work or hers has, over a marriage that has survived for over 48 years, seen us separated for probably as many years as we have been together.

Contents

Foreword

I looked at the definition of "work" in a dictionary before starting this to find considerable scope to occupy a life. Work: *n* bodily, intellectual labour; occupation; product of labour or artistic activity; *pl* factory; mechanism, engine etc.; *v* cause to function; toil; be employed; ferment; make, shape.

I started to write this, during a period of austerity, rising unemployment and job shortages because I felt very fortunate to have had a life of work that was so varied, fulfilling and interesting and left me with a gift of memories of people and places that I could not have obtained in any other way. It hasn't always been easy and it is probably fair to say that you only really find out how something works when it goes wrong but if you can resolve the problem you are better equipped to overcome the next setback. I have truly toiled at times, both physically and mentally in some unusual places and fairly extreme environments but can honestly say I have never been bored.

I hope any who read this will find something of interest and enjoyment and if it becomes a bore just close it and find some other "work" to pass the time.

PART 1
The Formative Years

If a definition of work is paid employment, I can probably say my working life started when I was ten or eleven years old. This was not a period of child labour but a chance given to me by my older brother Roy[1] to earn a little pocket money. On Saturday mornings, following in a family tradition as a village blacksmith, he would load a trailer with a portable forge and travel round the Essex countryside shoeing horses. My job, for which I was paid sixpence (one fortieth of a pound), was to turn the handle of the portable forge to get the iron shoes red hot before they were burnt into the horses hoof to give a precise fit, prior to nailing them on. To those not from a farrier background this is not cruel but produces the most evocative smell of burnt hair which I can sense even now. Another memory from that time was being lifted onto the back of one of the few remaining working cart horses and realising what immense, powerful animals they were. My legs stuck out, almost at right angles across its back and it would have been impossible to fit my feet into any form of stirrup. I wonder if all the knights of old were bow legged?

I assume I was formed, probably unintentionally, as a result of a Christmas or New Year celebration, as my mother was 41 when I was born, some 12 years after my brother Roy and 15 years after my brother Walter (Wally). In any event I was born on the 6th September 1942 in the small (one pub and a Post Office) Essex village of South Hanningfield, where my father was the village blacksmith. I have only vague memories of life in South Hanningfield because when I was three my father's worsening health resulted in him selling the business and we moved all of five miles to Wickford into one of a pair of semi-detached farm cottages in the London Road. At that time Wickford was an important market centre for the local rural communities. On Mondays the cattle pens were filled, all manner of livestock, including rabbits, before

---

1 Sadly lost to lung cancer in 1990, a week short of his 60th birthday.

myxomatosis, were traded, the auction rooms were full and the town's two pubs, the Swan and the Castle, did brisk business.

Although only a quarter of a mile from the town centre our house backed onto a dairy farm, and opposite was one large Victorian house surrounded by an orchard and scrub land – so, in my earliest years a very rural community. However, Wickford is also a stop and branch line connection on the Southend to Liverpool Street railway line into London. In 1945, and the immediate post war years, new housing was desperately needed to accommodate those made homeless by the blitz, and Wickford, with its direct links to London was ideally situated for rapid development into London commuter territory. Unfortunately this resulted in a town surrounded by ever-widening blocks of prefabs, bungalows and housing estates but little or no improvement to the town's amenities. Thus, by the time I was a teenager, the dairy farm had gone, Saturday morning pictures was no longer an option as the cinema had been turned into a Woolworths and virtually all other entertainment meant getting on bike, bus or train to somewhere else. On the plus side the youth centre and local cricket, tennis and hockey clubs were well supported and good places to participate in sport as well as great places to meet young ladies, with the added benefit of making lifelong friendships (to this day Anne is not above giving me a slap if I get too familiar).

Back a few stages. During my most formative years I was very fortunate to have a loving and supportive family around me. As a family we were also very fortunate to have avoided the worst of the anguish that two world wars could inflict. My father was born in 1900 and was just too young to serve in the First World War and during the Second World War, as a village blacksmith, was placed in a reserved occupation as well as being an air raid warden. By the time my oldest brother, Wally, applied at an early age to join the Royal Navy, the Second World War was virtually over. That, combined with our location in the country, meant we were saved from any real trauma. I have a vague recollection, while still at South Hanningfield, of being held at an upstairs window to see a doodlebug go down in the surrounding fields but no recollection of bomb damage and was probably too young to be told of the death or injury of any relatives or close neighbours. It's only in recent years that I found out that mother's younger brother, uncle Bill was awarded the Military Medal for conspicuous gallantry.

My early school years were passed, happily for the most part, at Wickford Infant and Junior schools. My mum left school when she was 13 to go into domestic service and presumably dad left at a similar age to start working in the family business, so their formal education was somewhat limited. However, mum was encouraged by her employers in her love of reading and passed this on to me at an early age. A wonderful gift. It saddens me that today, so much of children's time is taken up by television, computer games and communication sites, text messages, etc. that they don't have time to read a good novel and appreciate the wonderful depth and nuances of the English language. If, for no other reason than that she has made reading a book fashionable again, J.K. Rowling deserves her OBE.

My father, on the other hand, was more a newspaper and crosswords man but gave me one piece of excellent advice "measure twice and cut once", an aphorism that applies to almost every aspect of life. So, between them, they encouraged but never pressured me to do well and as I was naturally sporty (South East Essex Juniors football team and 100 and 200 yards athletics champion), which made one quite popular, I enjoyed my junior school days. Of course there were the almost mandatory whacks with a ruler for some perceived misdemeanour and I caught, as well as head lice, all the childhood illnesses of whooping cough, chicken pox and mumps[2] and can remember feeling very sorry for myself while rehearsing the school nativity play after being given an injection against diphtheria (thank goodness it was Michael Aspell and not me who fainted on the stage).

Looking back on it I suppose it was quite a healthy existence in comparison to modern day living. Post-war food rationing continued until July 1954, so overeating and junk food were not an option. Also, virtually all my meals were home cooked with fresh vegetables and fruit (in season) from the garden along with eggs from our chickens and the occasional rabbit, snared to prevent raids on the vegetable patch. Nothing was wasted and to this day all our vegetable waste is composted ready for next year's planting. In addition, as my parents had no car, I walked, ran or rode a bike all over the place, which developed an early level of fitness hard to attain from one or two hours a week in the gymnasium. Combine that with the toughening effect of having to wear short trousers (hard to believe) until well into senior school and with no heating in the bedrooms (coal, gas and electricity was also rationed), so that ice formed pretty patterns on the inside of the windows

2 My brother Roy, who was home on leave, while doing his National Service, caught mumps and took it back to Libya and put half the base in quarantine.

during the really cold days; all this helped to build a certain resilience into one's attitude to life.

As I said earlier, my parents never owned a car. I understand that while living in South-Hanningfield they had a pony and trap and in his younger days my father rode a motor bike. Back in the 1920s this had furnished him with a license to drive all vehicles, a fact put to good use when Roy was discharged from the army. Having driven trucks in Libya, on his return he bought an old car and L plates and took dad along as the experienced driver while practicing to pass his test. The amusing part is, that he then tried to teach dad to drive the car. A resounding failure.

My senior school years were spent at Chelmsford Technical School, initially located in the centre of Chelmsford in buildings next to the technical college and latterly relocated to a brand new school in Patching Hall Lane at the Broomfield edge of the town. My first choice of school had been the much longer established King Edward VI Grammar school, which both my brothers attended, but as I only scraped through the eleven plus exam it was the technical school that finally accepted me after an oral examination. On reflection I am quite glad that I ended up with a more rounded education at a mixed school rather than the all boys grammar and in the last few years have remade contact and started a very enjoyable correspondence with two of the girls from those far off school days.

One of the oddities of being in the centre of Chelmsford was that we had no proper playground or sports field, so were let loose at lunch time to run riot around the central park. Also we had an excellent cross country team because for most of our PT lessons, the master, who was close to retirement, would say "off you go lads" and then take it easy for the next twenty minutes. Those of us, like me, who actually enjoyed running, would run. Those who didn't would stop off round the corner for a fag or two and join us on the way back. I don't think it was because the master was blind in one eye that he never seemed to notice that half of us ended up splattered in mud and the other half were clean and tidy.

As a preparation for the future, Chelmsford Tech. served me very well. Academically I did rather well, coming top of my class for five years in a row, which came as a bit of a surprise to me as I certainly did not feel as though I was the brightest of my contemporaries. I also received the Turner Award three times. This was awarded for either leadership or sportsmanship during time spent in lower, middle or upper school. This also persuaded me that I should stay on into the sixth form to take A level GCEs, with a bias towards the sciences: chemistry, physics and pure and applied mathematics, although I did read all the books set for the English literature course just for the pleasure of it. Staying into the sixth form also developed some other opportunities as I advanced from house captain to head boy and also captain of sport in my final year. There were of course some downsides to positions of responsibility.

Never at ease with public speaking, I can still remember the apprehension of having to call upon the school to raise three cheers for the Lord Lieutenant of Essex during the annual prize giving. The problem was, his name was Ruggles-Brice and as he was popularly known as Buggles-Rice I was convinced I would get it wrong on the day. Whew, the relief when cheers rather than hoots of laughter rang round the hall. Another thing was wearing the school uniform, including caps and ties, which we were meant to do while in Chelmsford on the way to or from school. This was in the late 1950s, the rock and roll years, drain pipe trousers, boot-lace ties and hair styles which included a DA and Elvis quiff, so a challenge to the fashion conscious. The tie could be suitably modified using staples and the cap, if small enough, almost hidden if worn like a skull cap with the hair combed round it. The latter was not really an option once you became a prefect with a bright yellow tassel hanging down the back.

It was an exciting era to grow up in with a lively music scene developing in the UK. One of my class mates, Clifford (Cliff) Richardson wrote to an American music magazine in search of pen pals just after Cliff Richard had success in the music charts for the first time. His search was not in vain, he got sacks full of mail each day, including one from the Everly Brothers. Happy days.

Being born on the 6th September was, I believe, a definite advantage during my school days as it meant I was always one of the oldest in my class and it also meant that I was legally old enough to drink in my final year. Not that pupils were permitted to visit pubs in the lunch hour but as a preparation for our future working lives we decided a pint on a Friday lunch time was good training and worth the risk. Some precautions had to be taken; since a number of the teachers used to drink in The Clockhouse at the end of Patching Hall Lane we took a swift ten minute walk to The Compasses and tried to get back, sucking our peppermints, before they returned. I am sure it was noticed but nothing was ever said.

I left school with seven O level GCEs and three A levels and a completed application for a County Major, the grant that would make it possible for me to go to university to further my education. I suspect that I was no different from the majority of school leavers in that I had no clear idea of what I wanted to do next. Most of my close friends had already left school and had been gainfully employed for a year or two, a prospect that had a certain appeal, particularly as my father had retired because of ill health and although I never felt we were exactly poor, money was not plentiful. Also, as higher education was completely outside my parents' experience they had no real ideas as to the course I should take. In the end I decided a course being offered by South East Essex Technical College seemed a good bet. This was to study for an HNC in mechanical engineering through a placement with a local company, whereby you were paid a salary, worked for six months and studied for six months. The best of both worlds. I am not sure why I opted for mechanical engineering as I was never a Meccano or Lego person and, as my wife will testify, am very prone to having some bits left over or finding a "design fault" when building anything in kit form; I probably felt it was closer to the family tradition of blacksmithing than most other careers. As it turned out I never did do mechanical engineering, probably for the best, although it would have been most useful in the later stages of my working life.

Normally during the summer holidays I would try to get a paid job (see Part 2) for five or six weeks but after the stress of A levels decided I deserved a holiday before starting work (gap years hadn't been invented then), so I just did a bit of potato (hard) or fruit (tastier) picking instead. A week before I was supposed to start my new course I had still heard nothing from the college so I phoned and made an appointment to go and see them. On arrival it all seemed a bit of a shambles. Nobody could give me any information about the work placement and the college looked completely run down and lacklustre. As a consequence I phoned Essex Education Authority and asked what else I could do with my County Major and three A Levels. The answer was a full time degree course (B.Sc. General) in chemistry, physics and mathematics, external London University, at the South West Essex Technical College (Walthamstow). As I was now feeling more relaxed after my 'holiday' this seemed a much better choice so I said yes. They said you'd better get up there straight away, the course started two weeks ago. So much for detailed career planning.

Looking back on it I regret not applying to go to University proper, as travelling every day on the 251 bus from Wickford to Walthamstow (an hour and a half each way) was very limiting and did nothing for the social life. I ended up playing for the college badminton team, but always had to leave before the match ended in order to catch the last bus home. On one occasion this meant conceding a critical game, so I agreed to travel back on a team-mate's motor bike, as we only lived a few miles apart. It was the end of November; I kept my track suit on under my overcoat and believe I wrapped a scarf around my head as I don't believe crash helmets were compulsory then and Barry didn't have a spare. By the time we reached Wickford I was so cold I felt rigid. I believe Barry had to lift me off the back of the bike before I could get my limbs moving once more. Never again!

In the first year three subjects were studied and assuming adequate marks were obtained during the end of year exams (no continuous assessment), one subject could be dropped for the final two years. I found the content somewhat strange; the physics and chemistry did not differ greatly from the school A level courses, the maths on the other hand was almost totally new. Virtually all the course material was presented by the lecturers on a blackboard and, in the case of the maths, frequently at high speed with enthusiastic explanations flowing out as he went along. I soon realised that I could either take down the notes or listen to the explanations but not both as I was always about a blackboard behind. As a consequence I am sure the maths lecturer thought I was a complete dimwit. I was always about a week behind the subject matter of any of his questions, which contributed in no short measure to me failing the mathematics paper at the end of the year.

Failure meant that I would lose my grant until I passed the Part 1 examination(s), which would allow me to return full time for the final two years. In those days, I am glad to say, there were no tuition fees to pay and the grant was assessed, depending to some extent on your parents' income, to cover your living and travel expenses. I can remember my first year's grant was £365 (1961), which gave me a great feeling of independence as I could start paying my parents some housekeeping, as well as enjoying almost as good a social life as most of my close friends who were all working by then.

Fortunately, living in Essex, meant that jobs were not so hard to come by as they have been in more recent years and I managed to get work, including a day-release to attend college part time, at Ilford Films Selo works in Brentwood. The section I worked in was mainly involved in testing the quality of the sound recording strip placed on the edge of large reels of camera film used by the BBC and the film industry. The work was not particularly memorable but did leave me with an appreciation of Elgar's Enigma Variations. I don't know if it was just that the tonal changes in the pieces made them particularly apt for testing sound quality or that it was one of Collin, our section leader's, favourite records. It was an odd environment to work in as the test laboratory was located in the centre of numerous darkrooms with restricted access. This led to a number of intrigues and liaisons which perhaps should not have taken place, culminating in one woman's husband turning up at the main gate with a shotgun. Just as well security managed to calm him down. Nothing to do with me, I hasten to add. I restricted myself to chatting up Jean, the manager's secretary, in the lunch break. She had the most memorable blue eyes and her fiancé was safely in Africa doing charity work; however, I did get invited to their wedding after he returned, so couldn't have been too annoying.

What was memorable that year, 1963, was a winter with the longest sustained period of cold weather that I can remember. I believe it snowed and froze in January and didn't thaw again until the end of March. In contrast to nowadays, the old faithful 251 bus ran every day to get me to Brentwood and as far as I could tell the schools remained open the whole time. The walk to work from the top end of Brentwood high street, past the Girls Grammar school (although I didn't know it my wife-to-be was a pupil there at the time) and through the woods along Upper Common road was breathtakingly beautiful, with all the trees covered in twinkling white hoarfrost. It's a pity that at that time I had neither the means nor the understanding to take any photographs.

Success; a year later I had passed my Part 1 examinations and was returning to college full time. Later, I realised that repeating the first year was no bad thing. I enjoyed the maths and at the end of the year when the lecturer decided to introduce us to the joys of Fourier analysis (a Part 2 subject), rather than having us sit about idling, I was astounded to realise what a practical subject mathematics could be. Formulas could be produced that would, for example, predict the heat transfer rates across different surfaces; or the surge current when an electric motor starts up. Not something that would enthuse a lot of people but thirty something years on, when responsible for starting some very large pumps that kept tripping out on a new water treatment works, I had some idea what the problem might be and could talk the talk sufficiently to ask the experts for a solution.

I decided to drop the maths during Part 2 for the safer option of chemistry and physics. Also, for my final year, I felt the bus journey every day wasted too much time, so found a B&B with evening meal fairly close to the college. It is odd that, whereas I had rarely been late for lectures before, it was now not uncommon for me to have to rush in at the last minute. Or, could it be due to my much improved social life; out and about in her little Morris minor, with my new girlfriend Sylvia or walking back, late at night, from her lodgings in Woodford (wealthy family friends)?

One of the disadvantages of taking an external degree was that you had to cover the majority of the curriculum, as little insight was available as to the content of the finals. Also, which I felt was somewhat unnecessary, we had to travel up to London University on three consecutive days to sit all the written papers. Exhausting! I was fairly fortunate that the content suited me but by the middle of the third day Sylvia was in tears, convinced she had failed and was not going to sit the final paper. I am so glad I managed to persuade her not to completely give up on three years of hard work. She went in and later, on the 11th May 1966, came out of the Albert Hall and a presentation by HRH Queen Elizabeth the Queen Mother, clutching her pass degree. I came away on the same day happily in possession of a lower second-class honours degree and it may be significant that quite a high proportion of people, with better than a pass, had to re-sit Part 1 after a period spent working, between school and college. Maybe a gap year does have some benefits?

Mentally and physically exhausted I spent the days following the completion of the written papers totally relaxing with Sylvia at her parent's house in Brightlingsea. Apart from sleeping and eating a lot, we lazed about or took a little sailing dingy out around the Colne estuary or, I should say Sylvia did; I, as a complete novice, just did as I was told. Her father, Horatio, was commodore of the local yacht club and I think Sylvia had been schooled in lieu of a son, so I was in safe hands. I am not sure her father ever really approved of me but nevertheless I was shown great hospitality and true friendliness by all of the family.

My final month at college, in between preparing for and taking the remaining practical examinations was mostly spent, when not in the pub, converting years of playing solo whist into an ability to play bridge; a very enjoyable and worthwhile skill put to good use much later, on various jobs all over the World.

PART 2
Part-time Jobs

As well as my time as a blacksmiths "apprentice", after I turned 16, I had a number of part-time jobs, both during the school and college holidays.

These, in the main, required little in the way of experience and were taken purely to earn some money to supplement pocket money while still at school, or to stretch the education grant.

To deliver the Christmas mail, references had to be obtained to show you were of good character and were not going to dump the post in the nearest waste bin. I did this job several years running and assume the temps were given the rounds that the regulars least wanted. This was OK for the most part until one miserable year it rained nonstop. I was given a bike and the round took me about five miles out into the countryside around Wickford, mostly along unmade roads full of flooded pot holes to wood-framed bungalows where a major challenge was finding the right house and spotting the typically "Dunroamin" or "Chez Nous" house name. Thank goodness for the few kind souls who took pity on me when presented with their soggy letters and parcels and exchanged them for a cup of tea and a hot mince pie. At least in the late 1950s it was proper mail and not a load of junk that was being delivered.

In complete contrast, one of my first summer holiday jobs seemed to be spent in almost complete and glorious sunshine. I was employed as a general dogsbody at a salt-water swimming pool located a fifteen minute bike ride from home at Battlesbridge on the tidal limit of the River Crouch. Before the gates were opened the work involved weeding flower beds and paving slab pathways and general cleaning and tidying in and around the changing cubicles, which were arranged each side of the pool. The main task, once the public were in, was making sure the cubicles remained available, i.e. clothes had been placed in the basket provided and taken back to the safe storage area before swimming, and empty baskets were cleared out after people had changed back if they were too lazy to return them themselves. Not very demanding or well paid but then at 16 a whole summer surrounded by young women in bikinis definitely had its good points.

The next summer was essentially spent labouring for a company, "Maywicks" I believe, who had bought up and were renovating job lots of the prefabs that had been built to house the many made homeless during the blitz and the new families of returning servicemen. I learnt two things from this work experience. One: asbestos panels, which formed the main building blocks of the prefabs did not seem to be recognised as a potential hazard at that time but were very heavy. The technique to move them was to stand with your back to the panel, squat slightly, grasp the panel on each side, rise up and lean forwards. Thus the majority of the weight was on your back and you could stagger off to wherever they had to be moved to. Two: I was not as fit and strong as I thought I was. After a few days the foreman said I could have a break that day and go out with one of the lorries. The job was unloading stacks of bricks at two of the company sites. Easy, except that all the work was done by hand. The driver stood on the lorry and passed the bricks to me to stack on the ground. The only problem was he could press six bricks together to pass to me and after a short time I could really only manage four without dropping them. By the time I got home that evening my arms and shoulders were aching like never before and I ended the day soaking in the bath until the water went cold.

After that, I managed to find some work that was a little more technical and not quite so physical. First, with Ilford Films, in the pre-digital camera days, at their film processing factory in Basildon, a short bike ride away. The job involved feeding rolls of the public's developed colour prints onto a large, steam heated, highly polished, stainless steel drum, which, if done correctly, put the gloss finish on the printed photograph. I nearly didn't get the job because at the interview I said I could only work for six weeks, which meant they would only get four weeks useful work out of me, following two weeks' training. As it happened after the first day's induction the experienced operator went off sick for five days and I was left on my own with two drums to operate. While he was away I never once committed the cardinal sin of letting sticky tape go all round the drum (shutdown and clean up). When he came back, with only one drum to operate, I messed up two or three times. Lack of concentration or I had just stopped looking out for the numerous "glamour" shots included in the family snaps. Nothing really pornographic but I believe a censor was in operation and anything over the mark was cut out and kept in a "special collection" by the print section.

My last summer-holiday job, before my final year at university, was with the Marconi Company in their Basildon factory where printed circuit boards were manufactured. I was employed in the chemistry laboratory associated with the dissolution and recovery of gold strip and other metals from scrapped boards. The processes used some powerful acids and a main function of the laboratory was confirming the waste disposal units were working correctly. On my first day, the chief chemist asked me to make up some methyl orange indicator to replenish the dropper bottles. I consulted Vogal (the inorganic chemist's "bible") and in accordance with the recipe, made up a litre of solution. I was a bit embarrassed to find there were only two dropper bottles each of 50ml capacity, so I had a rather large surplus of methyl orange to dispose of, which I surreptitiously tipped down the sink. When I walked outside a little later all the waste unit holding pits were a beautiful bright red, pretty much the same colour as my face when I realised what had caused it.

Looking back on it now, when, for many young people finding employment has been a real struggle, I cannot remember ever thinking I would not get a job if I wanted one and presume I was fortunate to have been born in the relatively prosperous south east of England.

PART 3
Laboratory Years

3.1 Full-time employment

My first full-time employment was again with the Marconi Company, one of Chelmsford Technical School's "houses", and before the deplorable decisions made by the new management following Lord Weinstock's retirement from GEC at the height of the dot-com boom, was an institution around the Chelmsford area for providing jobs, housing and recreational facilities for its employees. I started in the Specialised Components Division Laboratories based in Little Baddow, a thirty minute bike ride from home. The laboratory, as well as providing analytical services, was key to the development of new wave guide materials for use in the company's radar and weapons guidance systems. This involved powdering, mixing, moulding and then sintering new combinations of ferrite-type substances with the inclusion of selected rare earth oxides. It was interesting work and to try and understand what was happening required the application of some of my recently acquired inorganic chemistry theory. Unfortunately the first two months in the new job was spent packing up the facilities for a move to a new industrial complex in Billericay, and the next two months unpacking and setting up in the new work place. The most exciting event was finding quite a large silvery looking ingot gathering dust in one of the storage cupboards, which I could only just pick up. At first we thought it was platinum and worth a fortune but after some investigation decided it was more likely to be only tungsten and therefore not quite such a temptation.

At the end of my final year (1965) at college and before being offered a job with Marconi I had walked around the same new industrial estate in Billericay to see if there were any likely work prospects, and at the very end of the estate happened upon Humphreys & Glasgow, the company that was to provide me with a career and gainful employment for the majority of my working life. Their hoarding pronounced them to be an International Process

Engineering and Construction Company and within the gates were the company laboratory and construction stores. This sounded interesting so, nothing ventured nothing gained, I walked through the door and asked if there was any possibility of employment. Nothing at present but if I cared to fill in an application form they would keep me in mind. Five months later, after being asked to attend a formal interview, I was offered a job in the laboratory at a higher salary and with what sounded like more exciting (world travel) and interesting career prospects, so I handed in my notice at Marconi. It was something of a shame that it was only while working my month's notice, after the move to Billericay was completed, that I became fully involved with the more interesting aspects of the work with Marconi. However, a very good spin-off from my first job was being able to join the Marconi Social Club where I was fortunate to end up playing in the Essex badminton league. On leaving Marconi one of my team mates asked me if I would like to join him to play in a much smaller club that was just starting up in Battlesbridge and as result I met a whole new group of people, many of whom are still among my closest friends long after my badminton playing days were over.

3.2 Humphreys & Glasgow – Billericay based 1966–1978

Humphreys & Glasgow was founded in 1892 by two Americans, Dr Humphreys and Dr Glasgow, to design and supply town gas plants, a relatively innovative concept, initially in Britain but as experience and reputation grew, all around the world. When I joined in 1966 the company was still privately owned, a most unusual situation for a major chemical engineering company, and under the control and direction of Mr Ambrose Congreve, the son-in-law of Dr Glasgow. This, at times, created a unique working environment, more of which later.

In 1966, the production of town gas had progressed from using coal and coke as a feedstock to the reforming of oil using processes pioneered by the company and which were being continuously refined and developed. The new reforming processes were further developed, to the extent that H&G became one of the first contractors to supply petrochemical and fertiliser plants to Eastern Europe and the Peoples Republic of China.

To that end the laboratory had three major functions: 1) To supply an analytical service either in house or contracted out, 2) A research and development centre for testing and progressing new process ideas and analytical techniques using the latest technologies available and 3) Supplying commissioning chemists to assist during on-site start-up of new plants designed and built by the company. To carry out these various tasks, some sixteen permanent staff were directly employed together with a part-time secretary and a cleaning lady, Mrs. Healey, who was a vital supplier of tea and coffee and sometimes homemade cakes and who worked heroically to stop the place becoming a complete tip.

As a starting place for what developed into a career in chemistry and chemical engineering-related subjects it provided an ideal mix. For control purposes the laboratory was included within the process department, under the direction of Dr Shapiro, who was the company's water treatment expert, based in offices located near Victoria Station, in London. Dr Peter Lemin was in charge of the day to day operation of the laboratory at Billericay and it is a testament to the friendships made in those early working years that I kept in touch and, sadly, only recently went to his funeral. The majority of staff were qualified to at least degree level, or equivalent, with those younger than me studying for an ordinary national certificate (ONC) or a higher national certificate (HNC) on a day-release basis, so a good pool of experience to draw on and a friendly and stimulating place to start a career.

At that time H&G had a very close working relationship with British Gas, responsible for the design, build and start-up of more than 50% of town gas plants installed in the UK and indeed, around the world. In addition, during the summer months, the company carried out routine shutdown and maintenance contracts on a large number of the existing plants, and this included taking samples of any deposits, scale, sludge, corrosion material, etc. in order to build up a picture of where and why any problems were occurring in the plants and thus improve the design. To this end, in my first four months, I was required to apply good old fashioned wet chemical qualitative analysis techniques, learnt during my degree course, to identify the composition of the hundreds of samples delivered to the laboratory. Quite satisfying, and as a new boy, did not, at first, expose my lack of knowledge of more modern instrumental analytical methods, which would be required a little later. On the down side it did bring exposure to some of the lab's more antiquated fixtures and fittings. The technique required the frequent passing of hydrogen sulphide (H_2S) gas, the rotten egg smell beloved by most schoolboys, through solutions of the samples. The H_2S was generated in a Kipps apparatus contained in a fume cupboard located in a confined corner of the lab and was highly poisonous. Also, in concentrations above 400 to 500 ppm it kills off the sense of smell, thus increasing the risk of over exposure. The danger and probable inadequacy of the extraction system was realised when we found Joe, one of our senior chemists, unconscious on the floor by the fume cupboard. Fortunately, after being dragged into the fresh air, he quickly recovered, seemingly with no long-term ill effects.

Health and safety was not much talked about in those days but, for sure, we all took more trouble to limit the risk after that. One further incident that has stayed in my memory all these years and is related to a sample taken from a town gas plant when a sample was brought in with a note attached saying it was scraped from the side of a vessel, where one of the men steaming it out, had developed a purple rash and what should they do. Preliminary tests, using a spectrophotometer, indicated it may be mainly benzpyrene – highly carcinogenic. At the same time a portion had been given to Ross, our senior analyst, to find out what inorganic material it contained. For some reason he decided to burn off the organic material in the open well of the laboratory rather than in a fume cupboard. When the rest of the staff realised where this thick cloud of acrid brown smoke was coming from he was threatened with death by more than one if cancer should visit them in later life. As it happened, Ross died of a heart attack while swimming in the river Danube, on one of our Eastern European assignments a few years later, so no comeback in this lifetime. However, when I found I had non-Hodgkin's lymphoma in 2010 it did make me wonder.

For the next ten years, life based in the laboratory passed without quite such dramatic incidents but was varied and interesting and not without its dramas. At any one time, approximately 50% of the staff were involved in research and development projects instigated by the Process Department based in the head office. These varied a great deal, from the regular testing of new catalysts being developed by companies such as ICI for use in the reforming processes used to produce, for example, town gas, ammonia, urea or ethylene; to new methods of treating sewage or factory effluent streams; to sulphur and pitch pelleting; to new heat exchanger technology and included one really off-the-wall attempt to extract tin from what amounted to the slag heaps (price of tin had just rocketed) from Cornwall's last operating tin mine.

The rigs for testing catalysts were assembled in our own workshop to quite a high specification as they operated under pressure and to high temperatures, 800 to 1000 °C, for weeks at a time while inputted gas streams were monitored for relevant changes in composition. It was an added bonus that Peter, our workshop manager, had in a previous life in Australia run his own garage, so at lunchtime it was not uncommon to see people doing their own maintenance inside the bonnets of their cars. This, of course, was in the 1960s when you could actually get inside the bonnet and make some sort of sense of what was in there.

One of our lengthier projects was a pilot plant for the alternative treatment of sewage, to speed up the process and reduce the space required for making raw sewage safe for discharge into a river. The plant consisted of a 6m^3 vessel where the raw sewage, after a course filter, was treated with flocculating chemicals and a series of columns filled with activated carbon for final polish and sweetening. This was located on a small treatment works on the outskirts of Billericay about half a mile from the laboratory. In cooperation with the municipal work force we ran the pilot plant and monitored progress by taking samples four times a day, seven days a week. The samples were taken back to the lab for analysis. It wasn't really that unpleasant, unless you were on-site when the staff were back-washing the sludge pits, then you really appreciated the perfume sprays located all round the works.

After a few weeks a real pattern of life in Billericay began to emerge. At weekends the course filters were usually clogged up with condoms and the concentration of salts in the incoming sewage peaked about two hours later in the day. Two things stuck in my mind about this job. The first was, in the summer during Wimbledon fortnight, if we were not too busy, I could slope off to the afore mentioned Mrs Healey's to watch the tennis for half an hour, usually accompanied by a cup of tea and one of those homemade cakes. The second was less enjoyable. While adjusting the height of a tongue dish on the vessel outlet I managed to uncouple it so that partially treated sewage started to spray all over me. If I let go I would lose a month's work, so with eyes shut, mouth shut and trying not to breath I eventually managed to do it up again. Then it was into my car back to the lab and straight into the shower with all my clothes on. I spent the rest of the day in a paper boiler suit while my clothes dried. Disinfecting my car wasn't that pleasant either.

I don't know if the process was ever utilised on a full-sized plant and I could never quite persuade myself the outlet water was drinkable but it was an introduction to the use of activated carbon in the water industry, which was to play a major role in some of my future jobs.

It was always interesting to get something new to play with. When a new concept test kit for improving heat exchanger designs arrived I was given the job of setting it up for operation and performing some trial runs. As I had never had anything to do with heat exchangers before, the manual and operating instructions sent with it proved to be a bit difficult to follow so it was suggested I phone the London office to talk it through with our heat exchanger expert. The company employed some very bright people and Jonah Tang was one of them, a real boffin with a brain the size of a planet, unfortunately I couldn't understand a word he was saying. Only when he arrived at Billericay and I realised that not only was he of Chinese origin but had quite a severe stutter was it possible to make any progress and I was eventually able to provide him with the data he required. In later years, after moving to commissioning, I needed Jonah's help on more than one occasion and he always looked the same, slightly dishevelled with evidence of breakfast or dinner on his tie, but he usually came up with an answer to the problem and was a great asset to the company. It's not always what you know but who you know that makes a working life so much easier.

A major requirement to working for H&G was to be available, as and when the need arose, to work on site. These assignments could last for one or two weeks or one or two years and be located more or less anywhere in the world. In particular, on a lot of the smaller pilot plant jobs, we chemists were of great benefit as we could multitask and not only operate the plant but take samples and carry out the analysis required to monitor progress as well. I was eased into this way of life, after about six months working in the Laboratory, with a trip to GM Edwards works, near Neath in Wales, to monitor the trial runs of a gas absorption process using iron chelating compounds. First impressions of heavy industry were not good. As we drove down the valley to the works, the whole of the hillside, on the opposite side of the road to the local steel works, was covered in what looked like rust; trees, rocks, grass, everything was red. Thinking about it forty-five years on we might be pleased if we still had a steel industry that could produce that sort of pollution. I cannot remember much about the job other than there were four of us from the lab plus a project manager from head office with a big chip on his shoulder, and the impression that it never stopped raining the whole time (about a month) that we were there. It put me off going back to Wales for years. I can also remember working quite long hours and rushing off to the Bernie Inn for a steak and black forest gateau before they closed. High living for my first experience on expenses.

At that time, a large part of the company's business was to design, procure, build and commission plants for countries in the Eastern Bloc. Another function of the Laboratory was to define the analytical procedures and methods required in order to start up and operate these plants and then procure and supply the necessary equipment. The final requirement was to send "experts", at the appropriate time, to commission the equipment supplied and train the local staff in their use.

3.3 From Russia with love

My next assignment in 1967, aged 25, was totally different from a few weeks in Wales. I was assigned to an ethylene plant located in Novopolotsk in the USSR. This was quite a daunting prospect; the Cuban missile crisis took place in 1962 and the Cold War between the west and the Soviet Union was still at its height. Also, although I had met Dawn, my wife-to-be, earlier in the year, as an unmarried man still living at home with his parents, I was unlikely to be given leave to return over Christmas, so would spend the whole of the winter behind the Iron Curtain. Pictures of the freezing snow enveloping Julie Christie and Omar Sharif in *Doctor Zhivago* came to mind, or maybe it was just images of Julie Christie that distracted me. One thing that didn't bother me too much, and perhaps should have done, was my complete lack of any expertise in the use and operation of chromatographs which formed the bulk of the laboratory equipment being supplied by us to the plant. To overcome this deficiency I was sent on a one-day induction course to the manufacturer's factory and much more importantly was to be accompanied for the first three months by Tom Jackson, our chromatography expert. Tom was married with children and had insisted that he be home for Christmas. After that he would move on to an identical plant being built in Kazan, almost as far east of Moscow as Novopolotsk was west of Moscow, to provide some expertise there. If this story ever gets finished and any one reading it finds it interesting enough to keep going, they will realise that this almost blissful ignorance of the plant and equipment to be commissioned is very much the norm rather than the exception.

I had about two months to prepare, which included being vetted and obtaining permission and a visa to enter the USSR. Apart from my father's time spent with a cavalry regiment in India, after the First World War, I don't think either of my parents had ever been out of the Country so could offer little in the way of advice as to what I should take with me. There was no such thing as wheeled luggage in those days so in the end I bought a trunk and, on advice received from the site that food was very limited, packed the whole bottom layer with dehydrated (new on the market) packet soups, my brother's army service mug (metal) to hold my soup, a couple of pairs of long johns, a good fisherman's wool pullover, thick socks and a good pair of boots (don't think safety boots were a pre-requisite then) and I was just about ready for the off. In truth, on my first assignment, deciding what to take in the way of tools, technical equipment and reference books was quite difficult. I was well aware that, as the only chemist and in the absence of the internet and emails, anything I might need I should have with me, however, books weigh heavy and a fully loaded trunk wasn't the easiest thing to drag halfway across the world.

I flew to Moscow on 27th September 1967, accompanied by another H&G employee who was on his way to the Kazan site. After being met and escorted to our hotel, an enormous building sitting on the banks of the Moskva river, we were told to be ready to be taken that evening for an introductory meal hosted by Techmashimport, our client. A good start, the caviar and vodka was dispensed with many toasts and "Nazdraves" to accompany our hosts' determination to drink us under the table. Around midnight a taxi dropped us outside our hotel, whereupon my colleague, Tony, fell out of the taxi into a heap on the pavement and I had to virtually carry him into the hotel to his room. Around 7am a loud ringing dragged me out of a vodka induced coma. It was Tony on the phone, panic stricken, he couldn't find his wallet, money or passport and was meant to be flying onto Kazan later that day. Remarkably, when we got down to reception to ask them to phone the British Embassy to report the loss somebody had found the missing items outside on the pavement and actually handed them in. What a relieved Tony, especially as the Russian currency, the rouble, was non-convertible and buying goods in their prestige stores such as GUM could only be done using western currency, preferably the US dollar. Strange that they should effectively put the dollar on a pedestal when competition with the USA was so intense: the Space Race and nuclear missile proliferation to name but two. The next day, after Tony's scare, I reported my presence in the country at the British Embassy and was pleasantly surprised to find they had Watneys Red Barrel on tap.

I was very fortunate to spend five days in Moscow. The norm was to be met by a courier and after one night to be escorted to your destination, either by train or plane. I arrived at the same time as our plant manager, along with the manager of the polyethylene plant, being built next to ours, who had arrived in Moscow for high level talks with Techmashimport. I was to wait until the talks were finished when we would all return to Novopolotsk. The courier/translator that accompanied them explained to me that if there was anything I needed I should ask but his first priority was to the managers and the second to their wives, who had come with them for the shopping. This meant I had the unique opportunity to roam around Moscow unescorted for a few days. I walked for miles taking in Red Square; the colourful Byzantine splendour of Saint Basil's Cathedral; stood in line for a view of Lenin in his glass topped sarcophagus; an art gallery within the Kremlin with a wonderful collection of paintings; into GUM, Russia's largest department store, to buy a fine fur hat for the coming winter with my US dollars and finally the zoo. Even today it helps a great deal if you can read the Cyrillic alphabet as virtually none of the signs or street names were written in an English script and it was a few days before I dared to use the Metro, which is a work of art in its own right.

I learnt a couple of lessons about the communist system during my days in Moscow. First, do not assume you can cross a major road anywhere you like. A traffic policeman stopped the taxi I had just jumped into and would not let us go until I paid a 50 Kopecks (100 kopecks = 1 Rouble = 25 new pence) fine, even though the taxi driver was trying to persuade him I was an ignorant foreigner. Secondly, don't expect fast efficient service in state-run hotels. On my first night in the hotel restaurant I made the mistake of migrating to the area of this large almost empty room where other guests were sitting. It took about twenty minutes to be offered a menu and then similar times for an order to be taken and then each course to arrive. I realised while waiting, that despite there being four or five waiters standing in the doorway, only the one designated to our area ever came near us and he was in no hurry to serve anybody.

After my holiday I duly arrived in the relatively new town of Novopolotsk to find that we were being housed in a large hotel located along one side of the town square. First impressions were of a drab, utilitarian town consisting of row after row of six-story apartment blocks, built to house the workers for the new industrial complex, already with balconies full of washing and balcony-rails rusting in the dank air. I was to learn later that this was pretty much the norm for all new-build Eastern Bloc cities. Inspiring architecture was not something to be wasted on the proletariat but, to be fair, after the devastation suffered during the Second World War, providing basic accommodation was the top priority. I was given a single room on the fifth floor of the hotel, with its own bathroom and toilet, a small wardrobe and just about enough room for a table and chair. Fairly shoddy by western standards but most things worked – just not always at the same time. I soon found that the cold water would often go off for a whole day, was sandy coloured with solid particles in it and the hot water was almost boiling, which made life difficult if there was no cold water. Another feature, common to much of the Eastern Bloc accommodation I have stayed in, was that there were no sink plugs. To this day, I carry in my sponge bag a rubber disc that I cut out on my first day on site, which will cover and seal most plug holes. On the plus side there was a filtered water dispenser on each floor, which provided water for drinking and cooking and the gap between the double window units made a useful cold store, that is, until it got so cold outside all my eggs froze.

We were given a fairly generous local living allowance in roubles to cover the cost of food and drink and general living expenses. Transport to and from work was by bus from outside the hotel and life soon settled into a routine, at least for the first few months, of ten-hour days Monday to Friday and a half-day on Saturday. I soon found, in keeping with the communist ethic, that it took far too long to get served breakfast in the hotel so took to using a coffee bar next to the hotel for a quick cup of coffee substitute, a sweet bread roll and a tub of smetana (sour cream). This worked well until one morning I was too late even for a coffee, so, following the lead of the man in front of me in the queue, asked for a glass of what I assumed was fruit juice from one of the large glass dispensers on the back wall. I gulped down half the glass before realising it was about 40% proof fruit juice. I jumped on the bus that morning with a real warm glow inside me.

Most evenings, along with the majority of the other expats, I would eat in the hotel restaurant where we accounted for some 50% of the customers and most nights were still there, enjoying a convivial evening, when the police came in at around eleven o'clock to turf out non-residents. On one of my first free Saturday afternoons I walked round the town and purchased a cooking pot and hot plate, along with some basic provisions, so that I had a means of heating my package soups and boiling an egg if I couldn't face the hotel restaurant menu, which was extremely limited and hardly ever varied. In fact getting a nutritious and varied diet, especially as winter progressed, was a serious problem. No fresh fruit or vegetables, except for potatoes, raw onion and borsch (beetroot and cabbage soup) and very soon the company was supplying large jars of vitamin tablets to try and keep us healthy. One thing you could buy in the local stores, which was very tasty, was bottled fruit, except that it was as good as a work out in the gym to carry these thick glass bottles back to the hotel. I still have a vivid memory of fresh oranges arriving in the hotel around Christmas time and, although the going rate was around one US dollar an orange, they were snapped up very quickly, some things are beyond price.

I learnt a lesson in appreciation that Christmas in Russia. Our company gave £100 to the site manager to treat us over Christmas. Unfortunately there was very little that we could spend it on. A goose was acquired and duly cooked for the Christmas day feast but very little else of a traditional nature could be found. On the day, two of our contract instrument engineers arrived bearing a great big hamper, which their boss had sent from England. Christmas puddings, dates, figs, crackers, marmalade, mincemeat, After Eights, shortbread biscuits, etc., etc. were distributed for all to enjoy and were much appreciated. I remembered this some twenty years later when, as deputy manager of the commissioning department, I had a team spending Christmas in a remote region of China, so after several trips to the local supermarkets, a box of goodies was dispatched to site a few weeks before Christmas day. I'm not sure I ever found out if it got there but they do say with Christmas gifts, it's the thought that counts!

Work for most of the first month was taken up with unpacking and installing the chromatographs that had been sent from England and after connecting to the required services, developing the methods for analysing the various gas and liquid samples that would be taken from around the ethylene plant as it came on stream. As I said earlier, I knew very little about chromatographs, so Tom's technique of opening the packing cases, hauling everything out, pulling all the labelled parts from their packets into a big pile, which he then proceeded to assemble was a little worrying but we very soon had four machines up and running, without too many bits left over, so my fears were groundless. The good thing was hardly any of our Russian counterparts spoke any English, so Tom could give me plenty of instruction, without it being too obvious I was being trained in situ, and knowing he would be leaving in a couple of months really concentrated the mind.

Fortunately, the staff in our laboratory, mostly young women, were very pleasant and did not try to score points or make life difficult for us. This was not always the case as we found when, as a favour, we went across to the polyethylene plant, built by Simon Carves, to help set up the chromatographs in their laboratory. The woman in charge stood behind us and as soon as there appeared to be the slightest problem she would be muttering, in Russian, "bad English instruments" – we had learnt a few words by then – to the extent that I felt like telling her, putting it politely, to sort out her own problems. But Tom was made of sterner stuff and persisted in showing her western technology was not so bad after all. After a while, as we got to know people better, we realised there were distinct differences in the local people's perception of the West and, as a consequence, their attitude towards us. Roughly they could be split into four categories. Those, like some of our young translators who appeared to be completely brainwashed by the communist doctrine and would not hear a word said against the regime they lived in. Needless to say they had to put up with a considerable amount of banter and "friendly" argument during coffee and lunch breaks. Next there were the young professionals and middle managers who were members of the Communist Party because they knew it was the only way they could progress in a state-run system and not, as far as I could gather if you talked quietly to them on their own, that they had any strong conviction that communism was the best thing for them. Then there were the ordinary (majority) workers who were reasonably content if they had a roof over their heads, money to feed and clothe the family with enough left over for a *cto* gram or two of vodka to keep the cold out. Finally, potential activists, who were after any English newspapers or magazines that we had received, that would give them an uncensored view of the outside world. Needless to say I was a little wary of contact with the latter for reasons which will become clear later. Reading this now, when information about almost anything can be obtained at the touch of a button, it is hard to believe how controlled the propaganda was back then.

Another interesting aspect of life in the USSR was communication, or lack of it, and keeping in touch with friends and family back home became very important to me. In the absence of email, skype, Facebook, mobile phones etc. this came down to the telephone and writing letters. My parents had no telephone then so almost all my calls were made to Dawn. This may sound simple but the only telephone available to me was on the reception desk of the hotel. An international call had to be booked at least a day in advance for a specific time so coordination was critical. At the appointed time I would hover round the reception desk or wait in the restaurant until I was summoned and even then there was no guarantee the call would get through the three or four exchanges en route to Rayleigh in Essex. The sad thing was, in six months of trying, I can only remember three or four occasions where we had a normal conversation. Either Dawn could hear me but I could not hear her or the other way round and shouting at the top of your voice in a cavernous hotel foyer was not the most romantic of settings. Therefore, letters became an essential and I was soon writing five or six a week on a regular basis to friends and family. Even this was not quite straightforward. First, we assumed, rightly or wrongly, that they may be opened and censored, so we were careful not to put in anything too disparaging about the conditions or the country and the way it was run. Also there was nothing regular about the postal service, letters would go missing or arrive all out of sequence, so we soon started to number each letter and I started to keep a simple spreadsheet of letters sent and received. One good thing about letters is, if not destroyed, they still exist 50 years later and I have just been reading through a bunch sent to my parents to remind me of the highs and lows of my Russian adventure. As well as letters, my brother Wally sent me a *Sunday Telegraph* each week and mum sent me the *Wickford Recorder*, which kept me up to date with the hockey club results – not sure how they managed without me? The *Sunday Telegraph* was new to me, the *Daily Express* being the family paper of choice, and certainly in the first few months, when I wasn't too busy, I would read the *Telegraph* from cover to cover and opened myself to an expanded world.

When I first arrived I was told I would need to find some hobbies to stop me getting bored. For the past seven years a large part of my social life had centred around a trad jazz and later a rhythm and blues club at the White Hart, in Brentwood, where we would stomp the night away on most Saturdays and a folk club held on Friday nights in the Rising Sun in Billericay, where I had met Dawn earlier in the year. The resident group, *The Free Kind*, at the folk club were close friends, Alan, Chuck and Sandy, so I had spent a lot of time listening to them play and watching Chuck trying to tune his guitar. Consequently, when on one of my first walks around Novopolotsk I came across a music shop selling all sorts of instruments, I decided that learning to play something was the new hobby for me. Now, although I have reasonable rhythm and am not too bad on the dance floor I cannot sing a note, at least not in tune and am probably tone deaf, I persisted with my new idea and had soon acquired a clarinet (Acker Bilk's *Stranger on the Shore* was a favourite), a balalaika (I *was* in Russia) and a mandolin. The only instrument I ever played at school was the triangle, for a very brief period (my teachers knew a thing or two), so I now had a problem, I hadn't got a clue what to do with them. Calls for help went back to England and a while later Chuck sent me manuals on how to play the clarinet and the balalaika (translated from Russian into English). After a couple of months I could trim a reed and play a scale on the clarinet and could read music enough to strum a few chords on the balalaika but a simple tune was still a distant dream. I am not sure my fellow guests in the hotel appreciated my efforts and it was a pity that, a few months later, when one of my Russian friends (they were all music teachers) offered to give me lessons, I was too busy and tired to practise. The really annoying thing is on my return to England I took the clarinet into the laboratory, where upon Vic, one of my contemporaries, said 'I have always wanted to have a go on one of those', picked it up and proceeded to blow the first few bars of "The Saints". Thus ended my attempts to become a musician!

The 24th, 25th and 26th of October were declared a public holiday to celebrate the 50th anniversary of the "Glorious October Socialist Revolution". Tom and I were invited to march in the parade through the Town, to "show solidarity with the workers" from the ethylene plant but unfortunately we had to decline as we were working in the morning. However, we did attend in the afternoon, at the Communist Party Headquarters for prize giving and interminable speeches praising the achievements of our new brothers and sisters. In the evening we were treated to some very colourful and entertaining performances of different regions' folk song and dance. The downside was that no food or drink was included, so by the time it ended around ten o'clock, we were starving. Surprising how good a slab of dry bread and salami washed down by a beer can be!

During the holiday period, the square outside the hotel was also the venue for a communist party rally which led to an incident that could have had very serious consequences. Following the communist party coup d'état in 1948, Czechoslovakia had become part of the Eastern Bloc and as a consequence four of the senior operators from the ethylene plant built in Bratislava had been co-opted, much against their will, to help commission the new plant in Novopolotsk. Now the Czech boys did not like the Russians much anyway and by this time, with no sign of their married status requests being met, they were seriously pissed off. Because of the rally, the shift bus, bringing two of them back from the night shift, had to park outside the square and when they went to walk into the hotel they were stopped by a policeman and refused entry. Words were exchanged and Stannic, who was a big strong lad and had been part of the Czech judo squad, picked the policeman up and threw him through the plate glass window of the hotel. Somehow the incident was smoothed over and no charges were brought but not forgotten, as was apparent a couple of months later. Each evening, around eleven o'clock at night, the hotel restaurant would be closed to non-residents and two policemen would walk round ejecting anybody who was reluctant or too drunk to leave. On this particular night I was next to Stannic, arms linked in a line behind the table, singing a last song of the evening, when he suddenly went silent and started to tremble. I looked up to see a policeman standing the other side of the table start to reach for his gun, at which point Stannic tried to launch himself across the table only to be held back by the human chain he was a part of. Fortunately the other officer restrained and persuaded his partner to walk away before anything more serious happened, but a close call.

Forming any form of social life or contacts outside of work proved to be quite difficult. Apart from the language barrier, in the town, entertainment venues were limited to the restaurant of our hotel, where a four-piece "oompah" band played three or four nights a week, a flea pit of a cinema, – once the winter arrived – an ice hockey and skating rink, and across the square from the hotel, a refurbished "Palace of Culture". By the time the latter had opened its doors I had made friends with Bob, who was of similar age to me and worked on the polyethylene plant. Saturday night was dance night, so we decided to give it a try. I cannot remember dancing much but we managed to make contact with the resident band whose members spoke a little English and were as keen to talk to us as we were to them. It turned out they were all music teachers, four men and a woman (the lovely Xania) in their late twenties. Bob had a cassette recorder back at the hotel with some of the latest western pop records on it, Beatles, Rolling Stones etc., which were not readily available in the USSR, so we soon had some new friends, keen to move on from Louis Armstrong and all that jazz.

By now, we had become aware that it could cause a big problem for local people if they became too friendly on a one to one basis with any of us. As is their nature, some of the men had started close relationships with local women only to find they suddenly disappeared. If they were lucky they would get a letter to say that she was all right but had lost her job or had been sent to work somewhere else. As a consequence we were very careful when our new friends came to the hotel. They never came alone, always in a group and we always left the door of the room open so that the *dezhurnaya*, the woman who patrolled each corridor (providing assistance if we needed anything) could see in. The James Bond in us also made us suspicious of a disc shaped bulge in the plaster on the wall of each room, so if our conversations were being recorded for the KGB I hope they enjoyed some early Beatles. Strange coincidence… I read in the paper this morning (26 April 2013) that contraband Beatles records were selling in Russia in the 60s for around 200 roubles each, approximately a month's wages, so the KGB could have been making a killing on the black market.

The weather up to the middle of November had been abnormally mild with a lot of rain which didn't help at work or any other social activity so it was something of a relief when the first snows came and the temperature dropped enough for the world to turn white and a proper Russian winter to begin. It was also the time for some of our new Russian friends, Valodia and Eugene, to introduce us to an outdoor activity centre sited in the middle of a forest, by the side of a lake, about a mile from the town. As well as a cafeteria selling drinks and snacks it was possible to hire skates, cross country ski equipment or snow shoes and probably take a sauna if you wanted to. The ice rink was formed by simply running a steam hose over a field of snow until it melted and then froze again. On our first Sunday we tried skating but the skates were fixed to a leather shoe, rather than boots, with no ankle support and after about an hour I couldn't stand up any more, so on the next visit we (Bob and I) tried the cross country skiing. This was much more to our liking and after a stuttering start the large wooden planks clipped to the boots started to feel more natural and our gait was developing into an almost elegant glide, to the extent that we were venturing further and further away from the centre into the surrounding forest. It was great exercise and very relaxing to be totally free of work for a few hours. The only problem being, as it got colder, lumps of ice started to form under my nose as my breath froze on my relatively newly grown moustache. I had to shave it off in the end, that's the moustache, not my nose. All went well for a couple of months until we came across a downhill slope cleared of trees. Now, the skis had no fixed heel and we had no idea how to turn or stop when going at speed. Bob went first and ended up in a tangled heap at the bottom. I followed when he had crawled out of the way, took off and landed head first in a snow drift. I realised then I was very lucky it was only my bindings that were broken and not my neck as, although it looked clear, the stumps of the trees were still in the ground sticking up under the snow. It was at this point it got serious. Bob could not put any weight on his ankle (turns out it was broken) and after a futile ten minutes trying to fix my bindings I started to freeze as I was only wearing a light cotton track suit top over a roll neck. Fortunately, on this day, we were accompanied by two of our Russian friends and a Welsh lad called Ron who was quite good on skis. Ron took off for the centre, which was three or four miles away, to bring back a sledge. The Russian boys more or less suspended Bob between them and started the slow trek back. I had no choice but to walk back, which is extremely tiring when you're sinking up to your knees in snow every few yards. Bob's plight was alleviated slightly when they crossed an army patrol. One of the soldiers took off his belt and bound the ankle, which was an act of great kindness, as I suspect he could have been put on a charge for losing part of his equipment. That was not the end of my cross country skiing but with Bob out of action I would not go on my own and was certainly more cautious after that.

In the run up to Christmas, things were speeding up at work, ethylene was being produced and we had refined and finalised the methods for analysing most of the specified gas and liquid streams to be sampled from the plant. In addition, with the help of Maria, our excellent interpreter, training had been given to all the laboratory shift teams in the use of the chromatographs and the taking and transfer of reliable samples to them. It was about this time that I seemed to acquire an additional work load. A room next to the laboratory housed most of the online analysers, which are machines that are permanently piped into key component streams around the plant, so that more or less continuous analyses and, in some cases, automatic control could be undertaken. For some reason I was given the job of assisting with the set up and operation of these analysers, even though their specification and purchase was included in the instrument group's responsibilities. I probably looked young and naive enough to be lumbered with a job nobody else wanted! Shortly afterwards an incident occurred that was of great concern. Because of the highly volatile nature of the streams being sampled, the machines, in particular two infrared analysers, had to be purged with nitrogen, an inert gas, to stop the risk of explosion. The nitrogen was piped in from the plant, rather than being supplied from bottles, as was the case for the laboratory, and one morning the whole room smelt strongly of hydrocarbons. As a precaution we shut down the power supplies and further investigation showed a knock-out pot in the nitrogen line to be half-full of liquid. Analysis of the condensate and vapour in the pot showed it to contain a high proportion of propylene. The site manager was informed and after further investigation it was concluded that under abnormal conditions during start-up the nitrogen line could get back-pressured with propylene which should never happen. As a follow up I wrote out a Problem Report which was sent back to the head office to try and ensure the correct solution was found and prevent any similar problem occurring in future designs. In this instance, I do not think the system worked properly because a few months after returning to England I heard that an infrared analyser had exploded blowing the front cover into the face of the section manager. Fortunately, although very unpleasant, he was not killed and thankfully the problem did not lead to a larger explosion on the main plant. Some years earlier there was an explosion on a plant built in Czechoslovakia that killed three people.

Perhaps, as a result of my increased responsibilities, I had a bit of a moan about my relatively low rate of pay and was surprised to find out that if I wanted to I could deposit some of my excess local (non-convertible) living allowance into a fund used for running the site and for which I would be credited in sterling. This I was pleased to do and stored up the knowledge of this practice for any future sites I might be sent to behind the Iron Curtain. Also, a few weeks later I received a letter from the company saying they were pleased with my work and would pay a pro rata 2.5% bonus on completion of the job. In addition, it was pointed out to me by some of the "old hands" that under current tax laws, if wages earned while working abroad were paid directly to a bank in, for example Jersey, they could be paid free of tax. After numerous letters to and from my bank and the company I managed to get this organised before the bonus was paid. However, the real bonus was that six months later, when Dawn agreed to marry me, Jersey made an ideal destination to choose an engagement ring.

Just before Christmas I was introduced to the Soviet Health System. I suddenly felt very unwell, with intense pains in my abdomen and was taken into hospital with suspected appendicitis. After further investigation, I am glad to say, gastric flu was diagnosed and after two days in bed I was sent home with prescribed medication to recover. Tom came to see me every day, very concerned that if I did not get back to work soon his promised Christmas leave would be cancelled. Good hygiene appeared to be a priority at the hospital, as all visitors had to put on a white coat and shoe covers before entering the wards. All very well until going into the toilets. Basic in the extreme, a Turkish squatter which looked as though it was frequently missed and a basket at the side to hold the used toilet paper, assuming some could be found; a cold tap, no sink or soap or towels so hands, if they were washed, got wiped on the white coat. Still, they sorted me out and later saved the life of another of our guys when he had a heart attack. Back at the hotel I was very thankful that one of the wives took pity on me and kept me supplied with rice puddings until I was well enough to leave my room. Also a very good reason for allowing a few married status positions within the site teams, because it is a universal truth, a man needs to be looked after when he is poorly.

I did return to work in time for Tom to depart, as scheduled, for Christmas, taking with him a bundle of letters and cards that would be free of any possible censor and therefore a chance to give a more open view of life in a communist state. Freedom of information was definitely controlled. I went to the local "flea pit" of a cinema several times and never once saw a film that showed the west in a good light. I particularly remember a 1958 film called *The Key*, billed as, the latest American? Blockbuster, starring Sophia Loren (probably why I went to see it) and William Holden. Set in war time England during the blitz everything was as drab and miserable as it possibly could be, the blackout in operation, food severely rationed, and nothing to lift the spirit at all.

Christmas, as such, was not celebrated in a communist country but at New Year gifts and cards with Father Frost on them were exchanged and people congregated around a large tree erected in the square in front of the hotel where they stood with heads bowed in silent contemplation?

It was about this time that a true Russian winter started. I knew it was getting colder when the lorry drivers who parked in the square overnight started clattering about at five o'clock in the morning lighting bonfires under their engines to thaw the diesel. However, when I walked out of the hotel to catch the bus to work and my nose froze as I tried to breathe in, I knew it was cold at a different level. Fortunately, standing for a few minutes just outside the door, allowed my body to adjust so that I could breathe without it being too painful and ,wearing gloves, a good fur hat and my long johns was a must. The temperature dropped to -32 °C for a week or two and then settled back to around -12 °C, which was quite pleasant with the sun out and no wind, as there was very little moisture in the air.

Also, about this time, things got really busy at work. We were making ethylene and starting to export to the polyethylene plant as well as trying to increase production to the 100% capacity rate so that the guarantee tests could be started. As a consequence, I was periodically asked to cover night shifts to reinforce the laboratory in the absence of any other senior personnel. One night as I walked onto the plant it was a scene of frantic activity with real tension in the air. Just outside the laboratory two men were hammering away at a large valve while others rushed in and out of the control room. One of the shift operators told me a valve on the line to the flare had stuck or was frozen closed and with no bypass pressure was building to a very dangerous level. In fact, he advised me to get all the women out of the laboratory and get off site as quickly as possible. As I turned to go the valve must have opened because there was a tremendous roar and a jet of flame erupted out of the flare, which was about half a mile away, like a massive rocket in reverse. A few minutes more and my working life could have ended there and this story would never have been told!

Time for a small lesson in the art of chromatography, as it existed in 1967. Basically the chromatograph is an instrument fitted with a column made of glass or stainless steel which could be filled with a range of packing materials. A small sample of liquid or gas could be passed through the column using a carrier gas to impinge on a detector. The packing material being chosen so that the different components in the sample were preferentially adsorbed and then desorbed so that they were separated and on reaching the detector were measured as an electrical impulse, which can be recorded as a peak on a chart recorder. The area of each peak is directly proportional to the mass of the component that created the peak and can, therefore, be used to calculate the percentage of each component in a sample.

Are you still with me? On this job one of our most difficult tasks was using the chromatograph to measure the calorific value of each batch of fuel oil that was shipped in, as 20 to 30 major components were separated, each of which had to be multiplied by a series of factors, including individual calorific values, in a complex calculation to give an overall value. Nowadays everything would, once set up, be calculated automatically using an integrator and computer program. Not so then, I had only a slide-rule and had to measure the area of each peak (half base times height) using a ruler and a magnifying graticule. The point of this story is that it was one of the few times that I was annoyed with the women in the laboratory, as in most cases they were quick learners and took care with their work. However, when running a fuel oil sample, for a reason I could not understand, they altered all the settings Tom and I had taken pains to derive and ended up measuring the area of tiny narrow peaks, which introduced considerable error into the calculation. It was important to me, as the value would be used to determine how efficiently the plant was running during the guarantee tests, which had to be completed before I could go home. When I pressed for an explanation, using our interpreter, they shuffled their feet and looked very embarrassed before confiding that if they started the calculation with a big value for the area of each peak they would run out of beads on the abacus before they could complete it. I could not be angry anymore but three days later a large desk-top calculator turned up, I suspect from one of their advanced technology institutes, so honour and equanimity were restored. Incidentally, the abacus was still used extensively in Russia at that time and if you could see and understand what each bead represented, it made a good way of knowing how much you had to pay in any of the shops.

Travel, for us, without escort and prior approval, was severely restricted and limited to going to old Polotsk, which had some fine older buildings but the range of goods that could be bought in the shops was still very limited. For this reason when the opportunity to go to Minsk, the capital of Belarus, for a long weekend was offered I jumped at it. On the first occasion, sometime before Christmas, some of the highlights were: a) being able to take a bath in hot crystal-clear water instead of a gritty, sandy coloured soup, b) making a phone call from my own room where I could actually talk to Dawn in a normal voice, I am just glad she was home when the call went through and, c) going to the theatre to see the Bolshoi (big) Ballet Company in a performance of *Peer Gynt*, which was a completely new experience for me but one I decided was worth repeating. On my second visit, in early February, I again went to the ballet to see a performance of *Giselle* and was rewarded with something quite wonderful. I know little about ballet but the principal dancers performed a duet in the second act which was spellbinding and left you knowing you had just witnessed something very special, like seeing Torvill and Dean skate to Bolero for the first time. I believe a Russian audience can be quite critical but at the end of the performance they rose as one, the applause was thunderous and very soon the stage was covered in flowers.

The journey home was memorable as well for different reasons. The flight was delayed because of thick fog and when we were allowed to go, as we taxied, I could only just see as far as the side of the runway. Once in the air, the pilot more or less hedge hopped all the way back to Polotsk where the runway was literally in a snow covered field illuminated by lit braziers along its length. To cap a relaxing weekend there was a note awaiting me asking me to go straight into work to cover a night shift as there had been a few problems and with Tom now in Kazan I was the only option. It did not take long for exhilaration to turn to exhaustion.

I had a disturbing meeting during my trip to Minsk with a young Russian woman engineer who was working on the polyethylene plant and staying in the same hotel in Novopolotsk as I was. Katerina was in her early thirties and we had formed a friendship a few months before after a dance or two in the hotel restaurant where we both ate most nights. She was trying to learn English and asked if I would help which I was pleased to do, as I was trying to learn Russian, so a good exchange. I did ask, in my limited Russian, if it would cause any problems, us being alone together and she said she thought not, so we went ahead. However, we were still very careful and if I went to her room we always left the door wide open and had her books in full view and other than that we would walk round the town together trying to talk while we shopped. Once confirmed, I told her when I was going to Minsk and she said it was her home town and by coincidence she would be there as well, so we should meet up and she gave me her telephone number. I was successful in making contact but Katerina sounded very upset on the phone and told me there were "big problems", a phrase I understood in Russian and could we meet in a café just outside my hotel. I never fully understood what the "big problems" were but she said she was in trouble with her work and in fact, that meeting was the last time I saw her, she never returned to Novopolotsk! I still feel saddened that it may have been our association that created the problem.

We often speculated why we were restricted in our movements and associations quite so rigorously and suspected we were in a sensitive military zone being fairly close to the USSR's western borders. A few weeks later I thought I would test the system and one Sunday afternoon jumped on a bus heading out into the countryside. All was well for about fifteen minutes when the driver suddenly stopped the bus in the middle of nowhere and made it quite clear, in both word and gesture, that I had to get off. I was not best pleased, it being the middle of winter, the surrounding countryside covered in snow and

I had no idea how often the buses ran. Fortunately, before I was completely frozen, a bus turned up to take me back to town and after being squashed in amongst a crush of *babooshkas* I soon warmed up again. So, confirmation that we were in a *hot zone* and at least I did not get arrested as a spy, but no more unauthorised adventures for me after that. Making the most of modern information technology I have just Googled "Polotsk and the Cold War" and was astounded to see a Top Secret CIA Report stating that the Borovisty air base 16 km North West of Polotsk was home to a squadron of attack aircraft defending the Nikolskoye base suspected of holding at least five ICBMs (Inter Continental Ballistic Missiles) which I think is confirmation of why our movement and contacts were so restricted.

The end of January and beginning of February was a very busy period at work and as I was now the only chemist on site I was on, more or less, 24-hour call while the plant was brought towards its full operating capacity. Ethylene was exported to the polyethylene plant next door and, on the 4th February, polyethylene was produced in pellet form for the first time. Shortly after this, walking around the plant to take samples had an additional associated hazard as the place was cleaned, tidied and freshly painted in preparation for a visit by Premier Kosygin. I was not included in the welcoming party but enjoyed the feeling of excitement and pride in a job well done that the visit created. On the 19th February I was very pleased to see Tom back on site in preparation for the start of a guarantee run, not that I was working any less but the stress levels reduced considerably with somebody else there to share the load. On the 25th February we received the even better news that the plant was to be accepted without completing a guarantee run, so an end was in sight.

Another hobby which kept me out of mischief through the winter months was collecting stamps which the USSR issued in great numbers each year to represent their different regions, history and achievements. They were very colourful and interesting, particularly those associated with the Space Race. Yuri Gagarin, in Vostok 1, had been the first human in Space in April 1961, closely followed by Alan Shepard, for the Americans in May 1961. In 1962, the Soviets successfully launched Vostok 3 and 4, followed by putting Valentina Tereshkova, the first women into space, in Vostok 6 in 1963. In 1961, the Americans started the Apollo programme aimed at putting a man on the moon, which led to John Glenn orbiting the Earth in 1962, followed by a series of Gemini missions through the 1960s before the wonderful zenith of the moon landing in 1969. What you did not hear about were the disasters and the numbers of people that were killed at the time; 90–150 Soviets in 1960 plus the pilot of Soyuz 1 in 1967, followed by three Apollo 1 astronauts also in 1967. Also, the Space Race may never have been, as it is believed that Soviet Premier Khrushchev was poised to accept President Kennedy's proposal to join forces in a space programme just before Kennedy was assassinated in 1963. Hard to believe there are now in excess of 1000 satellites whirling round the Earth, we will need traffic lights up there soon!

Back to the stamps, I started in a small way but after buying a catalogue made a real effort to obtain a complete set of those issued in 1966 and 1967. By dint of swapping stamps sent out from England and the use of hard currency to buy unfranked stamps from a dealer in Minsk I managed to complete the 1966 set and just missed out for 1967. The albums are still on a shelf in my study and looking at them brings back some good memories, which is perhaps their greatest value.

With an end in sight, I was given another example of how the communist system worked. Our excellent interpreter, Maria, a third year language student at Minsk University, was co-opted to come and work in Novopolotsk. As a thank-you for all her help I asked her if she would like to be my guest, along with a friend to avoid any problems, for a meal at the hotel the next weekend. She said she would love to but could not as she was going to Minsk to get married. I said, 'does that mean I will not see you anymore?' 'Oh no,' was the reply, 'I have to be back here for work on Monday morning.'

A memorable event occurred a few weeks later. Doug Thrift, our project manager came out from England to get all the relevant documents signed for completion of the job. He was due to arrive in the evening and we, along with our Russian counterparts, were invited to join together for a meal to celebrate. As he walked into the room there was a collective gasp of breath, his secretary was wearing the first miniskirt, with legs to do it full justice, which I and certainly all the Russians had ever seen. What an entrance, and remember we were at the end of a Russian winter were most of the women were still wearing thick wool stockings, padded coats and clumpy felt boots.

This event made me that much keener to return home as I now had even more idea what I was missing and I do not remember Dawn telling me she was into the latest fashions either. Another thing, when I left England all my mates were still bachelors and it had been a blow for me to miss my oldest friend Robin Self's wedding which took place in February. I think I was four years old when we first met and the Self family were to be at the centre of a large part of my social life throughout my growing up and teenage years. Wyn and Ces ran the local tennis club we all belonged to and operated an almost open house policy as far as all the boys were concerned. Robin's "kid" sister Sheila was my traditional-jazz dance partner for most of my late teens until she migrated up to London to train as a nurse and I have never been quite sure how we did not become more of an item, as there is no doubt we were quite fond of each other. Now I had been told Peter, another close friend, was getting married at the beginning of April, so even more reason to pack up and go.

As it turned out I arrived back home with about a day to spare before the wedding and remember the drive up to London, as the boys were mini-skirt spotting for me all the way there. The probable cause of more than one accident as drivers' eyes were drawn away from the road ahead. I was not to realise until much later that the miniskirt was responsible for the loss of the "giggle band" and one of the most erotic sensations known to man. An accessory that came with the miniskirt, certainly in the winter months, were tights. Up until then a well-dressed young woman would be wearing stockings and a suspender belt, so any young man trying his luck, if not rebuffed too strongly, might find his hand sliding up a silken leg, past the band round the top of the stocking onto the velvety warmth of an inner thigh. Go on, you know why it was called the "giggle band", if you got past there you were reckoned to be laughing!

Packing to leave was a considerable exercise in its own right; as well as two balalaikas, a mandolin and a clarinet I had also bought Christmas presents for most of my family, so now had a small piano accordion for my niece Jacquelyn, who was showing some musical talent, a cine camera, a model of Konkordski (the Soviet rival to Concord), seven fur hats, several Matryoshka dolls of various sizes, plus stamps, records, books, posters depicting the "fight of the people for a better future" and a load of other bits and pieces accumulated over six months. Also an engraved set of gold lined silver vodka thimbles, a parting gift of remembrance from the girls of the Gas Separation Laboratory, New Polotsk 1968. I even brought my skis, boots and skates back, though how I managed that I cannot quite remember. To accommodate all this I bought another large suitcase, as well as my trunk, which was now emptied of its packet soups. However, the good thing about having all this luggage was that any excess baggage could be paid for in non-convertible roubles and claimed back on expenses in sterling. At least I was not as bad as some of the men who packed cases with rocks, metal dumbbells, etc. and it was noted that on the next contract, there was a limit put on the excess baggage the company would pay for.

Under the terms of the contract, if the job was completed successfully our client would pay our return air fares, which they did but only if we flew Aeroflot. As a result, once safely back in the laboratory I completed my expenses claim and included the unused return half of my British Airways ticket. A few days later I got a phone call from the commissioning manager's secretary asking what she was supposed to do with the ticket, as nobody had ever returned one before. Oh dear I thought, the new boy is not going to be popular with the lads if they find out who subsequently put an end to that little "perk".

I had been back from Russia for three months when I was sent to Vratsa in Bulgaria for a few weeks, more of which in Section 3.5. After that I felt a well-earned holiday was in order, so Dawn and I flew off to Jersey to spend some of my bonus and, little knowing what she was letting herself in for, while there she agreed to marry me. On returning to the laboratory I was told my next assignment would be to commission the laboratory of an ammonia plant the company was constructing in Romania. Now at this time Harold Wilson was prime minister with a Labour government in power and the country was in a real mess, with inflation running at about 16%. After a few heart-to-hearts Dawn and I decided that a further separation of six months or more, while we built up savings for a wedding, would be meaningless with inflation at such high levels, so I asked the company if I could be excused as I wanted to get married. Their agreement had a profound effect on my colleagues in the laboratory as Harry Clayton, who was scheduled to go to Czechoslovakia, was sent to Romania instead and married a Romanian woman and Fred Ahrens who was subsequently sent to Czechoslovakia, you have guessed it, married a Czechoslovakian woman. In fact, I would think some 50% of my colleagues on commissioning jobs in the future were married to or divorced from women from the Eastern bloc.

3.4 Permalene trips

Starting in 1970 and continuing for short periods over the next seven years I was part of a small team involved in additive trials at a selection of ammonium nitrate manufacturing plants around the world (see Appendix 1), to improve prill (small round pellets) quality.

The patent for this addition process was owned by the Mississippi Chemical Corporation (MCC) of America, who formed a partnership with H&G, to try to sell licenses for the technology to fertilizer manufacturers in Europe and the Middle East. The additive, known as Permalene-34, was a mixture of aluminium sulphate, boric acid and diammonium phosphate used as a 0.5 to 2.0% additive to stabilize and harden the prill form of ammonium nitrate, which, without the additive, goes through a crystalline transition between 32 °C and 34 °C, hence the 34 in the name. The problem was that on a hot day, this is the sort of temperature range the sacks of fertilizer will cycle through, particularly when stacked in storage under the beloved black polythene, resulting in the prills breaking down into a powder and making it increasingly difficult for the farmer to spread on his fields.

Ammonium nitrate, as well as being an effective fertilizer, when in its pure form, is a powerful oxidising agent and was the main ingredient of terrorist bombs for many years. The Bishopsgate bomb, which devastated the City of London on Saturday 24th April 1993, comprised a tipper-truck packed with a ton of ammonium nitrate fertilizer detonated by the IRA. I walked through the city on the Monday evening following the attack and it was frightening to see how far the blast front had travelled, with street after street showing buildings with every window shattered. Thank goodness not too many of the offices were occupied on the Saturday!

I believe MCC developed the process, in the first instance, to stabilize explosive grade ammonium nitrate used in the mining industry, but after some terrible explosions during manufacture most plants in Europe were producing fertiliser based on ammonium nitrate combined with calcium carbonate to limit the explosion risk, hence the need to run trials to prove effectiveness.

For the trials in Europe a very neat test rig was built, comprising a stainless steel solution tank, pumps and pipework all of which fitted onto the back of a small truck, usually driven by Pete the pipe fitter, for transport from site to site. Before arriving a list of chemicals and test equipment required would be sent and as the chemist my first job was to confirm all the laboratory test equipment was available and fit for purpose while the rest of the team set up the plant equipment and started playing about with the solution dosing rates. The usual pattern after the first few days, was that I would go onto 13 hour nights as, being a chemist, I could carry out the product testing as well as keeping an eye on the, hopefully, stable dosing system before the rest of the guys came in on day-shift to make any alterations they thought necessary – all, of course, with the cooperation of the plant management and operators.

In theory we could complete a trial in about two weeks, which surprisingly, proved to be the case as far as our first destination, Barton-on-Humber, was concerned, although no great improvement to the product was made. It did mean though, that we made it onto our pre-booked ferry to Southern Ireland and our next destination, Arklow. Here things did not run so smoothly as the finished product was formed in a granulator, rather than a prill tower (the MCC method) and the first introduction of the additive had a remark-able effect. Cannon ball sized lumps of product were emitted which was no good to anybody and it took two or three weeks of trial and error to balance the system to a reasonable sized granule. The delay, for me, was good news, as there was no point in working nights, which gave me the opportunity to enjoy some real Irish hospitality. The Arklow Bay Hotel, where we were staying, seemed to be run entirely by young women with the exception of a barman and Hugh, the night porter, a great character and good musician, who apparently spent the winters playing in jazz bands in New Orleans and returned to Ireland only for the summer. After a few days Helen (*maître d'hôtel*) and her friend Mary (reception) looked favourably on our requests to be shown where the best local entertainment could be found and took us to some great pubs in the countryside where excellent Irish folk bands were playing. Terrific atmosphere, thick with smoke, the Guinness flowing freely, fiddle, whistle and bodhran leading some lively sessions with the whole bar trying to raise the roof on the chorus lines. It was not unknown for the party spirit to continue when we got back to the hotel where a piano in a basement room provided the music once Hugh could be "enticed" away from his duties to play a few tunes. My lasting memory of Ireland was driving into work one morning and seeing Hugh trudging along the side of the road. Q: 'Where are you going Hugh? A: 'Just along the way, no distance at all' Q: 'Do you want a lift?" A: 'To be sure.' A mile further on we pass the factory entrance and still no word from Hugh to stop. Q: 'Where are you going Hugh? You said it was no distance.' A: 'To be sure, it's just along the way and a beautiful morning for a ride.' This goes on for another couple of miles until we reach a small village where Hugh is happy to be put down. Q: 'We thought you said it was just down the road,' A: 'To be sure, but the distances are so different when you are in a car!'

One of the really exciting things about my job was being sent to a country that it was most unlikely I would ever have visited under my own volition. Shiraz, in Iran, was one such case and at that time I was not too sure where Iran was, until I looked on a world atlas. Our normal team of four was reduced to two, as the test rig was not being driven all the way to the Middle East and Ladelle Blanton from Mississippi had to be back in the USA. The fact that we flew out mid-November 1970, which was getting a bit close to Christmas, may also have been a factor. Anyway, Irvin, our project manager and I, left a cold grey England to arrive, via Tehran, in the rather splendid ancient – some 4000-year-old – city of Shiraz, also known as the City of Gardens and Roses and located in the south west of Iran. We were there while Shah Mohammad Reza Pahlavi was still sitting on the peacock throne, after a 1953 coup d'état orchestrated by the UK had made him the Head of State, so the country appeared to be more westernised than is currently the case.

We stayed in a modern hotel in the city and were driven each day to the fertilizer-producing complex, located some 40 miles away along a three-lane highway. This road had been built to provide access to the ancient capital city of Persepolis, where in 1971 the Shah hosted a great extravaganza to celebrate the 2500th anniversary of the Persian Empire. The vast amount of money spent on foreign dignitaries – Princess Anne represented our royal family – while the common people were starving, was a precursor to the Islamic Revolution, which started in October 1977 and led to the Shah being deposed in 1979 and Ayatollah Khomeini becoming the Supreme Leader. The only problem with travelling on this highway was that it was effectively a three-lane road with no apparent rule as to who had the right of way when overtaking. In the short time we were there we saw some terrible accidents; lorries smashing into buses and ripping the whole side off was not uncommon, which made the journey to and from work rather nerve-wracking. However, the landscape was like nothing I had ever seen before, with a series of dry flat plains, interspersed by mountainous ridges and pot-holed at regular intervals by *qanats* (irrigation wells).

Like Ireland, but for different reasons, the Permalene testing did not get off to a good start, mainly because the chemicals we were given to make up the additive were not of the finest quality and we ended up with a thick brown soup, rather than a water clear liquid. We persisted without much success for three or four weeks until, with Christmas fast approaching, Irvin called a halt and asked our liaison engineer to book us tickets for the flight(s) home. I can still remember – in the car on the way to the airport, three days before Christmas, our man gave us the flight tickets and imparted the news we were only wait-listed on the flight from Tehran to London. Irvin, who had only been married a few months, went wild and had a real rant at our client to the point where I nearly had to hold him down. Fortunately, we had no problem getting on the flight to London but not good for his blood pressure and in fact I heard the sad news, some years later, that Irvin died of a heart attack on the steps of Victoria Station.

Some happier memories of Shiraz were the formal gardens and visiting the tombs of Hafez and Saadi, two of the most revered Persian poets, as well as walking through a magnificent covered bazaar, permeated by the smell of strange herbs and spices and easy prey for the vendors of all the wonders of the East. I could not afford a Persian carpet but bought a table cloth covered in traditional designs, which we still have and as I sit here writing this I am being watched by a simple but beautifully modelled clay Ayatollah. The great mosque, its dome covered outside in deep blue tiles with gold star inlays and inside with small segments of mirror, so that the whole inside glistened like burnished silver was another wonderful sight. Finally, visiting Persepolis and looking in wonder at the ancient capital of the Achaemenid Empire, started by Darius 1 and completed by Xerxes the Great in the 6th century BC, was a most memorable experience for me, despite having read about the Persian Empire and the building of Persepolis in one of my school prizes titled "The Living Past", the reality gave a whole new perspective to one of the Middle East's great civilisations.

The next trial took place in 1972 at Rainham in Essex and being only 15 miles from my home it meant I could drive there and back each day, or so I thought, until after a succession of 13-hour nights I nearly drove into the back of a lorry on the A127. From then I moved into a motel near the factory with the rest of the team. The most memorable thing about this trial was that *it worked*. A definite improvement in prill hardness and quality meant the sale of a license was a definite possibility and a great encouragement to approach other manufacturers to run further trials. I still have an unopened 20kg bag of essentially *pure* ammonium nitrate from that trial in my garden shed and have, as a consequence, a slight concern that one day I might be visited by the bomb squad.

The next trial didn't take place until 1975, following lengthy periods commissioning fertilizer plant laboratories that the company built in Bulgaria and India. The most memorable feature was the location of the factory, built in an ugly industrial sprawl, at Porto Marghera on the mainland side of the causeway leading to Venice! The trip didn't start well – on the second day, I felt awful, sweating and nauseous to the extent that I stopped eating and stayed in my hotel room, convinced I had food poisoning or something similar. Twenty four hours later I felt fine, very strange. It was some years later, after a similar experience, that I realised it was a reaction to stopping taking malaria tablets, after returning from India. Actually, "Marghera", in the Venetian dialect means "marine swamp", so perhaps I should have carried on taking the tablets for a few more weeks. What really made the trip was the character of our liaison engineer at the factory, Mr Napoli, a gravelly voiced, chain smoking, hunchbacked raconteur, who spoke the Venetian dialect and was only too pleased to take us into Venice of an evening, to show off his beloved city. Venice at night, away from the main squares and well-lit streets can be quite confusing and scary, especially if your imagination is working overtime having recently watched the film *Don't Look Now* starring Julie Christie and Donald Sutherland, where the menace from a mysterious red-coated figure is tangible. Having said that, Venice in the right light, is one of the most visually stunning cities in the world with something of interest and delight round every corner and canal turn, that is, just so long as you do not fall in. That early visit certainly whetted (no pun intended) my appetite for more, and we (Dawn and I) have been back three times since, at different times of the year and have never been disappointed, apart from some less than inspiring food on our last visit.

The final Permalene trip took place in 1977, to Toulouse in France where, despite excellent cooperation and every effort being made by our hosts, very little improvement in the prill quality could be achieved. As a result, in my final report, I concluded that trials at plants where calcium carbonate was added to the ammonium nitrate for safety reasons, which was the norm for most of Europe, had very little chance of success. Whether or not management agreed with me that, somewhat sadly, turned out to be the last

Permalene additive trial that, to my knowledge, the company ever undertook. My abiding memory of Toulouse was lunch in the works canteen, which was a serious business and would last for at least an hour. First, all the workers would change from their overalls, some into suit, shirt and tie. I can still hear Ladelle (our American colleague) saying, 'gee, most of these guys in the States wouldn't even own a suit, let alone change into it for lunch at work.' Secondly, the menu was extensive, including frog's legs and snails on more than one occasion and lastly, wine was readily available but as an extension to the meal and not a main course like some of the liquid lunches taken in the pub, back in the UK.

3.5 Bulgarian experiences

Northern light eyes – quiet presence and soft aurora –
aren't you frightened?
The southern sun will put you on fire – with dark hands –
and you'll burn down
In the sunflower only and in the velvet bunches of grapes –
there coils the strength of growing ripe – in embers.
Northern light eyes – aren't you frightened?
Up to the sunrise only –
a single breath we've got.

My introduction to Bulgaria was a short visit in the summer of 1968, to help resolve a problem on an ammonia plant the company was commissioning near a town called Vratsa, situated in the foothills of the Balkan Mountains, in the north west of the country, midway between Sofia, the capital, and the Danube, which forms the boundary with Rumania. So, once again, back into the communist bloc but this time with nothing like the restrictions that I had experienced in Russia and, being in the summer, the available food was not too bad either.

As is sometimes the case the outbound flight was memorable, in this instance for a transit stop in Vienna. I was looking out of the window from the economy seats to see a red carpet and a welcoming party, with bunches of flowers, for somebody descending from first class. I recognised the curl, it was Bill Hayley of The Comets fame; virtually the founder of the Rock and

Roll era and exciting in that it was not so long since I had rocked in the aisle of my local cinema while watching *Rock around the clock*.

This was also my first introduction to an ammonia (NH_3) plant, which, in this case, was based on the steam reforming of a petroleum-derived feedstock called naphtha, to produce the hydrogen (H_2) molecules needed to combine with nitrogen (N_2) molecules to form ammonia. Naphtha is a mixture of different hydrocarbon (C_nH_m) molecules and when combined with steam (H_2O) at high temperature and pressure over a catalyst breaks down to form mainly hydrogen and carbon dioxide (CO_2), which has to be separated from the H_2. This can be done by absorption in a hot aqueous potassium carbonate solution using the Benfield process. The problem was that the process was not operating well enough for a guarantee test to be completed, so a team had been sent out from London to troubleshoot. My part was to check samples were being taken correctly and the proper analytical procedures were being followed, while various attempts were made to correct the fault.

The Benfield column is usually the tallest structure on an ammonia plant and consists of a series of bubble cap trays internally mounted at regular intervals up its length. To take the additional samples required at each tray level necessitated somebody with a good head for heights climbing up and down an external ladder two or three times a day. Since I was relatively young and fit, it probably explains why I was made so welcome by all the young women working in the laboratory.

In the end the answer to the problem was simple; the Benfield column was some 15% too short but as this would require a complete shutdown and major rebuild to correct, nobody wanted to believe it.

One of the good things about the visit was being able to travel more or less anywhere we liked within Bulgaria, so after working for two weeks without a break, it was agreed I could take a long weekend off. This enabled me to join a new friend, Collin Boggan, one of our process shift operators, on a trip to Varna, a major port and holiday resort on the Black Sea coast. Our route took us east through the centre of the country and on the way we passed through the Valley of the Roses; field after field of beautiful blooms and perfumed air. To this day attar of roses is one of Bulgaria's major exports. Another exciting find was looking down on the walled city of Veliko Tarnovo, located in the valley of, and almost completely surrounded by, the Yantra river. We had time only for a flying visit but the ancient capital was a place to remember for the future. During the journey we saw that Bulgaria was a very rural society with many of the villages appearing to operate on a collective basis with pigs in one garden, ducks and chickens in another, while others would concentrate on maize, vegetables, tomatoes or melons but with the ubiquitous grapevine providing shade over most of the cottages verandas.

At that time very few of the roads were of motorway standard and on stretches of road running through mile after mile of orchards it seemed natural to follow the example of our fellow travellers and pull off to pick a bag full of lovely ripe apricots or peaches. We assumed in a communist country the produce from state run farms was there for the taking by the people? Happily, at one point we came upon what appeared to be a new motorway, so Collin got his foot down and we made good progress for about five miles until suddenly it just stopped – no signs, no barriers, just no road. This probably explained why there was no other traffic on it and why it was not on our road map. Our only choice was to backtrack until we found an exit that would hopefully take us on to Varna.

Although we could stay only for two nights, our first impressions of Varna were very positive, with attractive tree lined streets leading down to the "Golden Sands" of the Black Sea coast, separated from the town by the promenade and well-tended gardens, which contained some much more attractive and imaginative restaurants than the usual state-run establishments. This short visit was a big help in deciding it would be a good place to stay and take Dawn when, five years later, I was asked to return to Varna for another assignment.

Alcohol can become a big problem when working away from home for long periods and after a few good sessions in Russia where the evening ended in a sort of "black hole" I did try to moderate my intake somewhat, however, on one of my last days in Vratsa this proved to be a little tricky. The Bulgarian shift operators that Collin worked with invited us to join them for a farewell lunch in the countryside. It was all very convivial, sitting outside in the hot sun at a table laden with bread and olives, *shopska* salad, salami, eggs, endless bottles of beer and wine and a very fine home distilled *slivova* (plum brandy), which was the main protagonist in the many toasts that were proposed and drunk. The only problem was that every time I took a mouthful the alcohol fumes travelled up my sinus and closed my eye. I got quite worried that the man sitting opposite me would think I was winking at him. Strong stuff! By the time the party broke up I was staggering, and how Collin managed to drive back and dump me at my hotel is a mystery. Even more remarkable was, a few hours later, the telephone in my room woke me from a drunken stupor and Collin was in reception waiting to take me to another party to celebrate the wedding anniversary of one of our senior process engineers. I felt as though I sobered up with each beer I drank and it was a few years later before *slivova* became an acquired taste.

Fast forward five years and preparations were being made for the assignment to the plants nearing completion of construction in the Devnia Valley near Varna. Where practical, the chemist assigned to a particular site would, in the period prior to his deployment, be involved in the specification and procurement of the laboratory equipment required on the site and the preparation of specific analytical procedures for inclusion in the plant operating manuals. This was a good practice because in this instance the company were building ammonia, urea and ammonium sulphate plants, all of which were virtually new to me, so any opportunity to gain some familiarity before arriving on site as the "expert" was very helpful. Another flash of insight came when I realised how careful one had to be when writing procedures that would be translated into a foreign language. In the early days of chromatography, hotwire or thermistor detectors were used without any cut-out protection, so a proper flow of carrier gas to the detector was essential to prevent burn-out. All the way through the procedure I wrote "*check* the carrier gas flow"; now in most English dictionaries the definition of "check" is retard; restrain; stop, well before *verify*, which was what I intended, so after translation my procedure would probably be telling the operator to do exactly the opposite of what was wanted.

Since this was a large job requiring a big crew, married status assignments were being allowed (a stabilising influence?), so when I was asked to be ready to go in March for six months, having learnt from past experience, I assumed nine months was more likely and Dawn applied for five months' extended leave from her work as a medical microbiologist at the local hospital. This, we thought, would allow her to join me from May to September for a holiday on the Black Sea coast. As it turned out my departure was delayed until the end of April and after Dawn sweet-talked her boss into letting her go early we were able to travel together. This was a good thing as Dawn had never flown on her own before and the transit through Sofia Airport, where all the signs were in the Cyrillic alphabet and few people spoke English, was quite daunting in itself without a big pile of luggage to worry about.

49

We were housed on the third floor of a six storey, relatively new but typical communist era, cast concrete block of apartments on the outskirts of the City. There was a lift which we used to move our luggage but soon learnt to avoid as the power supply was… let's say erratic at best. The apartment had a large lounge, two bedrooms, toilet and shower which contained exposed, flimsy power sockets and a crude, highly dangerous washing machine, plus a kitchen fitted with fridge and cooker and an opening onto a balcony for airing the washing. On arrival, our first inspection of the kitchen showed a very large juicy snail sliming up the wall followed by another on the work top and yet another on the floor. They got thrown over the balcony but, very strange, three storeys up with no plant pots or anything like that on the balcony or in the apartment. On our first Saturday afternoon exploration of the town in search of likely food sources all was revealed. We came upon a stall in the open air market selling nothing but large juicy snails and by then I had learnt that John Willet, the construction piping supervisor, who had occupied the apartment before us, had a reputation for his culinary skills. A few of his last supper had escaped the pot!

Other vagaries about the apartment were that the water heater had to be regularly cleaned out before the deposited silt reached the emersion heater and tripped out the power supply, which necessitated a trip to the basement to replace the fuse wire. The worrying thing was some of the fuses on supplies to adjacent apartments had a nail in place of the fuse wire, presumably to prevent the need for regular visits to the basement? We also had a storage cupboard in the basement which I padlocked and forgot to open before we left; I wonder if it is still there, that is if the block has not burnt down due to a power overload?

To get us to work a coach would pull up outside the apartments at around 7.30 each morning for the twenty minute journey to the Devnia Valley, where a vast complex of new chemical plants had been built, with contributions from most of the European nations. We would all pile onto the coach, with the French "*bon jour-ing*" and hand shaking all round, the Italian's talking loudly and the British returning a monosyllabic grunt as they slumped in their seats, particularly so, if recovering from a heavier than usual session the night before.

My first introduction to the main ammonia plant laboratory came as a bit of shock as there was a large room with some benches in it but virtually no services of any kind run in or connected up. The laboratory manager, Madam

Hartinova (Dima, to use her diminutive, as I got to know her better), was, via the translator, very apologetic but said her senior management placed little importance on the readiness of the laboratory in the grand scheme of things. This, I came to realise later in my career, was an attitude prevalent on many jobs, unless the laboratory function and its ability to perform specific tasks was clearly identified on critical path networks during the planning stage. In this instance, after doing my homework and discussing priorities with our senior process operators, I went to my manager to prevail on his Bulgarian counterpart to get something done. A few days later, to Madam Hartinova's great delight and after which I could do no wrong, we were allocated a general handyman to get everything run in, piped up and working. As in Russia, all the laboratory staff were female so it was quite nice to have another male about the place and, although he spoke no English, we managed to become good friends. Each morning when I went in, after a Turkish coffee and perhaps a *slivova* or brandy to celebrate somebody's birthday or name day, "my girls", as they were known to the envy of the instrument and piping group, would have more equipment unpacked ready for set up and training to start. I do not know whether it was because I was more mature or that I had been married for nearly four years but I found it much easier to find the right balance when working with all women than I had in Russia five years earlier. Having said that – it was still tricky, later in the job, trying to deflect the attentions of the Bulgarian plant manager's wife, who was also a chemist, without causing offence, especially as she was using poor Dima as a translator go-between. There are times when appearing to be a bit slow on the uptake and not understanding the language can be a good thing.

As well as getting the laboratory itself up and running another key requirement on any new job was to walk around the plant with a set of Piping and Instrument Diagrams (P&IDs) to find out where all the sample points are located, are they in place? Are they accessible and are they fit for purpose? This may sound obvious but when taking samples from a gas or vapour stream at up to 900 °C and 300 barg pressure, getting a representative sample can be the most difficult part of the analytical procedure. In addition, there are components within the various gas streams around the plant(s) that are highly toxic, for example hydrogen sulphide, carbon monoxide and ammonia itself has an Immediately Dangerous to Life or Health (IDLH) level of 500 ppm (parts per million). That is the maximum concentration from which one could escape, within 30 minutes, without any irreversible health effects and since most sample points, gas or liquid, have to be blown down before the sample is taken, it is vital that this can be done in a safe manner; also, that the people taking the samples are fully aware of where and why the danger exists. I can still remember being shown round the plant by one of the "old hands" and being told "if you hear a hissing noise in this area do not wave your hand round a flange/connection to find where the leak is because at 300 barg it could just slice your fingers off." Good advice and well heeded. One sample I never got used to taking, without my stomach churning, was from a platform on top of the high pressure steam boilers, which involved squeezing round some very large relief valves. If the valves had lifted they would have blown like a jet engine at take off and would almost certainly have burst my ear drums.

So gradually the ammonia plant laboratory was commissioned, primarily monitoring the quality of water from the various water treatment plants for the boiler water, steam generation and cooling water systems, until we were prepared, with growing confidence, to tackle a key element associated with the ammonia plant coming on stream. High pressure steam is generated to drive the turbines used to compress the ammonia synthesis gases to the high pressures needed before conversion to ammonia in a catalytic convertor. For this to occur without damage to the turbine blades, the boiler system and all the stainless steel pipe used to carry the steam has to be thoroughly flushed through, degreased and then chemically cleaned to remove any rust flakes, weald bead and loose metal particles that would impinge on the turbine blades and damage them. This is a tricky procedure using hot, inhibited, citric acid (3%) at a controlled pH which is circulated for up to 24 hours and is monitored continuously until the concentration of dissolved iron (Fe) reaches a plateau, which indicates all the loose material has been removed and you are now just dissolving the boiler and pipework. Time for flushing and passivation, followed by a few hours' sleep!

To confirm that the chemical cleaning has been successful, high pressure steam is blasted along the feed line to the turbines onto highly polished stainless steel target plates, until no pit marks can be seen. A very noisy procedure, usually done at night, but one evening I was taking samples from inside a small hut housing an on-line analyser when the nearby target plate holder snapped off and the jet of steam smashed into exposed pipework and vessels with a mighty roar. Bits of lagging and cladding were flying all over the site and logic told me to stay in the hut but the noise and vibration were so great my body took over and I just opened the door and ran. No real damage done and after a few more days of blasting the cleaning was accepted as successful.

While progress was made at work, we were also settling in to our new life in Varna. As spring moved into summer, Dawn, with a group of the other wives, would spend their days working on their tans on the beaches at Golden Sands or Druzhba, while their men-folk sweated in the progressively more corrosive atmosphere that was the Devnia Valley. Unless a critical phase was taking place at work, I usually had Saturday afternoon and Sundays free to explore and enjoy a major holiday area along the Black Sea coast. As in Russia, getting a regular supply of reasonable quality food, even in the summer, was not easy and most Saturday afternoons we would catch the bus into town clutching our "just in cases" (string bags everybody carried just in case they saw something worth buying). For instance, potatoes disappeared from the shops for months before the new crop was ready. My brother, Roy, who was by then a publican, sent us a large, catering sized, tin of instant mash, which kept us going, but if you could not survive without a chip you had to eat in one of the local restaurants, which never seemed to run out. Good quality meat was another problem. Scrawny chickens were available in the not-so-supermarkets but other meat was sold by the kilo in plastic bags, usually just a mish-mash of chopped up bone and off cuts. Very egalitarian but not very appetizing. One day we spotted a whole leg of lamb and by suitable gestures indicated that we wanted to buy it. Before we could stop him, to our horror, the butcher took a clever to it and chopped it into bone-splintered lumps. Another oddity was at the meat shop just down the road from our apartment. All the meat was frozen and having learnt the word for beef (*teleshko*) we would order and wait while a suitable size lump was carved off with a hack saw. It was not until we got it home, thawed and cooked it, we would find out if it was prime fillet or stewing steak. I don't think it was our lack of language because it seemed to cost the same whatever it turned out to be.

Local knowledge, acquired through the expat grapevine, after a few months told us where to go for those little treats that could not be found in the normal shopping outlets. For example, one of the pharmacies usually had good home cured bacon hidden in its fridge for sale at a suitably inflated price and not always in western currency, which carried a big premium on the black market. Another good piece of advice from the girls at work was to stock up with sugar before the end of summer because when the fruit and vegetable preserve and bottling season approached sugar completely disappeared from the shops, not to reappear for at least six months. I think I was down to my last bag when supplies returned and that was a lot better than most.

It would be wrong to give the impression that we were totally dependent on local supply for our wellbeing because, as in Russia, we could place an order with a Danish company that on a monthly basis trucked in supplies of all manner of goods, paid for in western currency. I felt it was part of the experience of living behind the Iron Curtain to limit these purchases to essentials such as good bottles of gin and whisky but the range was extensive and after a few months the whole block would vibrate on a Saturday night to the lads playing their Black Sabbath or Deep Purple LP's through state of the art Bang and Olufsen speakers.

One of the advantages of living in Varna was that during the summer it was possible to book a package holiday from the UK to the Black Sea coastal resorts, flying direct to Varna. This meant Dawn's mother could fly out for a holiday visit with little or no hassle and after registering at her hotel spend most of the holiday living in our apartment. The other good thing was the half-board holiday was operated through a voucher system which could be used in any number of restaurants around the resorts, which added some good variety to places we visited during her stay. A fond memory for her was during a trip to the beach with the wives, they were stopped at the side of the road with a puncture, looking forlorn and apparently with no jack. A truck stopped, three burly Bulgarians got out and after a few gestures and grunts one of them squatted and heaved, lifting the flat tyre off the ground while another fitted the spare. With hardly a smile or a word spoken they were back in their truck, clutching a few packets of western cigarettes (better than currency) and were on their way.

Before Dawn had to return to work in the UK we managed to fit in a couple of long weekends. One down the Black Sea coast towards the Turkish border, stopping on the way at the very picturesque old towns of Nesebar, sited on a small peninsula jutting far out into the sea and finally on to Sozopol, an equally picturesque coastal town; probably founded by the Thracians, further developed by the Greeks and Romans, before reaching full prosperity during the time of the Second Bulgarian State, which was stopped by the invasion of the Ottoman Turks. In both towns the cobbled streets were lined with very attractive houses, built during the Bulgarian Revival period, with stone-built ground floors and projecting bay windows and oriels to the upper floor, clad with weathered wood facing. Most of the houses had big cellars on the ground floor for storing wine or, in days past, for drying fish. Strangely, for such an important port, little or no fresh fish could be obtained in Varna, so, on seeing the fishing boats drawn up in the harbour in Nesebar, one of the highlights of the trip was bringing back a big bag of freshly caught sprats for a late supper on our return to the apartment.

Another trip we made, in the company of friends from work, was to the previously mentioned Veliko Tarnovo, which I probably promoted as a place worthy of a visit. The town had been built on and cut into the steep slopes and cliff faces rising up from the gorge of the meandering Yantra River and looks quite splendid from above. The main city walls and fortress have been sympathetically restored and driving around the city is not a good option, as it is made up of a maze of narrow cobbled lanes winding around the hills or creeping up and down the rocks with the help of countless stone steps. To make the most of available space, the houses have been built on one, two, three or four levels, depending on location, and walking around is not for the faint hearted as you can soon become lost or breathless, or both.

We enjoyed our stay, enhanced by joining the Mayday parade and experiencing the holiday atmosphere but, a highlight, a recurrent theme, was finding a street trader selling *luks* (onions), which we had not seen in the shops in Varna for about two months. We bought all that he had and were very popular when we arrived back and distributed some of our find to the deprived back at the apartments. It's interesting, writing this now, forty years on, how little we appreciate being able to buy almost anything we want whenever we feel like it.

Enduring friendships were made during our time in Varna, both amongst colleagues at work and social contacts outside of work. Sue and Kate, who were teaching in one of the most prestigious schools in Varna, soon became regular visitors to the apartments to join in some convivial bridge evenings. Well, they were convivial until we all drank too much and the games became a little too competitive. An indication of the quality of the students at the school was that, in the final two years, all subjects were taught in a foreign language, hence Sue and Kate's presence. At the end of the summer term, Dawn and I were invited to attend an evening performance of "Winnie the Pooh" by the English speaking students. After the show, a lovely young lady called Julia (English & Russian) made herself known to us, thus starting a friendship that has lasted more than 40 years. In the first instance she would meet Dawn and acted as guide to show her the sights and places of interest in and around Varna. Even then, her English was excellent, so she did not need to practice but after Dawn returned to England we continued our budding friendship by meeting for an occasional meal and lively, in-depth discussions about a whole range of subjects. I can remember the first time I went to pick her up, at her parents' apartment on Karl Marx street, her father, also in excellent English, took me aside and said, 'she is very young you know'. I am sure Julia didn't think she was "very young" but I got the message and when we returned to Varna and met her father again in 2005 I am sure he trusted me a little more than he did then.

Another reason for an enduring friendship to start was when Roy Turner, the H&G deputy site manager, was taken ill and confined to his bed. It was now Dawn's turn to minister to the afflicted and she helped to keep him going with nutritious soups and egg custards, which seemed to be one of the few things that he could stomach. One result of surviving, or should that be surviving on, Dawn's cooking was to establish a friendship that is still strong.

One thing that did surprise me was the friendships that developed into romances that ended in marriage. Perhaps not so surprising when a large group of young and, in some cases not so young, men with money to spend and testosterone levels running high are thrust into the company of some very attractive young women for a period of two to three years. However, under the communist system, as most of the women spoke good English and were well educated, they were not allowed to marry or leave Bulgaria without some strict conditions being met. First, the man had to prove that he was *not* married and then the state required a fairly sizeable lump of money to be paid, in western currency, to compensate for the woman's education and loss to the state. As this, on average, took about six months, after the job had finished and the men were back in the UK, or on their next assignment, I was surprised that at least eleven of the men in this situation persisted and married their loved ones. I sometimes wonder how many of the marriages were successful. Of course, on the other hand, a number of existing marriages were, as seems to be inevitable, wrecked by affairs and separation. Not that all the men left, John Willet married Maria and was last seen sitting on the veranda of their cottage on the outskirts of Varna enjoying a cigarette and a very drinkable glass of Bulgarian red.

Dawn had to return to England to go back to work in September and as we had been allocated a two bedroom apartment a very likeable process engineer and experienced ammonia plant operator from Yugoslavia, named Antal Vig, was moved in with me. A period started soon after that when, for the first time in my life, I started to put on weight to the point where I had difficulty doing my trousers up. Can anybody remember the figure hugging flares of the 1970s? This probably had something to do with sharing cooking duties with two of the instrument lads from the flat next door. Most nights we would get back from work, put a chicken or some such in the oven, peel a large pot full of potatoes (now back in the shops) and then settle down to drink our way through a crate full of the local bottled beer, as an aperitif, while the food was cooking. This was really to avoid wasting the beer because, fine when fresh, it would go cloudy after just a few days if left.

Antal was one of those progressive, entrepreneurial characters that pop up now and then in the contracting world. Realising that life would remain fairly one-dimensional in the communist-controlled, state-run industry in Yugoslavia, he had managed to extricate himself by freelancing his ammonia plant operating skills with western contracting companies such as H&G. His family home was in Pancevo, just outside Belgrade but, with foresight, he managed to move his family out of danger to an apartment in the UK, before the bombing started in the Balkan conflict during the 1990s. He would turn up in the H&G London office periodically after that and I still have a 500,000,000,000 dinar note he gave me, issued during the rampant inflation that followed the collapse of the country's economy, at the end of the war. Some years later a Christmas card arrived with a photograph of a very nice looking villa he had bought for his retirement in Sveti Stefan, in what had then become Montenegro. A good place for a holiday I thought until a few years later he told me the Russian Mafia had moved in and "made him an offer he couldn't refuse". The last I heard from him and perhaps with retirement deferred, was that he was putting money into a new venture to build multi-storey beehives (met the designer on a plane). The web-site looked really impressive. Good luck Antal!

At work, more and more of the ammonia plant was brought on-line to the point where my application for leave over Christmas was turned down, as this would occur during a critical period that would include the reduction of the ammonia synthesis catalyst; a key event requiring maximum input from the chemistry department. I did not really believe that such an important event would take place over Christmas and the New Year but not wishing to cause too much friction asked for leave a month before Christmas, which was granted. This proved to be an excellent compromise because, with a lot of hard work by Dawn, we managed to get the whole family to our home for a big get-together/pre-Christmas party, which was a lovely way to see everybody before my return to Varna. As expected, nothing happened over Christmas and New Year, apart from lots of eating and drinking and some good parties. One of our crew drank so much he actually turned a sickly spearmint green before collapsing during the Christmas day dinner. Pouring water into him revived him enough to take a swing at the plant manager, so his employment did not last much longer. New Year turned out to be a good night with parties going on throughout the accommodation block and ended with a conga going from apartment to apartment as the occupants' country of origin reached midnight. I remember seeing the New Year in at least four times but it could have been more.

Back to reality and after a few more sleepless nights the ammonia synthesis catalyst was successfully reduced and ammonia was produced, somewhat later than scheduled but none the less, to everybody's delight, for the first time on 21 January 1974. Now, it might be assumed that my job was nearly over but in reality the plant still had to complete a guarantee test to show it could produce its rated capacity of 1000 tonnes per day of ammonia and this was far from easy for a number of reasons. First, it was expensive with regard to raw material costs and second, there was limited ammonia storage capacity, which meant that other plants on the complex that required ammonia as a feedstock had to be built, commissioned and ready for operation. A practical and logistics nightmare as, in the case of the ammonium nitrate plant, it also required the nitric acid plant to be up and running and the ammonium sulphate plant, also built by H&G, required the sulphuric acid plant to be producing. Since most of the other plants were the responsibility of different companies, each with their own agenda, it was not an easy prospect.

In fact my work load increased considerably at that point because I now had to spend more time in the ammonium sulphate plant laboratory, which until then had been more or less ticking over. The women in the lab were all relatively young and inexperienced as far as an industrial chemistry laboratory was concerned, mostly coming straight from university and the chief chemist, Lily Ivanova (we still exchange Christmas and birthday cards), was only twenty, so a busy period. It was made particularly difficult as, with the balance of the component chemicals in the plant being all wrong during the first month, I had to constantly recalculate and rewrite a number of our standard analytical procedures before the women could perform the required analysis. One woman in particular could not seem to see the need to keep changing the procedures and when I asked her why she said, 'well I am a naval architect, not a chemist, so why should I worry about your stinking plant?' Or words to that effect. Ah well, the good old communist system at work again! About one thing she was right, it was stinking. Because the component balance was wrong a lot of solutions from the plant were being dumped into waste gullies that ran down the centre of the building. Large extractor fans sucked the fumes to the outside of the building. Unfortunately the laboratory air conditioning intakes were right next to the extractor fan outlets. As you walked into the laboratory your eyes started to stream and on some days it was almost impossible to breathe. I measured the concentration of ammonia at 300 ppm on one occasion and at that point told the women they should walk out and refuse to work in such conditions. They said that was not possible, so I made a formal complaint to my manager but it did not help a great deal so we kept going as best we could until the plant settled down and we made ammonium sulphate instead of throwing it down the drain. Now, I do sometimes wonder what triggered my non-Hodgkin's lymphoma in later life?

The whole Devnia Valley now became a bit of a health risk because as more and more of the plants came on stream the valley would fill with a mix of noxious fumes. Some mornings as the bus dropped down into the valley a layer of SO_2 laden air would catch in the throat and make your eyes water and at others a dense white fog would envelope everything as ammonia from our plant mixed with chlorine from a plant further down the valley. At least they neutralised each other to some extent!

It was at about this time that the commissioning department manager, Mr Jack Hawes made one of his periodic visits to the site to resolve any existing or future staffing problems. On most sites there is nearly always one group who can be guaranteed to be at the forefront of any scams or dodges that are going on and at Varna it was part of the instrument team, affectionately known as "the animals". A notice went round informing us that our presence was requested at 13.00 hrs in the lunch room. After a few pleasantries Mr Hawes, sucking on his pipe, said, 'Now lads, perhaps somebody can tell me how some of you are managing to put more local currency into the site fund each month than you receive as a local living allowance.' He knew full well of course that sterling could be exchanged on the black market at a much better rate (almost double) than the official rate that the company used to credit our accounts. Nobody volunteered to tell him but it was, of course, illegal and he made it clear it had to stop, or a very welcome perk would no longer be available to any of us.

Communication was not much easier from Bulgaria than it had been from Russia, so I was still writing a good number of letters each month and as I had no telephone in the apartment, at least once a week I would go to the main post office in Varna to book a call to speak to Dawn on a pre-arranged day and time. At the appointed hour it made sense to be at the post office at least half an hour early and be prepared for a long wait before being directed to one of the booths when the call was put through. A small advantage over the calls made from Russia before we were married was a modicum more privacy, although we still assumed, rightly or wrongly, that the call would be monitored and that we could, most of the time, have a two way conversation but still not an easy way to sustain a marriage.

When the chill winds of winter had passed on and with spring in the air, at the beginning of March, Dawn came out for a flying visit because, apart from my week at home before Christmas, we had been apart for six months and things were getting a little strained. Although lovely to be together again I think the short visit helped only to emphasise the separation and so, after completing a twelve month tour, I applied to leave the site and return to the Billericay Laboratory. This request was not received well by the H& G site management team, as we still had the Guarantee Tests to complete, or by the client because "my girls" in the laboratories seemed to be reluctant to let me go. The next few weeks were very stressful, certainly enough to give me a very stiff neck, until I made the decision to quit if my request was not agreed to. Fortunately management said that was not at all necessary and I could leave, without losing my completion bonus, as soon as a replacement was found. As it turned out I made the right decision because Malcolm Law, who came out to replace me, was on site for a further twelve months, before the job was wound up.

Once I knew that Malcolm would be arriving towards the end of April, life became even more hectic. At work, making the best preparations that I could for handover to Malcolm, as I knew ammonia, ammonium sulphate plants and site work in general was a new experience for him, as well as leaving Dima and Lily with any books or information that would make their jobs a bit easier and perhaps give them the confidence to take on the system a bit more. It was during one of our chats that Dima asked what I thought was a strange question; she said, 'How is it you English men are always confident that you are right?' Now this certainly was not true as, particularly during the first six months, I had spent many hours puzzling over how to proceed. She then qualified the remark by saying, 'You must realise that for most of the past two hundred years we have been a subject-people, firstly under the Turks, then the German occupation and finally Russia and the communist system; a system that punished failure and did little to encourage individual enterprise.' It made me realise there were some benefits in following in the wake of the British Empire.

It was also hectic at the personal level with parties to organise to bid farewell to colleagues and new friends that had been made during a memorable year as well as trying to organise my departure or more specifically what to pack and what to leave behind – surprising how much stuff you can acquire in a year. In the end I limited myself to an extra 20 kg, fitted into a large trunk which was no longer needed by our site secretary. I also had a present to buy and a party to go to as Lily had invited me to her 21st birthday party on the 14th April, which stayed in my memory for another food-related reason. Her parents, who still lived in the countryside, brought in a large earthenware pot of roast lamb. It was delicious, probably the best meat I had tasted during the whole of my time in Bulgaria and certainly surpassed some of the local delicacies, such as "nervous meatballs", an English description on the menu of one of our favourite restaurants that always made me smile.

I left Bulgaria on the 3rd May 1974. It was quite an emotional parting as Dima and a few of the other girls from work, including big Dorri and little Dorri, came to see me off and I ended up with another bag full of presents to carry. I was not too worried about paying for excess baggage as I had saved a wad of non-convertible local currency to pay for it, which I could reclaim, via my expenses, in sterling. So, when I got to the check-in desk and was simply waved away without any demand being made for payment for my excess I was a bit nonplussed, as it was illegal to take my wad out of the country. In the end I stuck it an envelope with a note to give it to a worthy cause and posted it back to site. They must have thought I was worthy because it was paid into the site fund and I got a credit in sterling. As a result of it being the first day back to work after the May Day holiday, when I got onto the plane I found there were only five other people travelling which explained why they were not concerned about excess baggage. The six of us soon became acquainted and with the willing compliance of the cabin crew a very convivial flight was had by all. A very enjoyable return to England, only to be ruined when I arrived at Heathrow to find an all-out transport strike taking place; frustration was not the word for it! I eventually managed to contact my elder brother who very kindly came to pick me up and take me home. You did not get the unions calling out the brothers to go on strike in Bulgaria!

3.6 Mangalore – India – Love it or hate it

In our case it was love, but more of that later. My first flight to India was quite eventful in its own right. Heading towards the boarding gates at Heathrow for my Air India flight to Bombay, via Lebanon, a tall bearded fellow strode past me followed by a gaggle of cameramen rushing to keep up. It was July 1975, and once airborne and settled down in economy with my newspaper, I realised from the photos and news story, that I was sharing the flight with Chris Bonington and a good number of his team who were soon to make the first successful attempt to climb Mount Everest's huge Southwest Face. That was not all, while in the transit lounge at Beirut Airport we heard a number of loud explosions from outside the building. It was the start of the civil war and ours was one of the last commercial flights to pass through Lebanese air space for more than fifteen years.

My first experience of India was arrival in Bombay in the middle of the monsoon season to find the airport hotel, where I was staying for one night, completely surrounded by flooded streets. The taxi driver negotiated the floods without too much trouble and in the morning after visiting the Indian Office, established in 1962, for an introduction and to drop off some documents, it was back to the airport for the internal flight to Mangalore. Coming in to land was quite exciting as the airport and runway looked as though it had been constructed by slicing a large red sandstone hill in half to give a flat surface raised above the surrounding countryside, but not much margin for error or overshoot, especially in the monsoon rains.

To accommodate the expat workforce, the company had taken over the Summer Sands Beach Resort at Ullal, in Karnataka state, about 13 km south of Mangalore. Blocks of mainly two bedroom bungalows, built around a swimming pool and a stand of coconut palms away from the beach and the Arabian Sea. It was an exotic location, situated in a relatively prosperous part of India, with two rice crops a year, coconuts in plenty and fish from the sea that could be caught by using large drag nets directly from the beach. So first impressions were good with no signs of the poverty or horrible stench from the slum dwellings that greet you on the drive from Bombay Airport into the centre of that city. Another advantage was being in a region with the best education record in India, a greater than 85% literacy rate.

The plants being built by H&G and now nearing construction completion were, as in Bulgaria, an ammonia plant and also a urea plant, so not altogether a new experience for me. Another good thing was that many of the crew were the same people that I had been working with in Bulgaria, which made settling into a new job so much easier. As my first visit was to be of short duration, to assess the state of readiness of the laboratories for commissioning to start, I shared a bungalow with Roy Turner, who was already well-established and living the life of the sahib, with his own cook, cleaning girl and driver.

Walking into the ammonia plant laboratory on my first morning was a pleasant surprise because, in contrast to Bulgaria, it appeared to be well equipped with most of the services connected and fully functional. After being introduced to and shown round by Mr Satanayarana, the chief chemist, I was fairly confident I would not have to worry too much about the wet chemical analytical procedures and could concentrate on setting up the chromatography systems, sampling techniques and the program priorities when I returned in a few months time. Before I left I did visit the piping group to "borrow" some surplus lengths of stainless steel pipe, with fittings, to make up portable cooling coils, which always seemed to be in short supply, once we were ready to start taking samples.

After two weeks, and still in the middle of the monsoon rains, I pulled my suitcase from the top of the wardrobe to pack for my return journey, only to find it had grown a carpet of green mould. A belated good tip was to suspend a light bulb inside the wardrobe, which goes someway to stopping your clothes going mouldy as well. I was dropped at the airport in good time to catch the flight to Bombay for the late evening flight to the UK. Unfortunately the incoming flight was delayed because of the monsoon rains and arrived at Mangalore about three hours late, where it made a very heavy landing. A cheery voice announced there would be a further delay for inspections to be made! Mangalore was a small airport with no air conditioning and little in the way of facilities, so by then I was not only sweating in the

100% humidity but also sweating on making my connecting flight back to England. I was not re-assured when I walked outside to try and find some breeze to see a man in shorts and wellington boots holding an umbrella to one side while using a torch to peer at the under-carriage of the plane. Inspection done; a short while later the announcement was made that we should prepare for boarding. What to do – risk the journey with little hope of making my connection or try again another day. In the end I decided to keep moving while I could and duly arrived at Bombay too late for the London flight which meant another hour or two trying to book another flight before searching for a hotel room. The joys of international travel become somewhat blunted at two o'clock in the morning and I am just glad the company was paying for it. On the plus side, a late evening flight the next day meant that after a few hours sleep I had the chance to see something of Bombay, which otherwise would not have been possible. Another reason for returning home without too much delay was my being scheduled to go to Porto Marghera in Italy for one of the Permalene additive trials and following that to Maastricht in Holland for some much needed training associated with the urea plant being built in India, under license to the Dutch company Stamicarbon.

Urea: NH_2CONH_2, is made by combining, under pressure, liquid ammonia and liquid carbon dioxide, a by-product of the ammonia synthesis process. The final product was made in a solid pellet form by dropping the hot, liquid urea through prill heads down a tall cylindrical concrete tower, where the droplets cooled and solidified into easily transportable pellets. Stamicarbon were providing all the required analytical procedures and although the chemistry was not so difficult, the physical nature of the process meant some expert guidance was needed with sampling techniques and good safe practice around the plant.

I remember Maastricht as having a quaint city centre with cobbled streets, some good bars and a mainstream cinema showing what I thought at the time were some very blue movies.

Back home some serious decisions had to be made. At that time, Dawn was a member of the Theosophical Society, formed in 1875 by a Madam H P Blavatsky "to encourage the study of comparative religion, philosophy and science". The Society's headquarters were at Adyar, near Madras in India, and partly as a consequence of reading about the country and its religions and studying the Society's literature, Dawn was very keen to come with me on my next visit. She had already established that she would be granted another five months' unpaid extended leave from work but, to avoid Indian Tax complications, I was being sent out on a tourist visa, with no married status benefits. I asked the company if they would agree to Dawn coming with me, if we paid for her air fare. They said yes and that they would make a bungalow on the Ullal site available to us, so after arranging her visa, jabs and antimalarial tablets amongst a few hundred other preparations we were almost ready for our next big adventure.

The call came in early November and as the plane descended towards Bombay the evocative smell of a million cow pat fires rose up to greet us. We have been back a few times since and it is always the same. Is there any other country in the world that has its own "perfume"?

I was soon hard at work and Dawn was establishing her credentials to becoming a proper memsahib by relaxing round the pool all day with some of the other wives, while staff from the Little Hut – the on-site restaurant – kept them hydrated with fresh lime sodas or fresh coconut milk. It is possible a few gin and tonics were taken but that was only to keep up the quinine levels and not often before the sun sank below the yard arm. Although I can remember a photograph of one of the women floating in the pool with a beer wedged between her fairly substantial frontage.

As I was meant to be on a relatively short-term assignment we did not take on a cook like most of the other families, so Dawn did spend some of her time being driven into Mangalore by Ragi (Mr A Raghuveer, our excellent driver, who we shared with one other family) to visit the market and other stores for the essentials or any more exotic items that might catch her eye. I think she enjoyed it because Ragi would escort her round the shops and then carry her brown paper packages (carrier bags were at a premium) back to the car before driving her to the ice cream parlour for a cooling milk shake. Actually, brown paper was an essential if you were prepared to brave the flies and "shite" hawks at the outdoor meat market, where bloody purchases were just as likely to be slapped into your hand if you had nothing to wrap them in.

As with most jobs, one of the priorities was to get all the water treatment systems up and running. A big problem was discovered when cooling water circulation was started through the heat exchangers, or I should say circulation was attempted. The local cockroach population had decided the tube bundles were a desirable residence *par excellence* and occupation was total, flow minimal. A big delay resulted while end plates were taken off and the tubes rodded out or jet blasted to free them of unwanted guests.

This indirectly led to another problem; the local water was very soft and was left in the pipework for longer than anticipated, without any evaporation to increase the salt(s) content and therefore the hardness level. Soft water can be quite corrosive to carbon steel pipes and before long pin-hole leaks were appearing all over the place. I was soon reading any information available on heat exchanger operation and the analysis required to make use of Ryznar or Langelier Index charts (something new to me) to see if the dosing of the circulating cooling water was effective in making the water less corrosive so the ammonia plant start-up could be continued without further delay.

As it turned out this hope was short lived because when the reformer was fired up a lot of the refractory brickwork collapsed, resulting in a complete shutdown while the cause was ascertained and repairs were made. I believe, as far as I was concerned, this caused management some embarrassment since, had I not paid for Dawn to join me, I would have been sent home to preserve the available time in the country on my tourist visa, as well as getting me off the client's books. A compromise was reached by asking if I would like to take some holiday, which I readily accepted, as it gave us the chance to see so much more of India than otherwise would have been possible.

Armed with our Fodor's Guide to India, a week of frantic planning then started. We found we could purchase an Indian Airlines Internal "Run-Around" ticket for 200 US dollars, the only restriction being we could not repeat the same journey. In the two weeks I could be away from work we had a few definite objectives: visit a game reserve, Delhi; Agra, the Kama Sutra in stone at Khajuraho and visit the Theosophical Society's headquarters just outside Madras, where big celebrations were underway for their centenary year. As well as that we would be away over Christmas which we did not want to celebrate in an airport lounge. Our first thought was a Kashmir houseboat but as this was a long way north, with the possibility of getting stuck due to severe winter weather conditions, local knowledge persuaded us the Gymkhana Club at Wellington, near "Snooty Ooty" (Ootacamund, apparently where the game of snooker was devised) in the Nilgiri hills in central Southern India would be a much better option. We got confirmation of all our selected flights on the Friday, for take off the next day to Bombay, where an overnight stop was needed before an early morning flight to Jaipur and the start of the holiday proper. I just had time to sit down at work, with our office manager, to select hotels at each of our stops and send off telexes to reserve accommodation and at his suggestion, book a tourist taxi to meet us at Jaipur Airport for the onward journey to the Sariska Game Reserve, via the Amber Palace. The only confirmation I received before leaving work was from the hotel at Agra, so we set off the next day with some trepidation as to when and where we would end up.

Our first experience was to set a pattern of good fortune or good service and efficiency that continued for most of the rest of the holiday. Walking out of Jaipur Airport at 8.30am we were met by our driver, holding a board with Mr LODGE clearly visible, who led us to his trusty "Ambassador" before whisking us into town to pick up the packed lunch he had thoughtfully ordered for us. By 10am we were well on the road to Amber, the ancient capital of Jaipur State and the stunning Palace, a superb example of 16th century Rajput architecture, which was our first stopping point. We chose to walk up to the Fort/Palace rather than pay a small fortune to ride on an elephant but it was still a pleasure to walk beside the great beasts topped by their glittering *howdahs*. Inside it was cool white marble with intricate lattice-work galleries and beautiful mosaics, leading out to the ramparts with fine views over the lake and plains below, patrolled by the circling Egyptian vultures. We were back on the road in time to reach the game reserve at Sariska, our overnight stop, in time for a late tiffin on the lawns, surrounded by wild peacocks, strutting their stuff.

The accommodation bungalows were basic but clean and tidy and after a tasty curry supper we were picked up in a Land Rover for a night drive round the reserve. I was a bit surprised when we stopped to have a rather muddy buffalo calf bundled into the back on top of our feet and assumed it was being moved to another part of the park. It was only after we were driven up to a clearing where the remains of a tethered goat were visible in the spot light that I began to realise that our calf was to be used as bait. Any feelings of guilt were quickly banished when a magnificent tiger came out of the jungle and sauntered up the spot light beam towards us. What a wonderful sight and a picture that is embedded in my memory and the bonus was, the buffalo calf came on the rest of the tour with us and ended up back where he started, in his pen at the camp. Sad to say, by 2005 tigers no longer existed in Sariska, mainly due to poaching to satisfy the Chinese market for the perceived medicinal benefits from their body parts. Happily they have been successfully reintroduced and are now multiplying under a better protection regime.

The next day our driver took us on a daylight tour, to see a different range of wildlife, before returning us to Jaipur for an evening flight to Delhi.

Having seen a tiger the night before I was quite surprised at how many local people were walking along the roads through the reserve, the women very obvious in their colourful saris, going about their business, with little or no protection, other than a stick or a hoe. I suppose fat sambar (local deer) are preferable to skinny Indians. On reaching Jaipur we were given a rapid tour of the main attractions, in particular the curious sculptures in Jantar Mantar, which is, in fact, a monumental,18th century observatory and the five-story pink facade of The Palace of the Winds overlooking the main street of the old city, from which the ladies of the royal court could be nosy without being seen. Jaipur is known as the Pink City for a good reason.

Arriving in Delhi early evening, we had two nights and nearly two full days to explore before an evening flight to Agra. But even in December, it can be an exhausting experience coping with the constant noise and hustle and bustle of packed streets, clogged roads and polluted atmosphere. We started by going to Connaught Place and the relative calm of Lutyens' spaciously laid out New Delhi, from where we could walk round without too much fear of getting hopelessly lost. One lasting memory was almost any available piece of grass or baked earth being occupied by little lads or, in some cases, not so little lads playing cricket using a miscellany of cobbled together equipment. This was followed by a, have no fear, cycle rickshaw ride into the labyrinth that is Old Delhi. Here we ventured into the bazaar and practiced fairly newly acquired skills at avoiding the blandishments of stall holders to buy. I do not remember being offered an elephant but I am sure it could have been found without too much effort. This was followed by a visit to the Red Fort and the mighty *Jama Masjid*, the largest mosque in India, completed by Shah Jahan in 1658 and although not as exquisitely beautiful as the *Taj Mahal* – the mausoleum built for his beloved wife Mumtaz Mahal – the mosque is still a wonderful tribute to the skill of Mughal architects, builders and craftsmen.

Our evening flight to Agra was delayed somewhat, so we did not arrive at our hotel until eleven o'clock, only to be told at reception no rooms were available. This was not good news, as the word at the airport was that there was a convention taking place in Agra and all the hotels were full. I thankfully produced the only telex I had received before leaving Mangalore, showing a confirmed reservation. "Very sorry Sahib, no rooms available". I then had a touch of inspiration and turned the register round on the reception desk, where it clearly showed our names had been entered but crossed out. I made it quite clear we were not going out onto the streets of Agra at nearly midnight and they had to find us somewhere to stay. We ended up on camp beds in an unused bar room, which at least had its own attached toilet and washroom – sanctuary after an extra long day.

The next morning, after a lazy start and a failed attempt to get us moved into a better room, we set out to gain our own impression of one of the seven wonders of the modern world, the *Taj Mahal*. To access through the grand red sandstone gateway meant running a gauntlet through the hawkers and hustlers outside the main entrance but the view of the *Taj* framed through the gateway was stunning and well worth the effort. Once inside, in the relative calm, it was time to absorb the true beauty and symmetry of the white marble multi-domed tomb, which shimmers in the waters of its reflecting watercourse leading from the gate, through ornamental gardens, to the tomb entrance. Up close, both its external and internal surfaces are completely covered with exquisite inlaid designs executed in some thirty-five varieties of semi-precious stones, which thankfully have not been defaced by graffiti or people scratching their initials into the surface in the hope of recording their own immortality. As a reminder of our visit I have just lifted my coffee cup from a marble coaster inlaid with a pretty floral design of just five stones.

From the *Taj* we made our way to the massive red sandstone Agra Fort, standing on the bank of the Yamuna River and once there, Dawn, who by then was not feeling very well, left me to explore on my own while she sat in the shade in one of the inner courtyards. The thing I most remember was visiting the small tower where Shah Jahan was deposed and imprisoned by his son Aurangzeb for the last seven years of his life, possibly for over-spending on extravagant building projects. The view through the small window in the tower was very poignant as it framed the *Taj Mahal* in the distance across the river and where, following his death, Shah Jahan was laid to rest with his beloved wife.

That night we had intended to visit the *Taj* by the light of the full moon – a special treat – but unfortunately Dawn had succumbed to the dreaded Delhi belly and could not move more than a few feet away from the bathroom so I went on my own. I spent that night and the next day dosing her with Imodium, trying to keep her fluid levels up and praying she would be recovered enough to make the early evening flight to Khajuraho, our next destination.

The Temples of Khajuraho
Above, half seen, in the gloom,
Strange works of a long dead people loom,
What did they mean to those who now are dust,
These rioting figures of love and lust?

from the "The Garden of Kama"
by Adela Florence Nicolson

Very fortunately, Dawn, although still feeling very delicate, was well enough to travel so we made it to the oasis of calm and tranquillity, in modern day India, that is Khajuraho. The magnificently carved and ornamented temples, some 85 domed structures standing on high platforms, are dedicated to and are a home to God in all his Hindu forms and incarnations. For the most part they were all built by the Chandella kings between 950 and 1050 AD but the surprising thing is they chose a site for their new religious and political capital that to this day has remained a complete rural backwater. It was probably the area's remote nothingness that saved the temples from destruction by the Moslem invaders and it certainly helped Dawn's recovery to be able to take a peaceful stroll round a rural village that probably looks much the same as it did 1000 years ago. One-room mud brick houses, women in colourful saris sweeping their yards… and I can still picture the donkey plodding round in circles to draw water from the well to irrigate the meagre crops.

We did, of course, visit a number of the temples to gaze in wonder at the skill required from what must have been thousands of dedicated craftsmen. All forms of life were depicted; from the hunt, to feasting, music and dance, but the sensuous, voluptuous forms engaged in the most intimate and extraordinarily varied portrayals of sexual intercourse make the temples truly a Kama Sutra in stone. I assume that the belief was that religious enlightenment could be attained through sexual ecstasy; a view probably somewhat alien to most people brought up in the Christian or Moslem faith, however, it did seem to be a popular venue for honeymoon couples and I suspect, with a better chance of success than a pre-wedding talk by the vicar.

We left Khajuraho for Madras where I had, for a different experience and a room for about half the usual price, booked us into a non-European style hotel. We had a very spacious suite, with bedroom and large bathroom as well as a lounge area. The menu was vegetarian only and as we did not have much idea what most of the dishes were and you could not order a "number

5 or number 8" but had to select individual components to make up a meal, our supper was not a total success. In the morning, after being given some advice at reception, we skipped breakfast and took a taxi to Simpsons, a grand emporium, left almost unchanged since the days of the British Raj, that sold almost everything that one could desire but best of all in the basement restaurant, bacon, eggs, sausage, baked beans and fried bread. Heaven, and the first meal that Dawn had enjoyed in the last five days. Fortified, we found a taxi to take us to the Theosophical Society's headquarters at Adyar, another oasis of tranquillity set in beautiful grounds, where we had a most memorable day. My first memory is sitting under an enormous and venerable banyan tree while surrounded by people meditating in the footsteps of the Lord Buddha. However, the pinnacle of our day came when, without any foreknowledge, we were able to attend an address by the Dalai Lama speaking on the occasion of the Society's centenary year celebration. After the Chinese invasion and annexation of Tibet, the Dalai Lama and many of his people were given sanctuary near to Dharamsala in the foothills of the Himalayas, in Himachal Pradesh, where the Tibetan Government in Exile is still based. He addressed a devoted and enthusiastic audience – many were Tibetan by their appearance – in a large marquee and very cleverly, I thought, emphasised his key points by suddenly speaking in English, the *lingua franca* of most of the audience, rather than using the translator.

With Christmas fast approaching it was time to head for the Nilgiri (blue) hills, which could be reached by flying to Coimbatore, a vast urban sprawl on the plains at their base and then taking a bus, train or taxi up to the hill stations. I had no pre-planned way of doing this and was going to play it by ear at the airport and it was "ear" that did the trick. While waiting for our luggage, I heard a very English voice discussing the drive up to Ooty, so rather cheekily asked him for advice as to the best way of getting to the Gymkhana Club at Wellington. After establishing that we didn't have a mountain of luggage, rather reluctantly I think but in the spirit of Christmas, he offered us a lift in his Land Rover. What luck!

The Gymkhana Club was a splendid reminder of a bygone era and, although all of the staff and most of the members were now Indian, I imagine the standards were much the same during the days of the Raj. The clubhouse was all polished wood, with hunting trophies looking down from around the walls. The staff still wore white gloves in the billiards and snooker room and guests were expected to dress appropriately for dinner, although now relaxed to smart casual from formal. We were housed in one of many small bungalows that surrounded the clubhouse and were allotted a steward to look after us. Our steward was in his late fifties and had started working at the club as a ball boy on the tennis courts some fifty years before and in that time had served minor royalty, ambassadors, maharajas and more than one major general, so very interesting to talk to if you wanted to learn something of India's recent history.

It was after being shown round the club that we realised, to our horror, that we were in a Dry State and there was no bar serving alcoholic beverages, which, approaching Christmas, was a very worrying oversight. It was possible for individual guests to apply for a liquor licence but so close to Christmas it was not going to be possible to complete all the formalities, so two or three sober evenings appeared to be in the offing.

Before leaving on our trip I had been given a name and contact number for a company, based in Coonoor, that was supplying the site with a very passable equivalent to an English cheddar cheese and told that I could expect a warm welcome if I made contact. India was not a country renowned for its cheeses and years earlier the wife of one of the tea plantation managers, desperate for a piece of decent cheese, started to make her own and as her expertise and fame spread, started a small business. When her husband died she stayed on for a number of years running the business, after taking on Colonel Bedi as her managing director, who subsequently bought her out when she retired to Frinton or Cheltenham. Contacting Colonel Bedi proved to be an excellent idea as he invited us to his home where he and his wife did indeed give us a very warm welcome. We spent Christmas Eve sitting round a roaring log fire (there could be frosts at night at that altitude), drinking a fine brandy and putting the world to rights. He also took pity on our predicament and we left clutching a bottle of brandy, so although we ate our Christmas dinner at the club without any wine or beer accompaniment, it was not altogether an alcohol free period.

As well as being surrounded by tea plantations and eucalyptus trees the club's immediate surround was the almost obligatory cricket ground, which expanded into a golf course. At that time my main sports were hockey, tennis and badminton but when the opportunity presented itself I would try my hand at golf. It was not a problem to hire clubs, etc., so on a fine sunny morning I set off with the obligatory caddy and, as I understood it, an *aggy-wallah*, a young boy who raced ahead of us to spot my ball and, in my opinion, a very worthwhile addition to the enjoyment of my game. The caddy gave me some useful tips about which club to take to rescue my ball from some of the difficult situations it found itself in but after a few holes I realised something odd was happening. On some of my better shots I would drive off to see, in the distance, my ball bouncing under a small bush or into the semi rough, only to find when I reached it, that it was miraculously sitting on a small tuft of sand on the edge of the fairway. I suggested to the *aggy-wallah* that, although he had my best interests at heart, he should not really be doing this. He looked at me in all innocence and said 'winter rules sahib'. What more can be said, I had one of my better rounds of golf and he received a good tip!

Sitting on the veranda of our bungalow taking afternoon tea and cakes was not always as peaceful as it might have been. We never saw the person occupying the bungalow two doors along, just heard him yelling, cursing and swearing in a plummy English accent. I should think completely gaga but still being looked after by a faithful but threadbare retainer, probably his batman, who would come out a few minutes later and slump into a chair muttering to himself. Poor man!

The return journey down to the plains, from Wellington to Mettupalayam, located some 5600 feet up in the Nilgiri Hills, was an unexpected but wonderful experience which sometimes comes your way out of the blue (no pun intended). We managed to book tickets on the Blue Mountain Railway, a miniature train, comprising three or four open wooden carriages, lowered rather than pulled down the mountain by a tiny bright blue "Thomas the Tank Engine" steam locomotive. In places the descent is so steep the line has a toothed central rail which the locomotive can lock onto via a manually operated cog mechanism. The journey offers some wonderful views as it winds down the mountain and, if you are feeling really adventurous, passing through some of the villages, you could hop off at one corner, buy a bunch of bananas and hop back on at the next corner all without the train stopping. The train has been used as a location set in the film *A Passage to India* and on at least one television programme about *Great Railways of the World*.

Our experience once reaching Coimbatore again was not quite so wonderful. Rather than wasting valuable time flying up to Bombay and then back to Mangalore we opted for an overnight sleeper train across the western Gats direct to Mangalore. Our plan had been to leave our luggage at the station, take a leisurely stroll into town for some sightseeing and a meal before the journey. Coimbatore was a large industrialised city that seemed to have outgrown its services and some of its sights were far from pleasant. Beggars without legs propelling themselves along the road on cut off rubber tyres, channels down each side of the road that were little better than open sewers, flies, filth and poverty. We had no appetite for food in such a place so returned to the station and its buffet. We then faced a dilemma; three or four hours to wait but with the only comfortable seating in the Ladies' or Gentlemen's Waiting Rooms. Dawn did not want to be left on her own, so I took her with me into the Gentlemen's, which did not seem to cause undue offence, so there we stayed. We gained some insight into Indian travel practices, when about half an hour before the train was due a very imposing Sikh gentleman got his bearer to bring in his suitcase, whereupon, he very discreetly, put on a fetching pair of pink pyjamas before walking to the train for his overnight journey. We just slummed it in our day clothes!

Our fare included a bed-roll each, which we collected before boarding and two bunk beds in a four-berth carriage. After introductions were completed with our fellow passengers and we had braved a trip to the toilet and wash-room, I took the top bunk and we were soon settled in for a good night's sleep as we clickityclacked back to Mangalore. Just as it was getting light I was shocked into wakefulness when I heard Dawn gasping 'what's happened to my face?' Most Indian trains do not have glass in the carriage windows, instead they have metal bars and a metal mesh that lets air in but stops people poking an arm through and nicking things. Dawn had spent the night with her face next to the window and by morning it was coated in a fine clinker-like soot layer that felt like sandpaper when she touched it (one of the forgotten delights of stream travel). A beauty pack it was not but after a trip to the wash room and she found she was not permanently scarred, equanimity was restored, although I do not think she could understand why I found it so amusing.

We got back to Ullal after a wonderful trip that I found most remarkable in that, with very little time to plan, everything had worked so well and not an App needed anywhere. Even better, we got back in time for the New Years Eve party held in the club house and the next day the company had organised to take the staff – ex-pats and Indian – on a picnic to St Mary's, an uninhabited island visited by Vasco da Gama on his way to India, off the coast from Mangalore. The trip was made in one of the large working *dhows* that plied its trade up and down the coast and I thought for many years afterwards what a terrific holiday it would make to hire boat and crew to sail all the way down and round the southern tip of India. Probably a bit past it now as the facilities would have been basic to say the least. A short time was spent at the Mangalore dockside while our Indian colleagues organised the loading of all the essentials, which included multiple hampers of goodies to eat and ice boxes packed with drinks, both alcoholic and non alcoholic, then people were slotted into the remaining spaces. Soon we were sailing away on a glorious sunny morning, some with a smile and others with a queasy apprehension, depending on how well one had partied the night before. I still remember coming into the island and seeing Sean Slinger, our commissioning manager Bert's young son, (released from boarding school for the Christmas holidays) perform a perfect swallow dive off the prow of the *dhow* and swim into shore. The island was beautiful, on one side coconut palms leading down to golden sands and the calm blue waters of a tropical lagoon and, surprise, surprise, ten minutes walk away on the other side of the island, the waves were crashing in from the Arabian Sea over an array of hexagonal basalt columns, just like the Giants Causeway. Very exciting and certainly a wonder of nature I had never seen before. I wonder if the Indian Tourist board has made the most of such a feature or whether the island still retains its isolated tranquillity?

With our enforced holiday, Christmas and New Year over, it was back to the serious business of getting the ammonia and urea plants up and running. Progress was good; on the ammonia plant degreasing and acid cleaning of the stainless steel pipework was completed without too many worries and the new refractory brickwork in the primary reformer was dried out very carefully so that temperatures could be raised, feedstock introduced and catalyst reduction started progressively through the various stages that lead to the ammonia converter, where it was usual to have an expert from ICI (the licensor) to supervise the catalyst reduction and the introduction of the first "make gas" to be converted to ammonia. My main task was to see that all the analytical methods required at each stage were ready, that the chromatographs were available and correctly calibrated for each gas stream to be monitored and that all the sample points were correctly installed and functional. Finally, that the laboratory staff understood what was required and were capable of carrying out the work. Always more difficult during start-up because non standard quantities of components in the various samples often required a rapid recalculation and adjustment to the methods provided in the operating manual.

An unexpected delay occurred once all systems were considered to be ready for ammonia production to start. Our client consulted a Brahmin priest to ascertain the most auspicious day for this to occur, resulting in everything being put on hold for two days. A chance to check and double check that everything was correct before a *puja* was completed in the control room and we were allowed to proceed. Success and congratulations all round!

No time to relax as far as I was concerned because once a steady production rate had been established on the ammonia plant attention was very quickly focused on putting the urea plant into production to produce some saleable product.

Over the next two or three months any problems were rectified and production rates were gradually increased in preparation for completing the guarantee tests. It was during this period that Mr Ambrose Congreve, the company's (H&G) chairman and chief executive, made one of his periodic visits. As was his practice at the time, all members of the team received a beautifully gilded invitation to join him in the evening for "cocktails" at The Club – one of the bungalows that had been converted into a recreation centre, with bar, snooker, darts and card area, plus a small dance floor. Also, as was his practice, he would then invite each member of the team in turn to sit with him and explain how the job was progressing and if there were ways things could be improved. Unfortunately, Mr Congreve, who was by then 69 years old, after a long and tiring journey around India, was not feeling too well, so did not arrive at The Club until about 21.30. By this time, the commissioning group, who were not known for their abstemiousness where free drinks were concerned, were well into their cups. One Eddy C, when asked for his opinions said something to the effect 'that it would save money if you stopped swanning around the world on these jollies'. This was not well received and the site manager was told to sack Eddy and that Mr Congreve never wanted to set eyes on him again. The problem was, Eddy – a vital link in a successful start-up – was 6 feet 7 inches tall and not easily hidden. For the next two days a team of runners with radios had to sweep the site in front of Mr Congreve to make sure Eddy kept his head down.

The next day on site I was to meet Mr Congreve again. I was happily working away in the chromatography room when he walked through the door. He sat down and after introductions were completed asked me a few questions about progress and whether I had any particular problems. All fairly normal, however, he then started to tell me a whole succession of Irish (his ancestral home) anecdotes, some quite funny as I recall. After about twenty minutes he made his farewells and moved on. All very strange I thought until I realised the chromatography room was one of the few places on the site that had air-conditioning that was working. It is nice to be appreciated sometimes.

Now for a remarkable coincidence: During my final assignment, in Ireland in 2004, I went on a literary pub crawl of Dublin (does alcohol consumption become more intellectual as you get older?). In the group were a very elderly Indian couple and on hearing a reference to Bangalore I asked if that was where they lived. The gentleman said 'yes, have you been there?' To which I replied 'no but I worked in Mangalore in the 1970s'. He then asked what I was doing there and I replied, 'commissioning an ammonia/urea plant'. 'Ah,' he said, 'Humphreys and Glasgow?' Astounded, I asked how he knew that. It turned out he was a senior executive of the Indian company that had produced the conceptual design for the plant and he still knew all about H&G. I don't know his name, but I am sure Mr Congreve would have known him and of all the bars in the world and of all the millions of Indians, what odds of such a meeting. Shiva's dance sends out some remarkable ripples sometimes.

During the following months I had to undertake two unexpected journeys connected with working in India. The first was to Ahmedabad, in Gujarat State, where H&G had built and successfully commissioned a urea plant, which, unfortunately, could not be induced to operate at full design capacity. The company had decided to send two of their senior engineers from London to help resolve the problem(s) but the presence of a chemist, with *some* experience of urea plant analysis would also be necessary and they seemed to think I could fulfil that role. The trip was memorable to me for two reasons that really had nothing to do with work. I arrived a few days before my colleagues and dined alone in the hotel restaurant on my first night. The lighting was, typically, very dim and I was halfway through my chicken Kiev before I realised the chicken was practically raw. Now this was particularly worrying because on the flight to Ahmedabad I had been reading a novel about a plane journey where the crew and passengers were stricken by food poisoning so virulent that death was occurring within a matter of hours. So far I had been lucky but that was not to last and halfway through the night I awoke in a cold sweat and was soon violently ill. I did not immediately panic and decided if I started to feel delirious I would phone reception to get some help. Fortunately, after an unpleasant twenty four hours, I felt stable enough to, very gingerly, return to work.

When I arrived at the hotel in Ahmedabad I had been told that I was in another Dry State but, as a foreign visitor, I could complete the necessary forms to purchase alcohol from a bonded store in the hotel. A bottle of gin and six bottles of beer should do for a start. When my colleagues arrived from England two days later we finished the beers and most of the gin on the first night and it was only then I found out I could only complete one order a month. What a disaster! Just as well it was not an extended visit. I cannot remember whether or not the problems were resolved, only that there did not seem to be too much wrong with the analysis that was being carried out, so within ten days I was on my way back to Mangalore. I did not have much time for sightseeing but can remember the city was famed for two mosques with interlinked shaking or vibrating domes, designed to limit damage by earth tremors.

Soon after returning (back home) to Mangalore I was told I had to leave the country, immediately! For some weeks I had been telling management that my tourist visa would soon run out, only to be told it was not a problem. Well apparently, with three or four days to go, it was. I was provided with a train ticket for an overnight journey across India to Madras from where I was to fly to Colombo, in Sri Lanka, where a hotel reservation had been made for me. Once there I was to go to a bank in Colombo, where I could collect sufficient money, that was being cabled to me, so that on my return to India I could pay my own way and no longer receive an allowance from the client. It was probably more to do with very convoluted Indian tax laws than my visa expiring but I was a little concerned, as I was not being asked to renew it before returning to India. All did not go smoothly. I arrived at the hotel to find virtually all the staff on strike, so in the morning I moved to the Holiday Inn across the road, where I had been directed in search of food. Next I made my way into Colombo to locate the bank where I could replenish my much depleted funds. This was very necessary as, in a time before credit cards and ATMs and after our unexpected holiday, my stock of western currency was just about sufficient to pay for one more night in the hotel and a taxi to the airport. Help! No funds available for a Mr Lodge and the same story when I returned later in the afternoon. What to do now? Back at the hotel I reserved a seat on the next day's late afternoon flight back to Madras, as I decided I would be better off without money amongst friends than stuck in Sri Lanka, and then had a very hot curry, which made me sweat even more.

The following day, before departing for the airport, more in hope than expectation, I made a final visit to the bank to be told at the counter, no funds were available for a Mr Lodge. After urging them to check again I was just about to leave when a head popped up amongst the myriad of clerks in the back room. 'Is that you Mr Lodge? I am having money for you.' What a lovely man! A flight and another stamp in my passport after re-entering India (perhaps it did make a difference) was followed by an overnight train journey back to Mangalore. I reached Ullal tired but happy to be back at what now seemed like home, to find Dawn, at the pool, quite unconcerned that we had been nearly destitute!

I think Dawn must have been really enjoying her life as a memsahib because when it came close to the time for her visa to expire and she still had five weeks of her extended leave of absence from work to run, she took on the might of the Indian bureaucratic system to extend her visa by a month. It is not that anybody was particularly obstructive but India has a lot of mouths to feed so multi-jobs rather than multitasking was the order of the day with lots of offices to be visited, forms to be filled in triplicate and more offices to be visited for signature and counter signature. I was quite impressed at her dedication to the task but with the able assistance of Ragi (our driver) she succeeded and happily stayed for an extra three weeks.

I should not be surprised at how people differ in their appreciation of their surroundings but never the less could not understand how some couples moaned about there being nothing to do in India and spent most of their spare time, if not going to the beach or into Mangalore for shopping or a change of drinking venue, around the pool or in the "Little Hut" or The Club. Dawn and I had the use of our allocated car (and driver) every other weekend and usually made the most of it with a trip to some local place of interest, there being a number of *bastis* – Jain Temples within an easy day's drive or just taking in the colour and scenes of rural existence while driving through the local countryside and villages: women in their multi hued saris, walking with great elegance, with a posture refined after many years of carrying heavy loads on their heads such as pitchers of water from the village well, the vivid green of the rice paddies being worked by water buffaloes, with attendant snow-white egrets poised for a meal to hop out – all interspersed between swathes of coconut palms and groves of sugar cane. Lakes and ponds covered in water lilies with dragonflies and kingfishers added dashes of colour to the picture. Many of the villages had a patch of ground for a playing field where the ubiquitous game of cricket was in progress or, more interestingly for me, *kabaddi*, a form of single breath tag rugby as far as I could make out, that I had never seen before, the rules of which Ragi tried to explain to me. Many years later, games from the Indian Premier League were featured on English television in a programme showing unusual sports from around the world, although I am still not sure I fully understood what was going on.

Another game that I am sure could have had a great future in India was darts. We had installed a dart board in The Club and the staff soon became addicted once they had watched a few matches so, like the communal television, I believe a communal dart board, promoted in the right way, could have been sold to villages all over India. With a bit more enterprise I could have been the Bernie Ecclestone of darts by now and writing this from my luxury yacht in the Mediterranean.

Another aspect of village life we were to experience was being taken to see scenes from the *Mahabharata*, performed by a group of travelling players. It was a big occasion with a stage and some seating being erected and practically the whole village engrossed once the action started. Unfortunately, as we could not understand what was being said and with performances lasting for over twenty four hours, an hour or two was all we could manage.

Before Dawn left I was delighted to receive an invitation from Mr Satanayarana, the chief chemist, to join him and his family for a meal at their home. It was a very enjoyable evening, made more pleasurable because both his young son and charming wife spoke excellent English, which prevented any embarrassing silences or misunderstandings. One slightly strange aspect, presumably in accordance with strict Hindu traditions, was that his wife did not join us at the table for the meal but kept appearing from the kitchen with yet more curried delights. We also found out that English was the common language used within the home. Mr Satanayarana and his wife had moved from North West India, where Hindi was the first language, when their son was very young but he now went to school in an area where Tamil was the principal language – hence English being used as the most sensible go between.

I was soon to experience a strange phenomenon. For the past few months Dawn had been working steadily on her sun tan, while I, busy at work, was still a whiter shade of pale, which seemed very unfair so a solution had to be found. The ammonia plant was built on a peninsula a road away from a fine stretch of sand and the Arabian Sea, so once things at work had settled down into some form of routine, a few of the other lads and I decided to spend some of our lunch breaks on the beach. Talk about mad dogs and Englishmen out in the midday sun, it was very hot! For my part I would usually jog (Lionel Deering still thinks I am crazy) along the beach near the water's edge – the only place you could put bare feet on the sand – for five to ten minutes, then into the sea for a swim and to cool down before drying off and a quick roasting, five minutes each side was enough, before returning to work.

Most days we had the beach almost to ourselves but on one particular day it was crowded with local people taking a huge drag-net out to sea. I still wanted to swim so waded out a few yards and dived through one of the big waves rolling in. All I could see was fish, big and small and then I could feel them all over my back and shoulders. Horrible! I could not get out of the water quick enough. When the net was hauled in we walked along the beach to see what the catch was like which was upsetting because, as well as a mass of fish of all varieties and sizes, there were two small dolphins. We tried to persuade the fishermen to carry the dolphins back to sea but to no effect and we were in no position to insist. I never found out what circumstances drove all the fish onshore, to this particular beach, on this particular day but the local people knew because a fleet of lorries arrived and soon a conveyer belt of people were carrying boxes packed with crushed ice down the beach and back again, full of fish. A welcome bonanza!

There were a few aspects of living in India that were not so pleasant. We soon learnt to keep all our food in sealed containers and to wash and wipe up any spillage immediately, or risk invasion by an army of tiny red ants. A couple of large cockroaches seemed to consider the roof space above our kitchen was their home but we learnt to live with them, especially after my efforts with a pea shooter were totally ineffective, and so long as there was no infestation by their offspring or smaller cousins. Air conditioning and mosquito nets were very necessary in the bungalow to keep insect problems to a minimum, and we were very happy to watch our resident geckos stalking and catching any that did manage to get in.

At another time we had the most awful smell coming from our toilet and shower room, which no amount of bleach and disinfectant would stop. Eventually, after investigation by some of the camp staff, we were told a dead cat had been buried in a shallow grave at the back of the bungalow, right below the air conditioning unit in-take. One problem we never did resolve was what was making all the noise in the roof space above our bedroom. Birds? rats? bats? – one thing I was sure of, after seeing a large black cobra in the garden behind the bungalow, I was not about to crawl into the loft space to find out what was up there!

It was not too many weeks after Dawn's reluctant return to England and her job as a medical microbiologist at Basildon Hospital, that I was told to prepare for my own departure, work successfully completed with very few loose ends to tie up, other than once more making my fond farewells to another group of new friends and acquaintances that I would probably never see again. However, there was one puzzle associated with my work that I took back to England with me. Once ammonia had been produced and production was being controlled at a steady rate, samples were taken from all around the plant in accordance with a prescribed schedule. Maintaining the correct ratio of hydrogen to nitrogen in the ammonia (NH_3) converter gas space at about 3:1 was essential for efficient production. The problem was, at random intervals, the laboratory analysis showed a ratio of closer to 5:1. When this happened I would check the analysis and the calibration of the instrument with a standard gas sample before reporting to the control room to see if there was a problem. The usual answer was 'nothing wrong here, your analysis must be incorrect, go away and try again', or words to that effect. The annoying thing was, if another sample was taken, in most cases the ratio was perfectly correct. A good practice on all our plants was to maintain a log book in the control room to record any changes made or unusual events, coupled with a written record of all critical instrument readings taken to a specified schedule. Therefore, as I do not like unsolved mysteries, before leaving I prepared a date/time record of the suspect analytical results compared to pertinent instrument readings and logged events. Although not definite there did seem to be some correlation between the suspect results and any procedure that changed the pressure in the ammonia converter, such as the addition of "cold shot", but still no explanation from the process operators as to why. Back in England, while on a visit to the London office I managed to raise the query with Frank Brown, head of the process department and company guru on all things related to ammonia plants. 'Ah yes,' he said, 'if there is a sudden increase in pressure more nitrogen is adsorbed onto the catalyst surface in the converter than hydrogen, therefore the ratio of hydrogen to nitrogen in the gas space will increase for a short period until equilibrium is once again established. QED.

I was never given the opportunity to return to India on a work assignment so was very glad to have experienced such a variety of the delights it had to offer early on in my career such that, with time, even the more frustrating and disagreeable aspects took on a fragrant hue. We have been drawn back twice since on holiday. First on a tour of Southern India, ending with five days over Christmas spent in a rustic beach-side hotel in Goa. I can still feel the warmth of the sun, sitting in a beach-side restaurant smoking a *beedi*, after a delicious meal of tiger king prawns, with "I'm dreaming of a white Christmas" playing on a more or less continuous loop in the background. The second holiday was again back to Southern India over the Christmas period where we included three memorable days cruising the Kerala backwaters on an eco-friendly converted rice barge.

3.7 Ambergate – Safety officer

My next assignment was to be a complete departure from my work as a chemist and to be truthful I am not sure why I was chosen or whether it was strictly legal, as I had no experience or qualifications as a safety officer. Off we go again.

The company had been given the contract to dismantle four streams of a redundant naphtha reforming towns gas plant that they had designed and built in the first instance, at Ambergate in Derbyshire. Two of the streams had never been used and at least one had been bought by another company, for transportation to another location and refurbishment for the production of hydrogen.

After production of towns gas was stopped the plant had been purged and made safe by British Gas and after standing idle for a considerable period was further checked by a team from ICI to confirm that it was safe for dismantling to start. I suspect the presence of a safety officer had been requested by the unions as another delaying tactic in an ongoing dispute with the management over pay and conditions; not uncommon at that time and when I arrived the work force was on a "go slow" about one thing or another.

As I was not a card-carrying union member or qualified fitter it was made clear to me that I could not use any tools, other than the multi gas detector I had brought with me, to check whether sections of the plant were safe for the dismantling process to begin. To this end I was assigned my own fitter to undo any nuts, bolts, flanges, etc. that I deemed necessary to get into the vessels and pipework. As most of my site work experience was gathered abroad it came as quite a shock to see a "work to rule" in progress, although progress is probably the wrong term to use. In the first few weeks I think my fitter undid more of the plant than the rest of the men put together.

My first useful contribution was checking the delay volumes. These are very large diameter pipe loops situated at the end of the plant, which allows the calorific value of the gas leaving the plant to be adjusted before going to the mains for distribution to the public. Although I could detect no gas in the pipes I decided, as an extra precaution to dip them with a long length of wood, which showed a two to three inch layer of oily condensate in the bottom of the pipes – possibly flammable once the guys start cutting through the pipes with welding torches. I reported to the foreman; job done, until, after a quick calculation, I decided his proposed forty five gallon drum was probably not big enough to drain all the liquid. I think two or three tanker loads were taken away in the end.

My second contribution was much more serious. By then I was working one stream ahead of the work force when I asked my fitter to uncouple a flange on the header that carries the naphtha to the reformer. As soon as he loosened a few bolts a stream of liquid started to spray out. It was clear from the smell this was not condensate but pure naphtha, a highly volatile and flammable liquid. The bolts, with some trepidation, were quickly tightened up. Fortunately, as we were a stream ahead, there were no cutting torches or grinders being used in the near vicinity and a potential disaster was avoided once a discreet and safe removal of all the flammable liquid had been made.

My third contribution was not anything like as hazardous but I did manage to clear the site for half a day. Towns gas is, within itself, colourless and odourless but because it is flammable and was then toxic it has an odorant injected into it before going to distribution, so that any leaks can be detected by a characteristic smell. The odorant of choice was a fairly evil smelling mercaptan held in liquid form and released from a small pot into the gas main before it left the plant. Even though the plant had been emptied and made safe I thought it a bit unfair to ask the fitter to remove the odorant pot, so, wearing rubber gloves, I climbed up onto the pipe track to uncouple it myself. There were just a few drips of liquid left in it but it only needed a few parts per million dispersed into the atmosphere to start a cry of "gas leak" and send all the work force running for the gates. Before they would return to work I had to give a presentation explaining that there was no gas leak and that the evil smell would soon disappear and would not make them impotent or otherwise ruin their sex lives. I actually thought it was quite funny but was glad none had dripped on to me, otherwise I would have been an outcast for weeks.

As well as giving me some insight into safe working practices and that you can never be too careful, the assignment or I should say, its location, gave me some lessons in personal survival. Ambergate is close to Edale, located in the Peak District National Park and the start of the Pennine Way. From past experience I knew it was an intriguing area to walk in and in anticipation, before leaving Essex, had packed my walking boots and rucksack. On a fine, sunny Sunday morning I parked in the fairly newly built Outdoor Activities Centre and headed off on a marked trail, climbing up onto the "Tops" and the start of the Pennine Way, with the intention of crossing to Kinder Downfall, a marked beauty spot on my map of the area. For any that have never been to this location it is like entering a strange alien world; at a height of nearly 2000 feet, a grit-stone moorland, covered in peat, criss-crossed by water eroded channels known locally as "groughs" (pronounced gruffs) – a name probably derived from the rough hard going they present to anybody, who like me, tried to cross them directly rather than seeking a marked trail. Still, after about an hour and a half of slithering and sliding in and out of peaty water-filled ditches I reached Kinder Downfall in time for a well earned sandwich. It was then that the problems started. As I set off on the return journey a misty rain rolled in and completely enveloped me to the point where I could not see more than twenty or thirty yards. I realised I could be in some trouble, as, against all the rules, I had told nobody where I was going and, although I had a map and compass, I was not sufficiently competent to use them with no visible points of reference to set a course by. After a brief consultation with my inner self I decided the safest option was to head more or less due west to bring me to what should be the nearest edge of the plateau where, hopefully, I could find a safe route to descend to lower levels. I survived and after about two hours of hard scrambling down the escarpment finally reached a road and relative safety. The only problem was, by road, I was now six or seven miles from Edale and my car. By the time I got back to my digs in the Red Lion, in Belper, I was exhausted and a hot bath followed by steak and chips and a pint, or two, were never so welcome.

My assignment as a safety officer came to a fairly swift conclusion in the end as the unions reached agreement with management, the "work to rule" was lifted and as much of the plant was dismantled in my final week as in the previous four. In hindsight were we fortunate? Would I have found that header full of naphtha if under pressure to release more plant for the men to cut into? I do not know but I am very glad I did!

3.8 Togo – The Mosquito Coast

After my sojourn as a safety officer and time out for the final Permalene trip (see 3.4) to Toulouse, I spent the next six months in the Billericay laboratory preparing analytical procedures and identifying the equipment and chemicals that would be required to provide a functioning laboratory for the government of Togo's first oil refinery. As it was my first experience of anything to do with the oil industry it was an exciting project to work on.

The product specification, that the refinery was required to produce, had already been agreed and for the product(s) to be sold, either internally or externally, had to comply with international standards. Particularly critical where, for instance, aviation fuel was being produced. To some extent this made my job easier because the American Petroleum Institute (API) and the British Institute of Petroleum (IP) both issued "Standard Methods for the analysis and testing of petroleum products". There were also companies, for instance Stanhope Seta, which specialised in the sale of equipment required to comply with the requirements of specific test methods. Coupled with a comprehensive catalogue this made the task of writing test methods and ordering the necessary equipment relatively easy. In addition the company made arrangements for visits to be made to the Mobil Oil Refinery at Coryton for induction in the use of some of the equipment and practical tips on safe sampling techniques; particularly useful when volatile liquids under pressure had to be collected and analysed.

I was not really expecting to go to Togo because when the plant was deemed to be ready for pre-commissioning to start I was still needed in England, so one of my colleagues, Harry Clayton, was sent instead. Also, since Togo had been a French colony, to limit any language difficulties, the expatriate workforce was divided between those supplied by H&G and a French contracting company with experience in refinery operation, who also supplied a chemist. However, after a successful commissioning phase it was decided that three chemists would be required to provide twenty-four hour cover during completion of the guarantee tests. Get yourself prepared for a rapid deployment to the West Coast of Africa. Hot, humid and with mosquitoes the size of sparrows, according to feedback from site.

By then I took care to keep my vaccination record up to date but yellow fever was a new and unpleasant series of injections that had to be endured before I could depart while at the same time trying to find antimalarial tablets that would not have the unpleasant side effects I had experienced previously. Eventually I was ready for my first, but by no means my last, experience of Africa and departed in October 1977 on a journey that, by today's standards was an epic in itself. From London we flew to Marseille, to refuel before crossing the Mediterranean Sea and then the wasteland but by no means boring landscape of the Sahara desert. First stop was Niamey in Niger where we had to go into transit while the plane was again refuelled. Stepping down onto the tarmac was like stepping into a furnace, the heat bounced off the ground and it was a relief to get into the transit lounge, a cavernous building full of chairs but with no access to any refreshments. Before entering, our passports were taken away and we were told to wait, so everybody sat around wondering what was going on. After about half an hour men in uniforms appeared, sat down at a top table and started calling out names to which people responded by going up and collecting what looked like their passports. In the general hubbub it was not easy to hear and after two or three calls for what sounded like "Mr Lodagee" I thought, that could be me. It was and I am glad I went to check, otherwise I could have been sitting in that room for days. The rest of the journey was a bit like being on a shuttle bus, first stop Ouagadougou, in Upper Volta, then Abidjan, in the Ivory Coast and finally Lomé, the capital of Togo, where I was met and taken on the short drive to the accommodation camp.

The camp comprised a large recreation building housing a bar, table tennis and snooker tables and a canteen, plus an outdoor swimming pool, surrounded by two-room Portakabins with a shared central shower and toilet – just about adequate so long as you got on with the man you were sharing with and you made sure the air conditioning was always on, otherwise the room was very soon full of all sorts of bugs, midges and mosquitoes. We were also supplied with insect spray and had a mosquito net round the bed but it was only after I had been there a few weeks I wondered why the French contractors were housed in married quarter bungalows and had a car each to drive about in? This disparity became even more obvious when on Sunday, our day of rest, I was introduced to Togo's possibly only golf club. For us, the British, this involved about a forty minute drive inland through tropical forest in a minibus to the club, where we could hire clubs and play a round; ending back at the club house, where, if it was working, we could buy a cold drink from a vending machine and a packet of biscuits for Sunday lunch. By comparison, the French guys would arrive by car and at the end of the round their wives would turn up with picnic hampers, cold beers and bottles of wine to complement the morning! Still, I do not think they experienced the same sense of adventure and camaraderie that we did!

One adventure we did not go on was to investigate where, while we were going round the course, the sound of the drums beating out of the surrounding jungle was coming from. We tried to get our driver to take us to see what was going on but he absolutely refused. Voodoo ceremonies were not something us white boys should venture anywhere near.

My first three or four weeks at work were spent on dayshift getting to know all the staff, familiarizing myself with the layout of the refinery and where all the sample points were located, the laboratory, the equipment and practising all the analytical methods that would be required during the guarantee tests, as well as trying to resolve any problems that were outstanding. I can still see the chief chemist, Mr Sogagee (I think), who was a lovely gentle man, standing in front of me when he was worried, rubbing the top of a greying, tight curled head, saying 'big chief we have a problem'. Fortunately only one or two proved to be real headaches. Once we were ready for the guarantee tests to start, being the least experienced of the expatriate chemists, I took the night shift, on the basis that everything should be running smoothly, without too many changes being made. Even at night the heat and humidity made it tiring work and unlike in India we did not have the luxury of an air conditioned chromatography room. I had to make myself two towelling wrist-bands so that I could mop away the sweat that kept running into my eyes while operating the equipment. Even the locals found it tiring. When one of the laboratory technicians spent an excessive amount of time leaning against a concrete roof support pillar, I walked over to see what he was doing and realised he was resting his eyes. As we did have a lot of work to do I gave him a gentle nudge and felt a bit mean when he almost fell over before waking up.

Togo lies in a long, narrow north-south strip on the west coast of Africa and Lomé, the capital and the refinery, were both located on the 40 to 50 miles of coastal strip, which makes the southern border of the country on the Gulf of Guinea, squeezed between Ghana to the west and the, as it was then, communist state of Benin to the east. The accommodation camp was located a short walk across the coast road from the beach, so was popular with the men who fancied a swim in the sea after work with the added attraction that there were often statuesque, bare-breasted young women to be seen frolicking in the surf and a couple of beach bars where cold drinks and local delicacies, if you were brave enough, could be bought.

Lomé was very colourful with a large central market selling all manner of exotic produce and products and I still have a set of beautifully carved ebony heads showing the in-vogue women's hair styles of the day. Of course, being a relatively poor country, not all the sights and smells were so pleasant but seeing the hides of freshly killed animals pegged out by the side of the road so that vultures could clean away the last remnants of flesh, I thought showed a certain resourcefulness. Another unusual experience was being called into the construction stores area to be shown two smallish pythons that had just been found, coiled up into balls like a Turk's head knot.

Just after I arrived some of the lads were planning a weekend trip to Benin to visit a village where all the huts were built over water on stilts. I was asked whether I would like to go but had a problem because my passport was still in Lomé, being processed. I was told this would not be a problem as they could get a letter from the authorities explaining the situation which would cover my lack of a passport. Armed with my letter we headed for the border only to be told without passport and visa they would not let me through. After an exchange of views I asked to see the officer in charge who was immaculately dressed and spoke perfect English; Sandhurst perhaps? After a further exchange of views about the merits, or otherwise, of my letter he just looked at me and with a polite smile said 'I will let you out but I will not let you in again'. I had to laugh and bid him an equally polite good day. Fortunately it was only fifteen to twenty miles back to the accommodation camp and thumbing a lift proved to be a well accepted means of travel. I never did get to Benin to see the stilted village but, on reflection, suspect he did me a big favour because I would not have liked to be stuck in communist run Benin without any proper documents or backup. Must have been crazy to even think about it!

The guarantee test went very well and with Christmas fast approaching once again, I was released to return to England. After Christmas, back in the Billericay laboratory, I received a call to say I had been invited back to

Togo for the opening ceremony of the country's first oil refinery. Thinking about the lengthy and arduous journey for what I assumed would be a half day of speeches I then made the decision to turn it down, something I later very much regretted. The refinery was a very prestigious project for President Eyadema who knew how to throw a party. The opening ceremony was one of the highlights of the celebrations marking his eleven years in power which went on for two or three days with very energetic and colourful traditional dancing and music, with food and drink in plenty. Evidently the president was presented with a bottle of refined petrol from the new plant, which was designed to handle 100,000 tons of imported crude oil a year and to produce 50–60,000 tons of refined petroleum products, 60% for export. Unfortunately the refinery stopped operating after just three years, I suspect for economic rather than technical reasons, as I never heard any call for a troubleshooting team to be sent out and I understand it was then converted into an import terminal. Hopefully that means there was still work for some of the laboratory and operations staff and not all the equipment went to the scrap yard.

3.9 Changing times

It was about this time that the advent of North Sea gas started to impact seriously on H&G's core business and as a consequence research and development projects and the analytical services supplied by the laboratory at Billericay were pared back until its future became a matter of great concern. In an attempt to avoid redundancies, Doctor Williamson, one of our senior chemists, after contacting friends from his time at university, promoted the idea that part of the laboratory could be converted to manufacture organic chemical intermediates. This proposal was accepted by senior management for a limited trial period, to see if, in part at least, the laboratory could pay its own way and so started a completely new phase in my working life.

We were led in fairly gently with contracts to produce organic buffer materials, these being compounds used in biological production regimes to maintain a stable pH range. Two of these: MOPS(3-(N-Morpholino)propanesulphonic acid) and HEPES 4-(2-hydroxyethyl)-1-piperazineethanesulphonic acid) as a final product, were nice white powders with no unpleasant properties. As the search for more business was expanded, this situation very soon degenerated until the laboratory became an unpleasant and potentially dangerous place to work. I suspect, as new boys in the market, a lot of the compounds we attempted to make were in short supply because the established manufacturers did not want to touch them. Particularly nasty was a lachrymatory substance, of which a faint whiff would set the eyes streaming, or those reactions where cyanide or bromine was used as an integral ingredient.

The bromination reactions presented a particular hazard, which even in those days Health and Safety would probably have put a stop to if they knew what was going on. The top storey of the laboratory had been fitted out with a line of five, large volume QVF reaction vessels and had a fairly antiquated overhead extraction system to the outside of the building. In addition a compressed air line ran the length of the building with plug-in Schrader coupling points at regular intervals. When bromination reactions were underway in two or three vessels at the same time we had to wear a full-face breathing mask to enter and attend to the production process. The problem was we had two choices: a hood with a long, cumbersome hose attached that you dragged in, with the end anchored outside the door – so, no positive pressure and not easy to move about without getting tangled, or a smaller line attached to the mask that plugged in to one of the Schrader couplings. Here, the technique was to take a deep breath outside the door, walk in and hope you could plug into the compressed air nearest to the vessel you wanted to work on before the mask fogged up and you could not see the plug-in point. Remember, most of the reactions required the liquid in the vessels to be heated and the top floor had a glass roof so it got very hot in the summer. The IDLH (Immediately Dangerous to Life or Health) level for bromine is 10 parts per million, so unplugging and plugging in at the next vessel was always a bit worrying!

A major problem was scale-up. To determine the production cost of any new chemical that we were trying to sell, a small quantity would be made to ascertain the efficiency of the process. Unfortunately when scaled up to a full production batch size the efficiency of the process almost always decreased, sometimes quite disastrously, from say 80% to 40%, so setting a competitive price for new jobs was very difficult. This was a serious hindrance in the attempts being made to keep the laboratory operating and another reason, as well as all the long names that I could never spell or remember, why I felt that anything to do with organic chemistry should be avoided if at all possible.

Thus, after two or three months, when I was asked whether I would transfer to the head office in London for a few months to help prepare a metering manual for a liquid ethane storage facility that was being constructed on Flotta, in the Orkney Islands, I did not to think too long before accepting, with the proviso that I had no idea what a metering manual was.

So, with some misgivings, after twelve years as a chemist based in the Billericay laboratory, I gave up my twenty minute drive to work for the hour and twenty minutes (on a good day) commute across London, to the offices around Victoria Station.

PART 4
The Move to Commissioning

4.1 Flotta – Orkney – Liquid ethane storage

I was not moved directly to the commissioning group but was seconded to the Special Contracts Division (SCD) a semi-autonomous group of the company set up to bid for smaller contracts without incurring the main company overhead. A successful strategy. Before moving to the London office I had been interviewed by Mr Norman Wilson, the CEO of SCD, to see if he thought I could manage the task of producing a metering manual and now, somewhat apprehensively, it was time to prove I could.

I was introduced and settled in to the team who were responsible for the design and procurement of equipment to supply the liquid ethane storage facility to a new North Sea oil terminal being built for Occidental on the small island of Flotta in the Orkney Islands. In the early days of the North Sea oil boom, the smaller, less profitable, fractions of gases that separated from the oil, such as methane and ethane would have been used to drive turbines for power or burnt off in the flare but the government soon decided this waste of resources had to stop. Thus a means had to be found to separate the ethane, store it and then export it and this, in turn, required accurate meters to be installed and approved to monitor the quality and quantity of the ethane exported so that Occidental could be paid and the government receive its cut.

From an island, the only practical way to do this was by ship, as a liquid. All gases have a critical temperature; the temperature above which vapour cannot be liquefied; in the case of ethane, 32.4 °C. They also have a critical pressure; in the case of ethane 47.5 bar; the pressure required to liquefy a gas at its critical temperature. To use such high pressures (some 47 times greater than atmospheric pressure) can be costly and dangerous, so a compromise of chilling the ethane to approximately -30 °C at a pressure of approximately 6 bar was the favoured option. To hold the volume of ethane expected to be produced from the main plant, with suitable redundancy, five large sausage shaped low-temperature stainless steel storage vessels were manufactured and covered in a thermal cement-like coating to minimise heat transfer. Ethane, under pressure, would be transferred from the main gas plant, to chillers designed and supplied by Hall Thermotank International, where it would be compressed and cooled utilising the Joule Thompson effect until it transformed into a liquid and was transferred into a selected storage vessel.

The internal volume of each storage vessel was accurately measured and each vessel was fitted with a float gauge, suitable for low temperature operation, such that the level of liquid in the vessel could be accurately monitored. The outlet from each vessel was connected via a manifold into a pipeline that ran down to the tanker loading jetty. This pipeline was fitted with a flow control valve and a flow meter calibrated for the transfer of liquid ethane. However, the principal measure of the quantities being transferred was to be based on the reduction in level from a selected storage vessel.

To compile the metering manual following a synopsis of the principal of operation of the ethane storage facility, certified drawings of each storage vessel together with the associated certified instrumentation had to be assembled. Calibration certificates are required and there are rules about how long before use the calibration can apply and how long after the start of use recalibration is required. As an aside, I was recently asked whether I would like "Smart" meters installed for my domestic gas and electricity supplies and when I queried whether they would come with any form of certification as to their accuracy I got the impression the fellow I was talking to thought I was crazy. Do they ever read low? A project for *Which* perhaps.

After a few months' liaison with manufacturers and discussions with the engineers in the office, who knew what they talking about, the first draft of the manual was ready for review. Further revision and update was followed by a review by Occidental until the manual was deemed ready for approval by the appropriate authorities. To my surprise it was approved with very little revision and so my sojourn in the London office came to an end.

I had not long been back at the laboratory when I got another call from SCD. The company were required to provide a commissioning adviser for pre-commissioning and start-up of the plant and since I now knew more about it than anyone else and had some plant experience already, would I be willing to take on the job? Since the situation and conditions in the laboratory had not improved any while I was away, there seemed little reason not to start on a new phase in my career.

The journey to Flotta was not altogether straightforward and would take the best part of a day – early train from Wickford to Liverpool street, underground to Heathrow, jet to Glasgow and a forty-seat propeller driven flight to Kirkwall on Main Island, followed by a taxi and ferry crossing to Flotta. So once again I was to be living away from home, for an unspecified period. I spent the first few weeks, mainly in the company of Bill Sutherland, the H&G construction advisor, who showed me round the site and introduced me to all the Occidental staff and personnel that I would be working with. He also explained a mass of company procedures, all new to me, required to maintain the correct paperwork flow between site and head office for any equipment items that were still arriving or were needed or were stored awaiting installation. After a few weeks Bill decided he could safely escape, or Occidental decided they did not want to pay for both of us, whichever, I was soon left to go it alone.

Once a section of the storage facility was deemed to be approaching construction completion I would make an inspection against the Piping & Instrumentation Diagrams (P&IDs) and data sheets to give approval for hand over for pre-commissioning to commence. This would result in a "But-list"(snagging list) being produced for all the corrections required, large or small. I do not know if it was because it was all new to me or I was more aware of the low temperatures the equipment would be subjected to but my first inspections were quite rigorous in that I got off the walkways and included a close view of the material stamp on the individual bolts, nuts and flanges on the pipework round the vessels. I was a bit shocked to find that a good 50% of the items installed were not of the correct low temperature stainless steel required. I do not think this made me too popular with the Occidental piping supervisors who were responsible for the installation because all the incorrect items had to be replaced. It also made a lot of work for me, long "But-lists" and rigorous re-inspections.

One of the early pre-commissioning activities required on most plants is to flush through all the vessels and associated pipework with water to confirm there are no blockages and hopefully flush out any weld bead, scale, coke cans, gloves or other rubbish that may have found its way inside. The outlet from each storage vessel was via a u bend, a block valve and stainless steel control valve. Because of the flammable nature of the ethane the control

valve was welded, rather than bolted, onto the vessel to reduce the possibility
of leaks, however, the casing of the valve could be split and the ball removed.
This was done during flushing to reduce the possibility of scoring the valve
but it was still not easy to confirm all the rubbish had been removed. As I had
some time to spare – the completion of the main plant was behind schedule –
I acquired a plastic marker buoy of about the right diameter and had it pulled
through the outlet from each storage vessel. Four of the five vessels had scaf-
fold clips lodged in the outlet pipe. Quite a scary thought if they had moved
once the vessel was full of liquid ethane and stopped the valve closing off
properly. Also a lesson learnt for future jobs and the importance of blanking
off outlet pipework while construction work is still going on inside a vessel.

Following flushing the next pre-commissioning activity was to blow water
from the system with compressed air and then pressure test at about 1.5 times
operating pressure to check for leaks. This identified a major problem. A large
number of the valves fitted around all five vessels were leaking around the
plate that connected the valve handle to the body of the valve. It was very
strange because it applied to valves of all different sizes and to valves supplied
by different manufacturers. It was a big headache for H&G as they were
responsible for supply and most came with inspection certificates confirming
they were tested and fit for purpose. After much head scratching, communication with the London office and visits from senior piping engineers, it
was concluded that the most likely cause was the valves being non-standard
following the need to fit extension arms to the valve handles. This need arose
because of the low temperatures the plant would be operating at and the
extra thickness of insulation round all the pipework that the valve handles
would have to protrude through. Apparently, the valves were tested before
the additions! I was then impressed with Occidental's decision to provide a
much needed rapid response to the problem. Instead of returning the valves
to H&G for correction by the various manufacturers, after a trial run, they
stripped out all the valves in batches and took them to a local company for
repair. I do not know who paid for it but it meant a lot of extra work and a
busy time for me because once the valves were reinstated all the checking and
testing had to be repeated.

Flotta was quite an unusual place to work, being a small island, some four
miles by three, essentially featureless apart from a few stunted wind-bent
trees but with some soaring sea cliffs, home to guillemots, razorbills and
puffins, which were a joy to behold. Before the terminal was built with the

accommodation camp and associated facilities it was home to thirty or forty families, mainly crofters, with a church, school, community centre and post office cum general store, so a massive change to the island but, I believe, a welcome form of alternative employment for many, both from Flotta and the main island. It amused me to learn that thousands of pounds had been spent on a study to determine that heather brown would be the most unobtrusive colour to paint the oil storage tanks. It also surprised me when one of the local girls told me she had spent her weekend cutting and stacking peat round her cottage for next winter's fuel supply. Tough life.

Another lesson soon learnt was that the weather could be highly variable. On the rare occasions when the sun was shining first thing in the morning there could be a howling gale by ten o'clock and pouring rain by twelve with some variation on the same theme in the afternoon. One of the most worrying occasions was stepping out of the stores to find bits of roofing material, cladding and other debris flying about the site and after making a dash into my Land Rover to feel the back lift off the ground – 120 mph winds, fortunately for a limited period.

Before starting the assignment I had insisted I spend the next Christmas at home. True to form, as Christmas approached, the official line was that according to program this would be a very critical period, so I compromised and said that if I could be home for Christmas I would return before the New Year. The journey home turned out to be somewhat fraught. Flotta had its own airstrip – a single runway just about long enough, in favourable conditions, to allow a light aircraft to land and after refuelling (hand-pumped from a forty-five gallon drum) to take off again. Flying from here to Edinburgh saved four or five hours on the normal journey time so I was pleased when this option was offered to me. However, when the plane arrived the people getting off looked chilled to the bone and warned me the heating was not working. I pulled on my waterproof over-trousers (always ready to hand), zipped up the parker and, hood up, hoped for the best. It was freezing, even covered in as many layers of newspaper as I could find but the views were spectacular. I suspect we were flying at a lower altitude than normal because the snow-capped Grampians looked almost within touching distance. Best of all we reached Edinburgh in time for the connection to London so I did manage a few extra hours of Christmas shopping time.

True to my word I returned before the New Year only to find, as expected, that nothing of any importance was going to happen until after the holiday period, so I decided to see in the New Year on the main island. I booked into a B&B in Kirkwall and an hour before midnight was stationed in a packed high street, bottle of whisky in hand, waiting for the action. All started well as the hour approached; a friendly crowd with people toasting each other, a pipe band came marching down the street and then it started to snow – a vicious wind with the snow coming almost horizontally, swirling up the marching kilts, so that some serious damage could have been done. I just about saw in the New Year before beating a hasty retreat to my bed. Very fortunately, as I had gone to bed relatively sober, I got up reasonably early and after a quick breakfast booked a taxi to get me to the ferry terminal to catch the 9.30 back to Flotta. It was still snowing and the roadsides were banked up with snow but I was lucky to have a taxi driver who treated it as a challenge and got me there in time, even though it was a bit like going down the Cresta Run. It was a further two days before anybody else from the main island reached Flotta, so it was an expensive New Year for those who got stuck on the wrong side of Scapa Flow.

It was a very rapid learning curve for me as nearly all aspects of the job were new to me, the instrument control systems being no exception. One of the instrument technicians very kindly gave me a copy of his City & Guilds notes on Control Theory & Practice which helped a little during the pre-commissioning period and provided some light reading in my cabin in the evening. However, it was a fortunate change in personnel that saved us from real embarrassment. As start-up approached the Occidental senior instrument engineer, an American, decided he had made enough money to pack it all in and return to Thailand where he, so he said, was having a hotel built. His replacement was Tony Lester, one of the H&G instrument group I had worked with in Bulgaria and, incidentally, had married and was still married to Annie, his Bulgarian girlfriend. Up to this time the chiller package supplied by Hall Thermotank had been tended with great care by their representative on site, Bill Broughton, who had been waiting for some time for ethane to start operations for real. However, when Tony reviewed their Piping & Instrumentation Diagrams (P&IDs) he took me to one side and said, 'seeing as I know you, with the instrument control system as it is, I believe it will be impossible to start the chillers using the integrated control system.' I must admit I did not fully understand his logic but after his mis-givings were discussed with Bill Broughton, urgent telephone calls with the Hall Thermotank head office resulted in a small team arriving on site a week later with additional relays and other control devices that had to be wired into the chiller package. Well spotted Tony!

Entertainment on Flotta was limited to either the staff bar or the Bears Bar, where, unlike on North Sea platforms, alcoholic beverages could be bought and consumed. My venue of choice was the staff bar which was quiet but sociable and a good place to get to know most of the other senior staff and keep in touch with progress and gossip from all over the terminal. The highlight came once a month when the chefs were given the chance to show off their skills and produce food from a country of their choice, which was always well received. Burns night was particularly well attended and gave me the opportunity, for the first time, to taste the haggis, which was piped in with due ceremony. As an alternative, Friday night in the Bears Bar was dance night. After about a month I thought I might look in to see what was going on, however, I was given fair warning by one of the more senior staff that, in the almost total absence of female company, if a big hairy rigger came over and asked me to dance the politic thing was to get up and make the most of it. As it happened the situation did not arise but as more drink was consumed there were more and more lone males rocking and stomping round the floor. One thing that did impress me was, although crowded, the hall remained a fight free zone despite the floor swimming in beer and at least one stack of whisky tumblers crashing to the ground as an elbow got knocked. On my first day on site I was told that an absolute rule was that any fighting would lead to the instant dismissal of all parties involved, no matter who was deemed to have started or caused the dispute. This policy coupled with the restraining presence of a number of large security men circulating round the room seemed to work. I think some clever psychology was used as well in that all the security men were getting on in years, probably retired policemen, who stepped in without being aggressive and did not themselves present a direct challenge to the rising testosterone.

One other entertaining evening, which I was fortunate to be invited to, was a social gathering in the island's village hall. I was forewarned that there would be no bar so went prepared with a half bottle of Glenfiddich. The hall was a converted Nissen hut consisting of a large room, with chairs all round the walls, occupied mainly by women and children and a smaller outer room where most of the men congregated, talking and drinking from their bottles. As the evening progressed a lone piper provided some music which, as the bottles emptied, was enough to persuade a few of the men back into the main hall to join in the dancing. It was not the liveliest evening I had ever been to but an interesting insight into life in the local community.

One of the final checks made before any ethane was loaded into the storage vessels was to test the pigging system installed on the pipeline running from our battery limit down to the loading jetty. For any not familiar with terminology used in the oil industry a pigging system is not used to raise prime porkers but a quaint name, probably American in origin, for equipment to scrape the inside of pipelines and thus keep them clean and free of grease, sludge, in our case hydrates, or other deposits which would inhibit flow. In its most simple form the *pig* is a hard foam cylinder or rubber sphere inserted into a pipeline via a *pig launcher* and then driven by pressure down the pipeline until it reaches the receiving trap or *pig catcher*. Apparently original pigs were made of straw wrapped in wire which made a squealing noise while travelling through the pipe, sounding like a pig squealing, hence the name, which is still used despite the devices becoming much more sophisticated, to the point where they have featured in three James Bond films to get him into or out of a tricky situation.

In our case, for testing purposes, the line was carefully filled with water with air being vented from the top of any expansion loops (included to allow the line to flex as it cools down when being filled with liquid ethane) and at the pig catcher. When all was ready at the Jetty end the pig was launched. We did not hear a squeal but there was an almighty crack as the pipeline whiplashed off its supports down at the jetty. Very scary and very fortunate nobody was injured! Although the line to the jetty was not my, or H&G's, responsibility it was still a major concern so I sent a problem report to our head office asking for advice. Also, after my experience with the wrong bolts being fitted round the ethane storage vessels, I got hold of the piping drawings for the line to the jetty and did an inspection myself. Because of the very low temperatures the pipe would experience once filled with liquid ethane, the pipe supports were fitted into a sliding shoe so that that the pipe could move as it contracted or expanded. Approximately 40% of the specified supports were missing, which put additional stress on the support clamps that were fitted. After all the damage down at the jetty was made good and the missing supports were put in place, with some trepidation, another test pig was sent down the line. This time it held but there was still a considerable backlash which caused the whole line to shake violently. Being a chemist until now, this was all new technology to me and it is surprising how much you learn when something goes wrong. However, I was not fully convinced by the assertion that the "hammer" effect was only taking place because the line was filled with water and a small volume of trapped air, rather than being filled with liquid ethane when any small volume of trapped ethane vapour would turn to liquid as the pressure was increased by the pig coming down the line. I am glad to say subsequent tests, when ethane was available, proved the boffins to be right, not that they suffered the anxiety and apprehension surrounding the launch; nearly as bad as having to sink a six foot putt to win the Ryder Cup. A good outcome of all these tribulations was that I got to know the jetty supervisor, John Salmon, quite well. It helped that he moved from Gravesend in Kent to Orkney, so we spoke the same language and could understand each other when talking on the two way radios, without having to repeat the message two or three times. Also a friendship developed that lead to me enjoying my first experience of clay pigeon shooting on a cold and snowy day on the main island in mid-February.

On the 13th January, ethane vapour was made available from the main gas plant; the chillers were started and continued to run successfully and by the 19th January we were starting to fill four of our commissioned storage vessels with liquid ethane. It was an anxious time as the pressure increased and everything cooled down waiting to see that no leaks developed and the structure and control systems continued to operate without any defects. An unintended tell-tale that a vessel was full of liquid ethane was the stainless steel nameplate, which protruded through the vessel insulation, becoming covered in a block of ice. Better that than somebody putting an un-gloved hand on it. By the 2nd February we were ready to load the first shipment. I was in the control room double checking with John on the two way radio that the ship was in place and everything down at the Jetty was ready for us to open the outlet valve on the selected storage vessel when I called a halt to go outside and make a final check on the status of one of the valves; suddenly what I thought was a two way conversation was interrupted by a multitude of voices cutting in asking what the problem was. After a rapid walk outside I was soon back in the control room and after assuring everybody listening that we were good to go, the appropriate valves were opened and the first shipment of ethane was on its way to be loaded for export. Happily, everything worked according to design without any serious problems and that included the metering system which I was particularly pleased about.

I spent a further six to eight weeks on Flotta while the remaining vessels were commissioned, the loading procedure was successfully repeated, any outstanding Butt list items were rectified and all the required paperwork was signed off before a completion certificate was issued by Occidental and it was deemed appropriate that I could leave my first job as a commissioning adviser.

4.2 Head office based 1979–1989

Within a week of returning from Flotta I was asked and agreed to be reassigned to the commissioning department so, after thirteen years, cleared my desk in the laboratory and relocated to an office looking over Victoria Station in London with a bird's eye view of guests of Her Majesty being met by the state coaches and the Blues and Royals for transfer to Buckingham Palace. I soon learnt, on such occasions, not to open a window and stick my head out for a better view for fear of a response from the men with rifles on the surrounding rooftops. It always amused me, after all the pomp of such a visit, to see a man with a brush and shovel going round removing evidence left by the horses. I always wondered if he had a job title "sh*t shoveler by Appointment to Her Majesty".

I was very fortunate to be assigned to assist the commissioning manager, Mr Reg Prior, who was a gentleman of the old school, with a wealth of knowledge of the company and process plant commissioning. Indeed by the time he retired he had worked for H&G and the subsequent owners for the best part of fifty years, which is a record I cannot imagine will be repeated any time soon.

There were four main aspects to the work:

1. Ensure that we had sufficient staff, of the right experience and qualifications, to send to site to pre-commission and commission the various process plants the company had been contracted to design and build, as and when necessary.
2. Prepare estimates of the equipment, staffing levels and associated man-hours required by the commissioning group to include in the cost estimate for any proposal for new work the company had been invited to bid for.
3. Control and coordinate a timely response to any problem reports issued by our site teams and maintain and update the company problem-reporting system.

4. Prepare, revise and update forms and company standards issued by the commissioning department for inclusion in the commissioning department desk manuals and ensure sufficient numbers were always available for allocation to new site teams, as required.

It was probably a good thing that, at that time, most of the work still involved a paper trail and finding my way round the various offices and getting to know all the department managers was essential and befriending their secretaries was even more important if a rapid response was required. I still do not think the pinging of emails with attachments to a faceless name engenders quite the same response.

The commissioning department maintained a core of ten to fifteen permanent staff on its books, supplemented by a group of young process engineers, usually extracted from the design team for a particular plant. An excellent policy as they gained hands-on practical experience to enhance their existing theoretical knowledge of the plant being commissioned, and we gained from having some very clever young engineers on the site. These, in turn, would be supplemented as necessary, by agency staff, particularly where instrument technicians operating a shift system were required. In the early days, on some of the big contracts such as Bulgaria, there were as many as sixty personnel on site for over two years, with perhaps a third of them on a married status contract, so it was almost a full-time job keeping tabs on their comings and goings, not to mention their expense claims. It helped that I already knew a number of our permanent staff from my time on site as a commissioning chemist but I soon learnt that it paid to be circumspect if a wife phoned in to find out when her husband was next expected home on leave. I know of at least one case where a man on a three-monthly leave cycle was only going home to his wife every six months and spent alternate leave periods with his second family in another part of the country. Not too surprising, I suppose, when enforced absence was the nature of the work and it should not be assumed it was always the husband who was playing away.

The most difficult jobs to staff correctly were those where a completely new type of plant was being constructed, for example, the Khartoum North Power Station where a lot of ex-Electricity Generating Board staff were taken on, based purely on a CV and a brief interview. I remember one incident where one of the men, fortunately for him, was home on leave when his living accommodation in Sudan was raided by the Religious Police. In a predominately Muslim country he, rather foolishly, had not only been distilling alcohol but selling it to the local people. The company could not condone such conduct, so he was summoned to the office and dismissed. I could not believe it when he got quite indignant and insisted he was within his rights to return to Khartoum to collect all his belongings. In the end we said that was his choice but nothing to do with H&G if he spent the next ten years in a Sudanese goal; not that, with his attitude, he was likely to have survived half that time.

I assume the company must have decided that I acquitted myself reasonably well on Flotta because over the next ten years (see Appendix 1) my time in the office was interspersed with more site assignments, usually as the lead or senior commissioning engineer. None were major contracts but they were of sufficient variety and complexity to build my experience and understanding of the company standards and operating procedures, my practical knowledge (Dawn cannot believe this) as well as man-management and client-liaison skills, some of which were sorely tested. I suppose, as my experience grew, it made my work in the head office a little easier but sometimes a little knowledge only makes you realise how much you do not know. At least I was starting to talk the talk and understand the terminology used by the different disciplines so that I could ask a sensible question of the people that did know.

The advent of North Sea gas and the subsequent demise of the regular contracts to build new towns gas plants meant the sales and proposals group were diversifying to an ever greater extent to win some new contracts. For each proposal that was bid, a preliminary set of Engineering Line Diagrams (ELDs) and Utility Line Diagrams (ULDs), together with a draft contract document explaining the extent of the company's liability would be prepared and issued with a provisional programme to each discipline, so that cost estimates of discipline man-hours and equipment costs could be made. As time passed, preparing these estimates became an increasing part of my responsibilities. However, other than knowing that the commissioning department's costs were usually between 6% and 12% of the total value of a contract, there did not seem to be any "scientific" basis for preparing the estimate, which I found very difficult to deal with. Therefore, I went back into the company records to compare actual costs (man-hours/rates for different disciplines) against the plant complexity based on the number of and content of different discipline items on the ELDs and ULDs for ten plants, of varying size, type and location, which had been built and commissioned over the past ten years. After considerable trial and error an "estimating procedure for predicting site pre-commissioning costs" was produced, together with a method for completing it, which seemed to fit the known facts and was reasonably reliable in predicting costs for future jobs. Initially this required a manual count of mechanical items, instruments, pipe-lines, valves, etc. from the ELDs/ULDs but as time passed and computers were used more and more by all the disciplines to store the data, a program was produced for the commissioning group to abstract and utilise data from the various disciplines to complete the pre-commissioning cost sheets.

As the company diversified it was not always easy to find any information for comparison purposes and I remember the hours spent on a very costly proposal for a paint and pigments plant to be built in Algeria. After more than a year of negotiations the company was offering to build a plant with the capability of producing ten different dyestuffs and six pigments (I cannot remember the exact numbers) with a guarantee that specified quantities of all the products could be manufactured within a one month period. At this stage the conceptual design was passed to the commissioning group for their input to the final bid package. Some people in sales group were not best pleased when I calculated, that with everything working perfectly, it would be physically impossible to clean out and make all the changes necessary to produce all the different products within the guaranteed time period. I think the bid was quietly shelved, which probably saved the company a lot more money than it had already spent.

Another function that I was given increased responsibility for was the control of the company's problem reporting system. For many years as a problem arose during pre-commissioning, commissioning or operation of one of the plants a problem report would be raised on site and sent to head office for resolution. It was the responsibility of the commissioning group to coordinate and control the issuing of a satisfactory solution to the problem. The process was operated through a card indexing system by selecting a primary key word, e.g. plant type, a secondary key word, e.g. mechanical and a final key word, e.g. compressor. For each problem report raised a new card would be made out with a cross-reference to the key words and specific contract number and the report would be filed in a lever arch file identified with that contract number. Over the years a considerable number of lever arch files began to accumulate in the commissioning department's storage area and it was another system that would readily lend itself to computerisation, but not during my time. It was a good system because it used a proven format for the quick resolution of a problem but also highlighted repeat problems or failures so that they could, hopefully, be designed out of future contracts. The tricky thing in some cases was deciding which of the key words was most appropriate and continuity and familiarity certainly helped. A good thing, from my point of view, was that it put me in close contact with most of the heads of departments and lead-engineers in most of the disciplines, which over the years makes a working life run so much easier. Fortunately, I did not have to hassle too many of them to obtain a solution to any of the problems presented to them.

For every new contract one of our senior commissioning engineers would be designated as the site commissioning manager with responsibility for all on-site activities as well as reporting to, and coordinating all the required interface with the head office. To this end he (I do not remember it ever being a she) would be issued with a commissioning desk manual which contained all the company standards, both procedural and technical that would be necessary to satisfactorily complete the work. Controlling the issue of these manuals, ensuring sufficient were in print and that they were updated to contain the latest issue of modified or new standards became an important part of my office-based role. A key aspect of the pre-commissioning work on any site was to break the plant down into smaller, clearly identified, sections or systems in order that the contained pipework could be seen to be flushed free of debris, e.g. weld bead, old coke cans, etc., if necessary chemically cleaned and both pressure and leak tested. In addition, all equipment would be functionally checked and instruments calibrated and loop checked, with the issue of appropriate, approved test documents. After gaining experience on a number of sites over the subsequent years I designed a pre-commissioning work sheet with an accompanying technical guide for preparing for and executing such activities, which was included as a company standard in the desk manual. In addition, on site, each completed system work sheet, once approved and signed off, was included in the document dossiers that were assembled as part of the required hand-over package to the client. A not inconsiderable amount of work – I can remember on the ICI Paints job it became necessary to hire an additional Portakabin to contain and assemble all the required documentation.

In 1983, a major change was to take place. For 44 years H&G had been under the direct control of Mr Ambrose Congreve, who was by then in his

76th year, but after a number of years of difficult trading, resulting in some forced redundancies, it was decided that the best interests of the company and its staff would be met by selling and thus allowing Mr Congreve to take a well-earned retirement. The company was acquired by the Enserch Corporation of Dallas, Texas which provided us with a much wider field of operations but also gave me a considerable headache trying to amalgamate all the commissioning department's standards and operating procedures with those used by Enserch; a procedure that had to repeated some years later when the company was acquired by another American company, Jacobs Engineering.

Depending on the workload, my time in head office was interspersed with further periods of site work or weekly visits to a site in a supervisory role, perhaps following a period assisting in the preparation of the plant operating and maintenance manuals. One of the most interesting and unusual was a contract with the Ministry of Defence (MOD) to build and commission a weapons testing facility for the Royal Armament Research and Development Establishment (RARDE) at Chertsey in Surrey, also unusual as it was only a short train journey away from the office. It comprised two very large test chambers, a Climatic and Altitude Chamber (CAC), a Complete Vehicle Climatic Chamber (CVCC) and a Central Plant Area (CPA). Each chamber was capable of housing a complete battle tank or helicopter, where their operational capability could be tested under the most severe conditions of temperature, pressure and humidity. One of the chambers could be sealed so that a vacuum could be created to simulate high altitudes and both chambers were connected to a range of different fuel supplies required to test the capability of selected vehicles under the differing operating conditions. Most memorable was the final acceptance and hand-over ceremony. All the "top brass" were assembled, from both H&G and the MOD, in front of the Altitude Chamber and after a speech or two the chamber door was slowly raised to reveal a Challenger tank back-lit by powerful lights with *Chariots of Fire* music broadcast from loud speakers all around the building – very impressive and one of those goose-bump moments as I had no idea what was going to happen!

4.3 Corfe – Dorset –The start of onshore oil production

In 1980, I was assigned as commissioning supervisor to oversee the start-up of a crude oil separation plant, one of Britain's first inland oil production facilities, located at Wytch Farm, near Corfe Castle in Dorset. The contract was awarded by Gas Council (Exploration) Limited, in collaboration with BP, to serve production wells (nodding donkeys) lying along the southern shore of Poole Harbour and was unique in many ways. The plant was designed to process well-stream crude to provide stabilised crude oil, pipeline gas, crude LPG and non-specific fuel gas and was, for the first phase, tiny, being required to process a mere 4000 barrels per day (bpd). In comparison, some of the plants I later visited in Saudi Arabia which were capable of processing up to 300,000 bpd, however, 4000 bpd was quite sufficient for my first experience of crude oil separation and the problems that arose were no less daunting. The plant was also located in an area of natural beauty and special scientific interest, so was limited to 6.5 metres in height and hidden away in a screen of woodland. It is certainly one of the only places I have ever worked where driving out of the gates at night I would see the roadside verge covered in deer, eating the newly sown grass. Another peculiarity at this stage was that the separated crude was to be driven away in tankers. To avoid accidents the original incoming road was extended to form a one-way loop system. Unfortunately some of the local farmers did not, or would not, recognise the one-way system, so you had to be alert for a tractor coming at you in the wrong direction. Just the same as the bullock cart drivers in India!

I was very fortunate to have a group of some of our very bright young process engineers working as part of the commissioning team, including one of the best, Chris Topham, who had worked on the design of a unique separator with specific size and height limitations for the plant. I did not always fully understand what he was telling me but he always seemed to find a solution to any problems that arose. I was very saddened to hear that Chris died last year, I believe of a brain tumour, and will be greatly missed by his family and colleagues in the now Jacobs offices where, with a shock of black hair turned grey he was still working as a very knowledgeable senior process engineer.

We only had one very difficult problem to resolve, which was, in part, due to the small size of the plant. The Bryan Donkin compressor used to compress the separated LPG vapour to liquid form operated with two banks of cylinders. One controlling at up to 50% capacity, which if exceeded allowed a second bank of 50% capacity to load while the first bank off-loaded and then started to load up again. For long periods the compressor would run quite happily at around 40% capacity but if there was a sudden surge, usually resulting from the line from the wellheads being "pigged" the second bank would load. Unfortunately, before the first bank fully off-loaded the relatively small capacity supply vessel would be sucked nearly empty and the second bank would off-load. Once into this cycle of operation the compressor kept loading and off-loading with a noise like a trip hammer until manual intervention got it back into some form of auto-control. Bryan Donkin assured us this type of operation would not harm the compressor and were adamant there was nothing fundamentally wrong with their control system. Fairly understandably, British Gas operations staff, who were responsible for the site, were not too happy with the situation and were demanding something be done. This put us between a rock and a hard place. In the end, after some weeks' trying to understand what exactly was happening, I decided to act and sent a problem report back to the office asking for a solution. The answer that came back was to replace the Bryan Donkin control system, which was not our responsibility, with one of our own design, consisting of a sequence of pneumatically operated solenoid valves that would allow a smooth transition during the compressor loading/off-loading sequence. The drawing seemed to make sense, so we decided to go ahead and a few weeks later the new controller arrived on site. The client made available a technician to install and make the necessary connections to the new controller, however, because of technical problems in the client's gas and LPG storage area, the compressor would not be needed for at least another twenty four hours. I took this opportunity to double check all the internal connections within the new controller and was shocked to find they did not correspond to those in the design drawing. After a number of hurried phone calls the necessary corrections were made and, to our great relief, once the compressor was put back into operation it ran very smoothly, which, in turn, allowed us to optimise the operation of other pieces of equipment and stabilise the overall performance of the separator unit. An added bonus was that our standing with the client greatly improved and later, I was given to understand, that within a couple of months of start-up the cost of the installation had been recovered.

A more quirky problem that arose was that after a shutdown and restart, for a short period until stable conditions were achieved, the separated gas and vapour would be sent to the ground flare resulting in a brief escape, before the flair fully ignited, of injected, foul-smelling odorant. This led to phone calls from irate local farmers demanding compensation because their cows were aborting or their milk yields were down. I do not think the farmers, who probably lost some of their land to compulsory purchase, ever came to terms with the need for oil production and probably never will, if indeed they are still farming. The surrounding land held even greater reserves at different depths and a few years later we bid for work to build new facilities to recover 60,000 bpd, unfortunately that contract went to another company. At its peak in 1996–97 Wytch Farm became the largest onshore oil production site in Western Europe, producing 110,000 bpd. Not bad from small beginnings.

4.4 Khartoum – Sudan – The Nile and its waters.

About a year after the rural delights of Dorset I was happily working away in the office when I got an urgent call to go home and pack a bag in readiness to fly to Khartoum the next day. David Osborne, the company's water treatment expert, whom I had known as a friend and colleague since the early days in the Billericay laboratory, was at Heathrow Airport when his father was taken seriously ill. I expect, as a lapsed chemist, I was the only person they could think of to take his place. The urgency arose because the company were in a joint venture to design and build the new Khartoum North Power Station and part of their responsibility was the water treatment system. Khartoum sits on the Blue Nile, just before it converges with the White Nile to join forces and flow on through Egypt. A very large proportion of the annual flow down the Nile occurs for just three or four weeks in the year when it rains heavily in the Ethiopian Highlands sending a torrent of water down the Blue Nile, resulting, before the Aswan Dam was built, in the annual flood in Egypt. This makes the building of a water treatment system very difficult because the water taken from the Blue Nile changes from relatively clean and clear (suspended solids as low as 10 parts per million) to a thick, brown soup (suspended solids as high as 85,000 parts per million during the exceptional flooding in 1978). The object of the visit was to test a range of flocculating agents, either on their own or in combination with the currently used primary coagulant alum or an alum/lime combination, to see which would be most effective at clearing the water of suspended solids especially during the time of flood, which had just started.

David returned to the office and handed over any equipment he had with him as well as method statements and gave me as good a briefing as he could of where I would be working and with whom, as well as what was expected of me. My journey to the airport was not improved the next day when I was asked to go via the office to pick up three packages of bid documents to be taken to our agents in Khartoum for a proposal to build a chicken farm or some such thing… total baggage 84 kg. I duly arrived in Khartoum at around 22.00 hours, via Geneva and Athens, to find the baggage reclaim area was one small room with a single conveyor belt along one wall. The room was packed as two jumbo jets had come in almost together and you virtually had to climb over people to see what luggage was on the conveyer belt. My problem was that there were no trolleys and I could not handle a large briefcase, a suitcase and three large packages, all together. It was also very hot and my nice tropical suit was soon soaked in sweat. Having got all my luggage together I managed to manhandle it, in three lots, through to customs and passport control and out into the arrivals hall where, thankfully, I was met by our agent. After a brief stop at the agent's office in town to drop off the three large packages, I was taken to the Hilton International Hotel, which was to be my sanctuary for the next week or two and very glad I was to get there.

The next morning it was back to our agents to sort out the bid documents before the drop-off deadline of 12.00 hours. We arrived at 11.40 and I was surprised that at least three other contenders, some of whom had sweated off the plane with me the night before, arrived after us. The opening of the tenders was an interesting experience for me; thirteen companies from all over the world, with prices ranging from £14,000,000 up to £32,000,000 to build chicken sheds. We were about middle of the road but after talking to some of the bidders back at the Hilton that evening, who all seemed to have a minister's son or uncle in their support team, I did not hold out much hope for our chances. If anybody who reads this is wondering how I remember all this, I have just found a letter I wrote to Dawn dated 15/7/81, letting her know I had arrived safely – a real old romantic me.

I do not think I was staying in the Hilton, probably the best hotel in Khartoum, because the company were feeling generous but because it was located west of the city on the south bank of the Blue Nile, within fifteen minutes walking distance of the main laboratories of the Mogren Water Treatment Works, which was to be my base for carrying out the evaluation programme. I was fortunate that the laboratory was under the leadership of Mr El Hag El Obeid, a chief chemist of considerable experience who had participated in a similar evaluation in 1976 and, along with his staff, gave me every assistance to complete the evaluation. A range of 18 poly-electrolytes from five different manufacturers had been selected for testing, to which was added the most effective product from the 1976 trials for comparison purposes. I found out on my first day that I would need to be up bright and early, as the normal working hours were from 7.30 until 14.30. However, I was permitted to work later if necessary in order to finish a test run.

One problem was that I had arrived during the month of Ramadan, which for a good Muslim means they are required to fast (no eating or drinking) from dawn until sunset each day. This is particularly onerous in a hot country, especially in a building with limited air conditioning, so by lunch time everybody was wilting and more inclined, although willing, to sleep rather than work. Also, from conversations I overheard, this situation was exacerbated by the tendency to spend a large part of the night eating and drinking in preparation for a day of abstinence. As a non Muslim these restrictions did not apply to me and the staff did offer to make me small glasses of mint tea but I felt guilty about accepting when they could not drink, so ended up drinking and eating very little for the first few days. That was until one afternoon, when most people had left, I nearly fainted and realised I was dehydrated and probably suffering from heatstroke. After that I took in bottled water and a small lunch pack from the Hilton each day. However, the working hours meant most days I would return to the Hilton in time for a few hours dozing at the pool with a beer and a club sandwich in the late afternoon sun, which was a real bonus. I remember one afternoon the peace was broken when the pool boys started rushing round collecting beds, towels, umbrellas, in fact anything movable. 'What's going on?' I asked, to which he just pointed at the sky. I just about got inside the building before what seemed like half the sand in the Sahara was dumped on us. I had never seen a sandstorm before; quite exciting!

Talking of the Sahara reminds me of another evening going into the restaurant to find it full of a group of young Brits. Being nosy, I soon found out they were on a trans-Africa trip and were parked up in front of the hotel having just crossed the Sahara and were ready for a touch of luxury for a change. It being a small world, it turned out one of the women knew Wickford, my home town, quite well as her grandmother lived just up the road. More chat

01 My father circa 1940

01a Author – formative years

01b Wickford Junior School 1952

01c Chelmsford Technical School 1958

03.2 Author circa 1968 – working in H&G Laboratory

03.2b Author circa 1969

*03.2c H&G Laboratory
party circa 1971*

03.3 Author USSR 1967

03.3c Russian stamp 1967

03.3b Letter home USSR 1967

Mr & Mrs. L. E. Lodge,
80 London Road,
Wickford,
Essex,
ENGLAND.

03.4 Iran 1970 – Shiraz postcard

03.4a Iran 1970 – Shiraz Ammonia Plant

03.5a "My girls" Bulgaria 1974 – Ammonia Plant Laboratory

03.5b "My girls" Bulgaria 1974 – Ammonium Sulphate Plant

03.5c Varna Bulgaria 1973 – Apartment block

03.5d Varna 1973 – Party time Dawn & big Eddy

03.6a The Gates of India 1975

*03.6b Ullal India
1975 – Our bungalow*

*03.6c At home Ullal
India 1975*

Mr. Ambrose Congreve

Chairman, Humphreys & Glasgow Ltd.,

requests the pleasure of the company of

Mr. & Mrs. A.F.Lodge

for

COCKTAILS

at the Engineers Association, Ullal,

on Saturday, 17th January 1976.

Time :
8-30 P.M.
RSVP Phone : 8301

Dress :
Lounge Suit

*03.6d Invitation to
cocktails – Ullal India
1976*

118

MCF, India: ammonia and urea plant

03.6e MCF India – Ammonia and Urea Plant

03.6f Mangalore India 1975

03.6g Taj Mahal India

03.6j Khajuraho temple India

03.6k Temple carving India

03.6l Khajuraho villager India

03.6o Road to Amber India

03.6p Amber palace welcome, India

03.6q Nilgiri blue train India

03.6s Mangalore India

03.6t Mangalore India

03.6u Fishing fleet India

03.6w Mangalore ammonia-urea plant

03.8a Snake catcher – Togo 1977

*03.8b Accommodation huts –
Togo 1977*

03.8c Lome – Togo 1977

03.8d Tannery workers – Togo 1977

03.8e Market day – Togo 1977

03.8f Refinery acceptance celebration – Togo 1977

*03.8g Togo Oil Refinery –
Opening day 1977*

*03.9 H&G Laboratory 1978 – Author
drying MOPS*

*03.9a H&G Laboratory 1978 –
Author working*

*04.1a Flotta 1978
– Liquid Ethane
Storage Vessel*

04.1c Flotta 1979 – Ethane away

04.1b Flotta 1978 – Author working

*04.2a Climatic Test Chamber at
RARDE – Chertsey, Surrey*

04.3a Wytch Farm Dorset 1980

04.3b Wytch Farm Dorset 1980

04.3c Wytch Farm Dorset 1980

04.5 Stowmarket ICI Paints 1982

04.7a Old Nile water intake, Sudan 1982

04.7b New Nile water intake, Sudan 1982

04.7c Nile water treatment – Burri Power Station, Sudan 1982

04.9a Sulpel Plant – Yanbu Saudi Arabia 1986

04.10a Gas Platform load-out, Lowestoft

04.10c Gas Platform in position, North Morecombe

04.10d Gas Platform, North Morecombe

04.10e Leaving H&G & BP Miller project

*06.2a GAC
Water Treatment,
Norwich*

*06.2b Author at
work, Norwich*

*06.2c Instrument
Technicians,
Norwich*

07.0 Validation group lunch 1995

07.3a Bridge evening, Vigo Spain 2002

07.3b Pinto replica, Baiona Spain

07.3c Sailing day, Baiona Spain

07.3e Mussel beds, Ria de Vigo, Spain

07.3f Sailing day lunch, Spain 2003

07.3g Inside apartment, Baiona Spain 2002

07.3h View from apartment balcony, Baiona Spain

07.3i Baiona Mariner & Parador

07.3j Hams & cheese restaurant, Baiona 2002

07.3k Niamh centre, relieved to see us, my 60th birthday party

07.3l Dawn & myself, 60th party, Baiona Spain 2002

07.3m Genentech Production of Retuxan, Porrino, Spain 2003

La planta de Genentech España en Porriño está siendo ampliada y reformada con vistas a la obtención de autorización por parte de la Food and Drug  Administration de EE.UU. (FDA), que se espera tenga lugar a comienzos de 2004. Una vez obtenida la autorización de la FDA, Genentech España proporcionará a Genentech una capacidad complementaria de producción de cultivo celular a granel de Rituxan® (Rituximab), un anticuerpo anti-CD20 para linfoma non-Hodgkin de células B, CD20 positivo, folicular de bajo grado o en recidiva o refractario (Rituxan lo comercializa Roche en Europa como MabThera).

07.4a Dawn site seeing, Dublin 2004

over a meal and a few beers established that what the women really wanted was the luxury of a proper bathroom and shower, so I offered them the use of my room. An hour or so later, wondering if they had taken up residence, I went up and knocked. The door was opened to a scene from the proverbial Chinese laundry; steam billowed out through the door and it was obvious the women were not ready to leave just yet. I guess they took full advantage of my offer by nipping back to their trucks to get two weeks' laundry done while they had the chance. I did not really mind but would probably think twice before making the same offer again.

Looking back I can think of two occasions which meant I was lucky to leave Sudan with nothing but relatively good memories. On my first day off from work I decided to get some exercise with a good walk. I started along the bank of the Nile, which always had something interesting to offer, be it *dhows* in full sail fighting upstream against the flood or sacred ibis, a bird I had not seen before. I am not a twitcher but always like to see what a country has to offer in the way of wildlife and species that are new to me. It was the sight of a very colourful bird, later identified as a red bishop, that turned me inland along the side of a cornfield from where I decided to continue in a wide circle round the back of the hotel. This took me through a scrubland forest, with not much of interest in it until I came to a dirt road that led me out into a small shanty town, its most surprising feature being a graveyard of Morris Minors, not one of which looked as though it was roadworthy and not a popular car to be seen on the streets of Khartoum. They had probably all been dumped as it was no longer possible to get spare parts in Sudan. Later in the day, back at the hotel, one of the waiters asked me where I had been and when I explained my route he said, 'you must not go into the Al Sunut Forest it is full of bandits.' Ignorance is bliss, I guess it must have been the bandits' day off as well!

The next incident, I suspect, could have been more serious. Water out-takes from the Nile were quite complex structures, the pump being mounted on a floating platform to accommodate the very big differences in water level throughout the year. David had asked me to take some photographs of a pumping station to help with the design for the Khartoum North Power Station. The intake for the Mogren Water Works was a short walk from the hotel, so late one afternoon I set off with my camera to get the required pictures. On arriving at the pumping station I walked up and down the bank to see which angle would give me the best detail and was just about to pull my camera out of my jacket when a soldier appeared out of the bushes at the side of the river and waved his Kalashnikov at me. I did not need telling that I should move on and was so thankful my camera was not visible as I could have been arrested and ended up in a Sudanese goal; not a happy prospect. The long, bitter and ongoing war with the Christian south of the country had made essential services an obvious target, it had just not occurred to me they would be closely guarded.

Another non-work experience in Sudan was a trip to Omdurman to visit a camel market and to see whirling dervishes performing their religious devotions. The camel market did not disappoint with many beasts being examined and haggled over in a colourful display. Unfortunately, because of the coincidence with the month of Ramadan the dervishes were not whirling, so I had to wait until many years later, on a holiday to Egypt to experience such an intriguing spectacle. With time to spare I took in most of the main tourist attractions including the fort from where General Gordon came to a grizzly end after refusing to evacuate the occupying Egyptian troops from the garrison; one of the few defeats of a British Empire force during the reign of Queen Victoria. Most surprising was being taken into an ancient pyramid shaped tomb, the walls of which were covered in hand painted scenes and hieroglyphs very similar to those in tombs in Egypt, and it did make me wonder whether the ancient kingdom of Kush pre-dated Egypt in this form of preserving life after death.

After fourteen days all eighteen poly-electrolytes had been tested, either on their own or in combination with alum and/or alum/lime addition to see which gave the best final water clarity after settlement of suspended solids from Blue Nile water during the time of flood. It was therefore time for me to pack my bags and leave Sudan, little thinking that within just over a year I would be back again.

It may be of interest to note that the White Nile, coming from the lakes plateau of Tanzania, Kenya, etc. makes up 72% of the Nile flow during the dry season and probably got its name from opalescence in the water, resulting from a higher colloidal solids content. Also during October, November and December it actually backs up the Blue Nile. However, during the flood period, 90% of the Nile flow comes from the Blue Nile, out of the Ethiopian Highlands and this provides 84% of the average annual Nile flow.

It was somewhat unfortunate to be told, before my report was completed, that the first choice poly-electrolyte was being withdrawn from the market but the information gathered was still a good basis for the design of the facility to continue, despite the additional difficulties raised by Khartoum sitting at the confluence of the Blue and White Niles.

4.5 Stowmarket – Suffolk – ICI Paints

In 1982, I was once again asked to leave the office to supervise a small team responsible for the pre-commissioning and commissioning of a plant the company had built for ICI Paints, only this time it was located in Suffolk, about an hour and a quarter's drive, on a good day, from my home in Essex. To start with I attempted to do the journey from my home daily but soon realised I could not do a ten hour day on site as well as the travelling, without the risk of falling asleep at the wheel. To reduce the risk of this happening I booked into a local hotel on Tuesday and Wednesday nights, which also greatly improved my contribution to the daily programme and review meetings, despite not being able to see across the site hut for cigarette smoke, to which I was not a contributor! I only really mention this because the hotel was a bit like Faulty Towers. It was managed by the son of the owners who, although only in his late twenties, already had a serious drink problem; probably even more of an occupational risk here than being a commissioning engineer. Anyway, it was not unusual for him to collapse behind the bar at around 9.30pm, at which point it was not uncommon for one of the regulars to carry him upstairs to bed. What really surprised me was being introduced to the honesty box system that was being operated. If you wanted another drink after the "departure" of the manager you went behind the bar, pulled yourself a pint and put the money in the box placed there for that purpose. It seemed to work perfectly well and could not have been seriously abused because the bar remained open for the six months or so that I was a guest and probably lost less than it would cost to employ a bar tender.

The plant consisted of a large number of supply tanks that would hold the required solvents, pigments and other raw materials that were the trade secrets of ICI Paint's resins production. These were linked by a complex piping manifold to both weighing and heated and cooled mixing and reaction vessels, which were in turn linked by another complex piping manifold to thinning tanks, filtration sets and product storage and distribution tanks. The facility had a computerised process control system, designed to ICI's specification, to give maximum flexibility to the product range and batch sizes.

One of our main tasks, after confirming the installation was complete, in accordance with the design P&IDs (Piping and Instrument Diagrams) was to flush through and leak test all the tanks, vessels and pipework to ensure they were clean and free of obstructions before solvents or pigments were introduced. One of our senior commissioning engineers on the site was David Heywood, easily recognised as "Colonel Sanders", who I first met in Bulgaria and more recently had worked with on the Chertsey site. As we became busier and busier he asked if it would be possible to hire his son on a short term contract as local labour, as he had been out of work for the past six months, although qualified as a garage mechanic. I had realised by then that the commissioning life can be a difficult balancing act as far as family life and children's education is concerned, so was happy to agree. It proved a good choice as he was a quick learner and made friends easily so he soon knew just where to go and who to see to get the job done. It was not until some years later I found out what an interesting life David had led, first in the army in Egypt, then as a district officer in Kenya, responsible for an area half the size of Wales but best of all a side-line of writing short stories that he got published in a number of magazines. I particularly liked one about a dung beetle, which captured the magic of those wonderful insects to a nicety.

I learnt a lot on that job, not least about the quantity of paperwork that is generated and the best way of dealing with it in order to achieve a successful handover to the client, although I only managed to slip the additional Portakabin that was needed to hold it onto the site when their project manager was on holiday.

It was soon after the completion of this job that my wife's company decided to move from Stock in Essex to Occold in Suffolk and were encouraging as many as possible of the more senior staff to move with them. Dawn was fairly keen to go as she enjoyed her work and was moving up the career ladder but it was a big decision, not least because it would put on hold any thoughts of starting a family for a few years yet. One thing I realised from my time at ICI Paints was that, if she agreed to go, she could not possibly drive backwards and forwards from Essex to Suffolk every day and a base near her new work place would be a necessity. Thus a second home was acquired and our love affair with the village of Hoxne was started. It still goes on and although we are both retired we still live a split life and Dawn spends at least half her week in the tranquillity of the cottage and surrounding countryside.

4.6 Dharhan – Saudi Arabia – Onshore and offshore GOSPS

This was another job that was a new experience for me and was totally unexpected. For many years H&G had been black balled by all the Arab countries after completing a contract in Israel. In fact a number of our staff had to apply for new passports after working in Israel to avoid complications when travelling through the Middle East. So, it came as a complete surprise when the company were invited by Aramco (Arabian American Oil Company) to bid for work in Saudi Arabia. The brief was to visit some of Aramco's onshore and offshore facilities and to advise them on the necessity for and the type of emergency breathing apparatus that should be deployed on these facilities. A problem with crude oil extracted from The Gulf is that it contains sulphur (sour crude) and can give off hydrogen sulphide, which is very poisonous even at low concentrations when breathed in.

I suspect sales and proposals group were not quite sure what to do with this invitation to bid when it arrived. It was little more than a study that would not lead to a major contract, so not worth spending too much time on. On the other hand the opportunity to work for Aramco should not be ignored. Looking around they probably thought a lapsed chemist, who had some experience of wearing breathing apparatus coupled with on-site plant experience, might be the man for the job. This involved a trip to the Hague, to Aramco's European headquarters, for a detailed briefing of what was required and then a period in the office putting a programme together, estimating man-hours and coming up with a bid price. Management suggested it should be at least a two man job and that the cost should include for one of our company safety officers to accompany me.

The itinerary in Saudi Arabia was to include visits to the following sites:

1. Dhahran   Aramco offices
2. Ras Tanura   Refinery
3. Abqaiq   Crude Oil & NGL stabilization & purification plant
4. Shedgum   NGL purification & sulphur recovery plant
5. Zuluf GOSP-2   Offshore gas/oil separation plant
6. Berri   NGL purification & sulphur recovery plant

Back in the office, one of my first tasks was to visit the company library to find an atlas to show me where these places were and estimate how long it would take to travel to and from each one. It quite amused me that the most up to date atlas the company possessed went back to the days of the Empire and still showed half the world coloured in pink. I also applied for copies of the relevant British Standards that specified respiratory protective equipment and escape breathing apparatus to give me a proper definition of what was required.

Further to the briefing it was expected that no more than a week would be required in Saudi Arabia, with no more than a day required to carry out a survey at each location. Following that, time would be spent back in the office, carrying out a survey and cost comparison of the range of emergency breathing apparatus available from different manufacturers, with recommendations for future use. All to be summarised and assembled into a final study document for distribution, following Aramco approval, to the various locations visited. I think five other companies had been invited to bid and being completely naive about such things, I probably put in a price around half of all the other bids. Anyway, much to my surprise, we got the job.

The journey to Saudi involved a flight to Holland in order to catch an overnight flight on Aramco's own wide-bodied jet. It was a very comfortable journey as alternate rows of seats were missing to give more space and we were liberally supplied with free drink, I guess to make up for the abstinence that was to come. Also, it is the only flight I have been on to be woken with, what I thought was a glass of orange juice, only to realise it was bucks fizz. I am not sure "a hair of the dog" really works!

We duly arrived in Saudi to be taken to the Aramco headquarters in Dhahran where we were introduced to a Mr Gus Leysens from their loss prevention group, who was to be our liaison throughout the visit and a Mr Willy ter Stege, the study engineer, who had flown in from Holland and was going to accompany us on the site surveys. The first priority was to get us fitted with security passes, which involved a visit to the Saudi controlled Administration Centre to get photographs taken, together with forms supplied by Gus Leysens. I was soon to learn a valuable lesson about how things work in Saudi Arabia when I was summoned to see the office manager about a serious problem. He rather forcefully told me the signature on my form was a forgery, a very serious matter. With some trepidation I told him that I had only just arrived and if I could go and get Mr Leysens he would explain. I shot out of his office and grabbed Gus, who had only been in the job himself for a couple of months and when I whispered forgeries he went somewhat pale. After phone calls were made to the group manager's secretary, who had supplied the forms, we were allowed to leave pending further investigation. Suspicions were raised because the signature on my form looked different from that on Mr ter Stege's form. In fact they were both "forgeries" because a number of the Saudi Arabians in senior management positions were, let us say, not too zealous about being at work. To keep things moving it was not uncommon for their secretaries to sign documents on their behalf. In this instance the secretary that signed my form was different from the secretary that signed Mr ter Stege's form. The happy ending was that neither Mr Leysens nor I ended up in prison and the next day we were issued with security passes.

An amusing follow on to this was an announcement by the religious authorities to the effect that the large number of young foreign women working as secretaries and personal assistants was creating a moral dilemma for the country and that their contracts would not, in future, be renewed. A week later the edict was rescinded, I suspect because senior management realised the whole organisation would grind to a halt if it was implemented.

The Aramco operation was so large that their headquarters in Dhahran was run like a small town (essentially American), within a foreign country. Enclosed within its own security fence was a housing estate, consisting of accommodation bungalows, supermarkets, all sorts of recreational facilities, several large canteens or dining halls supplying food 24/7 as well as office blocks and site services. It was large enough for women to be allowed to drive themselves within its confines but not outside and dress in "reasonable" western attire. A visit to the supermarket was interesting for what it stocked and was allowed to sell. For instance, there was a whole aisle dedicated to kit for home wine making, demijohns, bubblers, filters, fruit juice concentrate; the only thing not on sale was yeast but that is not the hardest thing to bring into a country. Also, a whole array of newspapers and magazines were on sale, as long as you did not mind buying them after they had been through the censor, which mainly seemed to consist of black felt tipped pens being used to cover any view of women's legs or décolletage. The pen was liberally applied and half the women pictured looked as though they had grown big black beards!

I know Saudi Arabia is a wealthy country but some aspects of their attitude to waste I found annoying. In the canteens, which mainly operated a buffet style system, it was noticeable that a group of Saudi men sitting together would each go up and bring back plates piled high with food. They would then pick at bits and pieces before leaving 60% to go to waste. In a country where pigswill was not an option this was particularly aggravating.

Back to work. The first two days were spent in Dhahran being given a more detailed briefing of the programme and specifics about the breathing apparatus already being used together with written details of the current training and maintenance procedures being employed. This information gave us a big problem. Throughout their entire operation, Aramco used a combination of American manufactured Scott 30 minute air packs, Scott "Ska-Paks" and Scott "Scram" sets, which were serviced at monthly intervals and on some sites MSA/AUER mini filters, which could not be serviced. Altogether some 3000 Scott breathing sets were deployed throughout their facilities and we could not see how, whatever recommendations we made, they would ever change to a different manufacturer or product.

The next day we raised this concern with Gus Leysens and after some hesitation he told us their main concern was with the AUER mini filters. A small filter, designed to absorb hydrogen sulphide (H_2S), with a three to five minute capacity, that plugged into the mouth, together with a nose clip. These filters fitted into a small belt pouch and had been issued, for emergency escape only, to selected personnel on around half the Aramco sites. Aramco, who called them "stick it in your gob and go sets" were not sure about the validity of using these filters but were under pressure to issue them to all sites without them. For this reason they had called in external "experts" in the hope that they would raise sufficient doubt about their deployment to have them removed from service. I was very glad we had asked the question because we now had a much clearer understanding of what we were looking for and why we were there; however, we were also determined not to let this knowledge affect the integrity of our study.

We had just five days to visit all five locations, including travel, which meant a maximum of four or five hours gathering information and surveying each site. It was very intense, with a similar pattern being established at each location, usually an interview with the operations manager or superintendent, the loss prevention superintendent and maintenance superintendent. This was to establish what type of breathing apparatus was available and where it was located, other relevant safety devices, such as H_2S detectors and wind socks and "permit to work" procedures in particularly vulnerable locations, as well as any incidents that had been recorded in the past. This would be followed by a walk round the site taking notes of both good points and bad points which would be reviewed and discussed each evening before summarising for entry into the final study document. Where possible we also tried to get a quiet word with some of the shift operators or maintenance group to see if they had any particular concerns or worries they would like to be considered.

Each site we visited gave us more experience and a better understanding of what to look for. It also made me realise that there is value to be had from bringing in external experts because, although generally very safety conscious, some good practises used on one site were not always incorporated on the others. One or two incidents occurred during these visits which I think are worth a mention.

At Shedgum there was not much market for the sulphur separated and recovered from the crude oil, so the liquid sulphur from the Clause units was pumped into the desert where it solidified into brilliant yellow football pitch size blocks about two stories high. Quite a sight and a good job there was no shortage of desert to put it in.

Before boarding a helicopter to fly out to the gas oil separation platform, Zuluf GOSP-2, our bags were put through a security check and a camera was found in Willy ter Stege's briefcase. Now, although he was an Aramco employee, rather than just holding the camera onshore until he returned, they decided he was a sufficient security risk that he had to be accompanied for the duration of the visit. Like a lot of Dutch men Willy was large, six feet four and probably around eighteen stone so I was quite amused, after a wait of about twenty minutes, to find a suitably "sized" escort, this fresh-faced, apologetic young man nearly as wide as he was tall, roll up to do the job. My first experience of helicopters, noisy uncomfortable things at best, was not improved by being squashed in with two giants.

At Berri we had just been introduced to the plant manager when a red telephone rang – Is this an exercise? 'Sorry lads you will have to evacuate, we have an emergency.' As we walked out through the gates I could see a big black plume of smoke rising at the other end of the plant but I was very impressed with the calm orderly way everybody was checked off as they walked out to their assembly points. Fortunately it was nothing too serious and a short while later we were checked back in, still with time to complete our study, albeit with a heightened sense of anticipation as we approached the flare area where the fire had been.

Back in Dhahran we showed the first draft of our observations, remarks and recommendations for each site visited to the loss prevention group, and I could tell from their reaction that they were quite surprised and not displeased at some of our findings. I was quite impressed myself!

After studying both the British and American standards pertaining to emergency breathing apparatus we were able to state that the MSA/Auer mini filter respirator did not comply with the minimum requirements and should not be issued as they were not of the self-contained type. That is an apparatus where the wearer carries his own breathing atmosphere with a duration of not less than five minutes. However, on all the sites visited we made recommendations about locations where additional self-contained breathing apparatus should be sited and emergency breathing apparatus should be carried.

Back in the London office we spent three or four weeks carrying out a market survey and cost comparison of breathing apparatus before making our recommendations for the best equipment currently available. In fact much of the British/European manufactured equipment was better specified and considerably cheaper than the American equivalent but I would be surprised if Aramco changed their policy to any great extent.

Finally, after another trip to the Hague and a number of revisions to satisfy Aramco's requirements, the study was approved and accepted. I was delighted to find that my first (and only) proposal was completed within budget and made 10% profit.

About a month later I was happily sitting at my desk when I got a call to say Aramco, at additional cost, wanted me to travel back to Saudi Arabia to present my findings at all the sites we had visited. Shock, horror; I had done enough small scale presentations of the commissioning group's capabilities to know it was definitely not my forte but could not really see how I could refuse. My equanimity was not improved after flying out to The Hague with the first draft of a presentation. They basically told me if I presented like that in Saudi all the guys would get up and walk out. I did not think it was that bad but was glad of their advice to use just bullet points in my overheads and concentrate on key points from our findings at each site. At least, when I eventually made the presentation in Saudi, the guys did not get up and walk out and in the end I did start to relax a little. The good thing was I did not get bombarded with too many awkward questions and did not detect too much hostility at our findings and recommendations.

One outcome of this experience was that at annual staff appraisal time I invariably asked to be put on a "Presentation Skills" course but, in truth, I do not think it is something I will ever learn to enjoy.

4.7 Khartoum – Sudan – Burri power station

It was just over a month after completing the work in Saudi Arabia that I was once again asked to leave the office to join a small team being sent to Khartoum to prepare a report on the status of and requirements for obtaining funding from the ODA (Overseas Development Administration) for the continuing operation of Khartoum's Burri Power Station. The British Government had found over the years that it was sometimes more effective to provide aid via a third party, rather than directly to the recipient and when possible that third party should be a British company. After a number of years of this service being provided by Babcock and Wilcox it was time for a change and Humphreys and Glasgow had been invited to provide a report showing evidence of their capabilities to take over the task.

I was included in the team to assess the training requirements as well as the analytical services and chemical dosing requirements to keep the power station operating efficiently and effectively over the coming years. I was not too surprised at being chosen to assess the analytical requirements because, following the demise of the Billericay laboratory, I was one of the few chemists left in the company but training was something altogether new to come to grips with. At least I had some idea what to expect in Sudan, or so I thought.

The journey out was uneventful and this time I was not lumbered with large boxes of bid documents to contend with. Even so, the baggage handling area was no less sweaty and stressful and by the time we reached our hotel I was glad of a shower and the luxury of air-conditioning even though the refinements of the Hilton had been replaced by a three star hotel in the centre of town.

My first day at the power station I was introduced to the chief chemist and his head of laboratory, a (let's say) Miss Suliman, recently graduated from Sheffield University with a degree in chemistry. The laboratory was a fairly dismal place with very few external windows and although well staffed did not appear to be a hive of activity. The next day I began to have serious misgivings when I asked Miss Suliman if I could see the laboratory's log-books and latest analytical results as she told me they were kept by the chief chemist and he was not expected to put in an appearance until tomorrow or the day after. A little more probing determined that the chief chemist was a very busy man whose duties took him away from the power station on a regular basis and was a very hard person to pin down. When I eventually saw the record books I was even more shocked to see the only results recorded on a daily basis appeared to be the boiler feed waters conductivity and this came from the Mogren Water Works, courtesy of Mr El Hag El Obeid. Further investigation ascertained that the laboratory was quite well supplied with equipment and chemicals, in fact the cupboards were full of boxes that had never been unpacked. I was only there for a brief period, on a fact-finding mission, so could not do too much but when I asked Miss Suliman if she would like a hand setting up some of the equipment she seemed highly delighted at the prospect of doing some work. However, I could also sense she was apprehensive about doing anything without the consent of the chief chemist. I felt really sorry for her and in fact the rest of the staff because it can be pretty soul-destroying turning up to work every day with nothing really worthwhile to do – especially when you are newly graduated and keen to put your knowledge to good use, and helping to keep your capital city's lights on is quite important! This being something successive governments in Britain will need to do if they are going to avoid a complete disaster in a few years' time. Without sufficient power, in a progressively modern world, nothing works, and to close down perfectly good gas- or even coal-fired power stations without sufficient redundancy is a complete abdication of the government's duty of care.

Back in Sudan in 1982, a walk round the power station with some of my colleagues showed me why so little analysis was being done. Despite the stores containing adequate amounts of water-treatment chemicals, for whatever reason, no boiler dosing treatment chemicals had been used for years, to the extent that the boiler tubes were so furred up the boilers were in the process of being shutdown so that tubes could be cut out and replaced in order that sufficient steam could be produced to drive the turbines to generate electricity. It also made me realise that whatever training regimes were currently in place or were proposed they would be of limited value if senior management did not utilise the knowledge and resources being made available to them. How to put that diplomatically in my final report was my next problem.

Two non-work related excursions I think are worth mentioning. The first was an invitation to join in a celebration, probably Her Majesty the Queen's official birthday, at the British Embassy. It was in the afternoon so we went more or less straight from work without any lunch as the invitation stated that food would be provided. On arrival we found that marquees had been set up in the grounds and a Sudanese military band was playing, for our entertainment, some stirring martial music, not always in tune but with great enthusiasm. After some introductions to embassy staff and other guests we were veering towards the food tents when, almost without warning, the heavens opened and the first rains for about six months inundated the whole event. We rushed for shelter and tried to grab some food in passing, as it soon became obvious the celebration would have to be abandoned. A great shame and in fact we struggled to get back to our hotel because many of the roads were very soon under water.

As my main point of contact, I spent a lot of time talking to Miss Suliman trying to understand a little better how things worked and somewhat intrigued to find out how a young Muslim woman from good family, her father was a government minister, had been given the freedom to go to Sheffield University. After some initial shyness she did confide that one of her biggest worries was that in the near future she would be expected to agree to an arranged marriage at which time she would have to give up work and lose all her "Western" freedoms. When I knew that I was leaving I asked if it would be appropriate for me to take her to dinner somewhere, by way of a thank you for all her help. She said it would not be appropriate but the next day invited me to meet her family at her family home for afternoon tea; an invitation I was glad to accept. She apologised that her father could not be present but arranged for an uncle to come to the hotel to escort me. It quite amused me that her uncle turned out to be a sixteen year old boy and the whole experience was a little bizarre. Tea was served in the garden and, apart from uncle, I think I was the only male there, trying to make polite conversation after being introduced to mother, assorted aunties and cousins, collected in little groups whispering behind their hands. However, I was treated with great kindness and I am glad I went as it was an experience I am never likely to repeat.

The outcome of our visit, once the final report was submitted, was the award of a contract to H&G, by the ODA, to provide backup services to Burri Power Station for the next three years and my final input was selecting and interviewing a suitable chemist to be part of the team sent to Sudan to try to ensure the equipment and chemicals provided by British Aid money was put to good use. From reports sent back I know that some progress was made and good practices were put in place although I suspect it was an uphill struggle. However a good lesson was learnt with regard to the soon to be commissioned Khartoum North Power Station.

4.8 Libya – AGOCO oil and gas facilities

My next excursion out of the office was one I was very dubious about going on and the strange events that occurred during the visit did little to dispel that feeling. However, in retrospect, once safely returned to England, it was an experience I would not have wanted to have missed and much better to have gone in 1983 with Colonel Gaddafi at the height of his power, rather than into the lawless shambles that now exists.

I am not sure why I was chosen for this assignment as I had little or no experience of the task in hand, perhaps nobody else who was readily available was willing to go. The Arabian Gulf Oil Company (AGOCO) was a Libyan government-run organisation that had taken over all the disparate – some English, some French, some American built – oil and gas production facilities in the country, to be run under state control. A company based in Malta, rather oddly named Christian International, was contracted to supply maintenance crews and artisan labour to the AGOCO sites and had been asked if they would like to bid for a contract to perform a complete maintenance function. Realising it was too big for them to handle on their own they approached H&G to go into a partnership arrangement. Since nobody in H&G had any idea what was involved it was decided a rapid survey of some of the facilities to assess the current status of the plants and existing maintenance programmes was required and it was at this point an ex-chemist with no maintenance related background was asked to go. Before leaving I sat down with our planned maintenance group and prepared a check sheet listing the key facts about the various plants condition and current status that would be required to make an informed decision about whether or not to bid for the contract.

The first step was to fly to Malta where I would be met by somebody from Christian International who would organise my visa for entry to Libya and then introduce me to one of their foremen who would accompany me on the flight to Tripoli and the journey around a selected number of sites once in the country. A sign of things to come was the plane filling up with smoke as it touched down in Malta. Fortunately, I was near an exit door and we all disembarked without any sign of fire. Then, after collecting my baggage and passing through customs, I was glad to be met by a young man who had a taxi waiting for me. However, as we walked outside I was introduced to another guy whose first words were, 'don't tell the boss'. Pardon? It turned out he had dented his taxi the night before and then got drunk but he had brought the other young man along to drive and he did give me a letter from Christian International explaining the programme and that I would be staying in the Hilton Hotel (getting better) until my visa and flight to Libya were organised. On the way from the airport to the hotel, somewhere in the dock area, my taxi man ordered a halt and said, 'come with me,' and headed off into a local bar where he said, 'these are my friends, have a drink.' Oh no! Fortunately it was only one drink and then we were off again, further into the dock area, when another halt was called and he said, 'give me your passport, I have to arrange a visa.' What to do now? I do not like parting with my passport at the best of times and these circumstances were far from encouraging, however, it did not seem likely that I would become part of the white slave trade and I did have my letter of introduction so reluctantly handed it over. I watched him disappear into a building that had no indication it was anything to do with Libya or its government and he shortly reappeared without my passport whereupon we proceeded to the Hilton without further stops.

I spent three enjoyable days at the Hilton, which gave me a chance to see a little of Malta, before my passport was returned complete with new visa and an Air Libya ticket for departure the following day. I was met at the airport by Freddie, who was to be my companion and guide for the next couple of weeks and a group of guys returning after R&R in Malta. I was glad of their company because the embarkation form was only written in Arabic and would have been impossible to fill in on my own, similarly at Tripoli Airport all the signs were in Arabic so I just followed the rest of the guys to passport control. Everybody else passed through without any problems but when it came to my turn he took my passport, examined it then put it to one side and gestured for me to go and wait while the rest of the passengers were checked through. I sat there in some trepidation, wondering whether I was going to be arrested for having a forged visa, made worse, in the days before I had a mobile phone, as I had no means of communicating with anybody outside to let them know what was happening. Eventually he took my passport into an inner office and after a few minutes returned, stamped it and to my great relief gestured for me to come and pick it up. Also, to my great relief after collecting my lone bag and passing through customs control Freddie was waiting, as I had no idea where we were going after leaving the airport. As it turned out the company had a bungalow, which they used as a staging post to put up men waiting for connecting flights en route to their various places of work all over Libya. Unfortunately there was some sort of strike going on with the internal flights, so the bungalow was overflowing with men. I was assured I would have a bed for the night and would not have to sleep in the corridor and then, even more bizarrely, spent my first night in this Muslim country drinking "sadiki" (Arabic for friend and an illegal, almost pure alcohol) and watching some of the most pornographic videos I had ever seen. I was quite relieved to find, in the morning, that our flight to Benghazi was operating, as I am not sure I could have survived another evening in the bungalow.

Our programme was to visit five sites with no more than a day at each one to gather information. Three were scattered along the Mediterranean coast and two were inland on the edge of the Sahara. First stop was in Benghazi at AGOCO's headquarters to get an overview of their operation. The most useful thing to come from this visit was a letter from their senior management saying I was to be given every cooperation at any of the sites on our schedule. As for their HQ, although everybody made the right noises, I could find nobody who knew or was willing to give me specific answers to the questions I was asking. Perhaps I was asking the wrong questions!

At our first stop after Benghazi and a courtesy call to the camp manager we were passed over to the accommodation manager to organise where we were to sleep that night. I could immediately detect ill feeling between this man and Freddie, who regularly travelled to all the sites as part of his job. On being shown my cabin it was immediately obvious the place had not been cleaned and in fact the sheets were filthy. Now, I do not mind roughing it but there are limits, so I went next door to see Freddie, to find his room was in much the same state. He explained he had trouble with this man on a previous visit because the man was homosexual and had been entering the cabins and trying to interfere with some of the men supplied by Christian International. Following conversations with some Scottish lads on one of the other sites I realised that this was not an uncommon problem and one of the nastier aspects of working in Libya where expats had very limited rights and could easily lose their jobs or even end up in goal if they protested too strongly. I resolved our immediate problem by going back to the camp manager and explaining, as diplomatically as I could, that sleeping in dirty sheets was not being given *every* cooperation. He apologised and had us moved.

Apart from such incidents our visits soon established a good rhythm, I became more confident I was getting useful information and the check sheets started to fill up. It also became obvious there were big differences between the sites; some were old, run-down with a very limited future, others were almost brand new. Some had well-established planned maintenance programmes, others almost none with equipment rotting where it stood. The last two plants visited, on the edge of the Sahara, were typical. One was almost brand new and the other was at the end of its useful life, to the extent that the pipeline carrying oil back to Benghazi was so corroded in places that the main pumps could not be used and only lower pressure stand-by pumps could be used to transfer the oil. I wonder if the CIA knew that, I expect so. To reach the new plant involved a jeep ride across the desert; there was no proper road and the route followed a line of pylons carrying the power lines. Funnily enough, although on the edge of the Sahara, dew could form at night and freeze onto the insulators carrying the power lines resulting in power outages as an unforeseen problem.

I thought my time at this Site would be limited because a jeep to take me back was arranged for 14.00 hours, so when the plant manager said he could take me at 16.30 I readily accepted his offer. We duly set off at the appointed time and were about half way back when "bang", a tyre blew out. Now, all round the Site were safety notices saying if you are driving into the desert make sure you carry fuel, water and a spare tyre, so I could not believe it when the plant manager, of all people, told me we did not have a spare or any water on board and, although the sun was going down, it was still about 40 °C and the small bottle of water I carried in my briefcase only had a couple of mouthfuls in it. I was greatly relieved when we spotted men working on one of the wellheads in the far distance and even more relieved when he produced a two way radio that was capable of contacting them. They were carrying a spare and in about fifteen minutes arrived in their jeep to get us out of trouble.

These two plants were the last on the schedule and, as I had a British Airways flight booked to return me from Tripoli to London two days later, the next morning I was more than ready to board the aged Fokker Friendship for the flight to Tripoli. Somebody must have had my interests at heart because when we put down at an intermediate airstrip in the middle of nowhere, I was given to understand the connecting flight had been delayed for 30 minutes so that I could catch it. It was not very full and after it had taken off I followed the lead of some of the other passengers by pushing the back of the seat in front forward, took my shoes off and stretched out to enjoy a relaxing journey. A few minutes later a magnificent peregrine falcon, wings spread, suddenly appeared on one of the seats in front. It peered round the cabin then fixed those golden eyes on my toes which I had just been wiggling with pleasure. My feet came off that seat at the speed of light. It was a small comfort to realise that the bird's owner, a Bedouin chieftain by his robes, although he had removed its hood, still had it attached to his arm by a thong. Still a beautiful sight.

I reached Tripoli just in time for my passport to be taken away to obtain the required approval from AGOCO that I had completed my work and that they had no reason to withhold consent for me to leave the country. The next day approval was obtained just in time for me to be rushed to the airport to catch my flight. Made it, I thought, until after booking in and getting my boarding card, I was required to take all my luggage for inspection and customs approval. This involved going into a vast room packed with non-nationals with piles of baggage all trying to reach a bored customs man to get his chalk cross of approval. After 40 minutes of incredible frustration, by which time I thought the gate had closed and after everything I had missed my flight, I got my bag accepted and taken away, only then to find, when I stepped outside into departures, the flight had been delayed. Thanks be to God!

I arrived back in England on a late November afternoon, after a memorable but not very pleasant trip, to find my bag had not been put on the flight. It had gone to Jordan instead. Oh joy! The biggest problem, as all my work sheets were in my briefcase, was that I was in my shirt-sleeves, with any warm clothing packed in my suitcase and it was cold! It was a relief to reach home and the suitcase turned up a couple of weeks later. I suppose I should be thankful the piece of petrified wood I found in the desert never got spotted before I left Libya, or I might well have been arrested.

The other thing I was thankful for was that I heard no more about the job or the contract, as I had no desire to return to Libya any time soon, although at that time I did think I probably knew more about the status of AGOCOS facilities than almost anybody on Earth.

4.9 Yanbu – Saudi Arabia – Sulphur pelleting plant

Before leaving the Billericay laboratory one of the last research and development projects I was involved in was running a very small test rig to drop liquid sulphur through various sized nozzles into a swirled water bath to see if uniform sized spheres of solid sulphur could be produced. The idea being that small spheres or pellets of sulphur could be more easily stored and then transported for use in other manufacturing processes than enormous blocks of sulphur. Eight years on this concept had been developed and scaled up to working plant size and marketed as the Sulpel Process, a number of which had been sold around the world to organisations where sour (sulphur bearing) crude oil was being processed. The latest one to be nearing construction completion was located at Yanbu on the Red Sea coast of Saudi Arabia and as all our commissioning group with previous experience of these plants were busy elsewhere I was once again required to leave my nice office job and head into the unknown.

An operating manual had been produced for the plant, which gave me a reasonable idea of the process and how the equipment was meant to function and before leaving I had a number of sessions with Tony Blenkinsop, the chief design engineer/project manager for the process to clarify anything I did not understand and to make some detailed notes on setting up the pelletiser and detailed pre-commissioning notes for preparing the Sulpel plant for operation. This included the preparation of a trip and alarm schedule on A4 size paper (for ease of use on site) combining as much data as possible from the P&IDs and Instrument Process Logic diagrams. Finally a visit was made to the manufacturer of the dewatering screen for a demonstration of what adjustments could be made to modify the screen's operation.

On arrival in Yanbu, I was pleasantly surprised to find I would be staying, to start with at least, in the Holiday Inn. On my first night I was sitting in the hotel lounge drinking an exotic fruit cocktail – no alcohol allowed – when a quirky, related incident occurred. A man walked in clutching a brown paper bag which slipped from his grasp and smashed on the tiled floor. Almost before a pool of liquid started spreading across the floor and before the faint whiff of alcohol could reach my nose, hotel staff arrived with dustpan, brushes and mops and in an instant, as if by magic, all trace had gone. The incident never happened and the purveyor of our old "friend" sadiki had avoided a hard term in prison.

Another oddity was that on arriving back from work, hot and tired, I could only relax at the hotel pool on Tuesday, Thursday and Sunday as only segregated bathing was allowed. I do not know how entry into the sea was controlled and do not remember being told it was men only when making enquiries about joining a SCUBA diving course but I am sure the sexes would have been kept apart somehow. Or, like driving, it was a male only activity. Something else that surprised me and I do not know why it should, was to find a wetlands nature reserve on the shore, within easy walking distance of the hotel, which was a pleasant place to visit.

For reasons I cannot remember, probably delays to the overall refinery programme, H&G's construction supervisors had returned to England and when I arrived as the company "expert" mechanical completion certificates for some key elements of the Sulpel plant had not been completed so were still the responsibility of the main contractor, Chiyoda Petrostar Ltd. (a Japanese company) who were very keen that they should be accepted by PEMREF (Petromin Mobil Yanbu Refinery Co. Ltd.) as a first priority. This made my task of starting up equipment I had never seen before very stressful, as while this situation prevailed they were very formal. If I wanted to discuss something about the best way to proceed, "you are the expert, tell us what to do", was a favourite phrase. Two pieces of equipment caused major problems.

The sulphur elevating conveyer was designed to carry sulphur pellets from the outlet of the dewatering screen vertically to discharge into a product chute leading into one of two available Prill Silos. The belt, some 650 mm wide, was made of a flexible flame retardant anti-static material with inset pouches capable of transporting 28 metric tonnes per hour of sulphur pellets. The belt had a bottom-mounted, motor-driven drive pulley and ran round two full width support rollers (one at top and one at bottom) with stub-type return idlers. According to the manufacturers operating manual the rollers were shaped so that the belt would automatically centre itself when in operation. However, a tension screw was included so that slight adjustments could be made if, after a period of observation, the tracking was not perfectly central. After completing the pre-start checks as required in the vendor's manual and completing the necessary pre-commissioning check-sheets for motor rotation, alarm and trip compliance, etc., I pressed the start button. The belt rumbled into life and then immediately, without time for any slight adjustments, shot off the support roller at the top point of its travel. At least the emergency stop button worked and once I had climbed to the top of the

Prill Silos it did not appear as though too much damage had been done. However, why the conveyer had behaved as it did was still a complete mystery. Chiyoda, without too much comment, brought in a large crane and hauled the belt back into position. Once again I went all round the installation checking the dimensions and location of the various elements of the conveyer and after reading the fault finding guide in the operating manual adjusted a number of the guide rollers at the top end of the belt to, hopefully, keep it in place. Only one thing to do and that was try again. This time the belt did not immediately come off but tracked slowly to one side while I worked hard on the fine adjustment screw to keep it place, at which point it tracked slowly back in the opposite direction and the fine adjustment was reversed. I kept it running for ten to fifteen minutes with the belt in place and although I felt sure something was not right I could not see any obvious fault. After demonstrating to Chiyoda their only concern seemed to be that it would run long enough to get a mechanical completion acceptance from PEMREF, which was duly obtained so everybody, apart from me, was happy!

The other piece of mechanical equipment to cause problems was the dewatering screen. The Sulpel unit was housed in a three-storey open metal framework with equipment located so that gravity flow could be used wherever possible. After completing all the necessary pre-commissioning checks and establishing that a ten to fifteen minutes dry run would do the screen no harm the start button was pressed. This time the piece of equipment itself appeared to be working perfectly correctly, unfortunately as well as the screen vibrating, the whole support structure, walkways and hand rails, were vibrating as well. My suggestion that, when the screen had water and sulphur passing through it, further adjustments could be made that would reduce the vibration seemed sufficient for PEMREF to accept it mechanically with the proviso that the structural vibration should go on the Butt List. An added difficulty with problem solving in Saudi Arabia was telephone communication with the London office was somewhat limited as Saturday and Sunday in Saudi were normal working days with Friday as the day off. However, after relaying my vibrating structure problem the suggestion came back that adding weights to the support frame of the dewatering screen might help. Before doing this I managed to borrow a meter from Chiyoda to measure the vibration frequency at various points all round the screen and the support frame, then placed sandbags around the frame, as additional weight, to see if this would dampen the vibration and repeated the readings but with seemingly little improvement, even after days of trying. In between times I completed all other checks and tests that I could to satisfy myself and the client that a construction completion certificate could be signed off. Once this was done it was decided that I should return home for a few weeks as no firm date could be given for when the unit would be needed to process sulphur.

Back in the office I took all the marked up drawings and vibration readings to our structural department and a few days later a very nice boffin phoned me and said it will vibrate. The support structure has a sympathetic frequency with the frequency of vibration of the dewatering screen and there is nothing you could do about it. When you are working on your own, trying to operate equipment and a process that you have never seen before it is very easy to blame yourself when something does not work properly, so I felt much happier about returning to Saudi when given this news. The company then produced drawings to include some additional large girders into the support structure that would resolve the problem, which were sent to Chiyoda for installation before my return.

On my return I found I was reporting to PEMREF, not Chiyoda, as construction completion had been achieved, so I immediately started all the pre-commissioning checks and preparations for putting the Sulpel unit into operation. Following my experience as a commissioning chemist I always carried a small tool kit with me and to this had been added a surface contact thermometer, a wire brush – an essential, so I had been told, for clearing sulphur fines from clogging the dewatering screen and, strangest of all, a couple of corks pulled from my better-quality wine bottles, as we thought it may not be possible to find any (corks that is) in Saudi (always plan ahead for the environment you are going to). A key part of the process was for liquid sulphur, held in the Pelletiser head, to fall through fine-bore nozzles into the body of the Pelletiser filled with swirling solution water (water plus additives), where the sulphur streams broke up into pellets and solidified. Around the body of the Pelletiser were ten swirl nozzles through which water flowed to rotate the solution water, ideally at 10 to 12 revolutions per minute with no vortex. The highly technical method for doing this was to place a cork on the surface of the water and adjust the valve position on each swirl nozzle until the correct swirl pattern was achieved.

One good thing was that after all the modifications to the support structure around the dewatering screen had been put in place it could be operated without making your teeth chatter if you were anywhere near it. Success, for a short while at least. During this period, in conjunction with the PEMREF operations group, all the liquid and solution lines were flushed out; steam lines were blown out and any blockages in the lines, traps or filters were cleaned out and cleared. A sulphur lorry was brought in to demonstrate that the vibrating discharger and retractable loading spouts from the Prill Silos were positioned and operating correctly so that lorries could be loaded without problems, once sulphur pellets were being produced. In this instance the lorry was sent away full of a load of accumulated dirt and rubbish from the hopper.

During this visit I was no longer offered the luxury of staying in the Holiday Inn but was moved into one of the accommodation camps; Camp 3, after complaining about the very poor facilities available in Camp 1. However, this move put me in touch with a larger section of the work force where I made contact with a group of lads from the Philippines who made the most of the Friday day of rest to go snorkelling in the Red Sea, in search of clams or other delicacies they could not get in the works canteen. While at home, by chance, I watched a television programme about diving in the Red Sea, which highlighted its many wonders but also the many dangers, such as stone fish, the beautiful but poisonous lion fish, the sting ray and the extremely venomous sea snake. Not put off by this I had packed my snorkel and a pair of rubber shoes, bought after an unfortunate encounter with a sea urchin while on holiday in Greece, so I thought I was well equipped to make the most of such an opportunity to join them. After a couple of very enjoyable excursions they decided to change the venue and headed off-road across the desert to an entry point miles from anywhere. Entry to the sea was via a walk across a reef covered by very shallow water, so the rubber shoes were essential, but once over the side into deeper water the fish and coral were amazing. It was like swimming in a wonderfully stocked aquarium and perhaps because it was so remote the fish took almost no notice of our presence. After a couple of hours I was back at the vehicle taking in some much needed fresh water with a picnic lunch when two of the lads out on the reef edge started shouting and waving. They had found some gem coral but in the process of trying to reach it had brushed against some fire coral which can be very painful and almost instantly causes the skin to blister. I began to walk out to see what was going on and was about half way to them when I felt a sharp stab into my left ankle just above the rubber shoe. I immediately turned back as it was almost instantly painful and by the time I reached the car my leg was swelling up and the pain was excruciating. I did not know what had stung me, stone fish perhaps or sting ray but I did wonder if my life was going to come to a sudden end on a remote reef somewhere in Saudi Arabia. By now the leg was swollen almost to my knee so it did not take too much to persuade the lads to pack up for the day and get me back to a hospital. Once there, my leg was examined and x-rayed because, although two prick marks could be clearly seen, I think they thought I had twisted it. In any event there was no talk of giving me any sort of anti-venom and after a few hours I was sent "home" with some much needed pain killers. It is not pleasant being ill in almost complete isolation from family or friends and I spent the next twenty-four hours in agony, not really knowing what to do with myself. Fortunately the swelling did not go above my knee and gradually the pain lessened and the swelling went down until I felt fit enough to hobble to a phone to let Dawn know what had happened.

Back at work, PEMREF had introduced molten sulphur to the sulphur storage vessel on the 21st August 1984, at a rate of 80 tonnes/day, so it was likely to be half-full by the 1st September and the pressure was on to complete all the pre-commissioning checks on the Sulpel unit in preparation for the introduction of sulphur. I also completed a series of Site Commissioning Memoranda (SCMs), explaining the principals of operation of various sections of the unit and then walked the plant with groups of PEMREF's operations staff describing how everything, hopefully, was going to work. Also a repeat check was made, in conjunction with the PEMREF Instrument and Electrical Group, to confirm all the alarms and trips were operating correctly.

By mid-September, sulphur had been successfully introduced, the whole unit was in operation and with sulphur pellets going to storage, some fine tuning could begin to improve the pellet size distribution and the dewatering operation. Certain elements needed constant attention, the dewatering screen needed to be wire brushed at regular intervals to prevent fines building up and blocking the screen and the elevating conveyer was still not tracking correctly, requiring fine adjustments to be made to keep it central. A constant worry!

The Sulpel unit was at the very end of the refinery area and a good twenty minutes walk from the offices and rest area, so once down there, particularly with so much to do, I tended to stay there and missed out on tea breaks, etc. A peculiarity of the location caused a hot, dry wind to blow out of the desert towards the sea most afternoons, which dried sweat almost instantly so that you did not realise how much moisture you were losing. I certainly did not, until one afternoon I felt terrible and once back at the office was told I probably had heat stroke and that I must return at regular intervals to drink plenty of water and cool down a little.

It was another health issue that, in the end, resolved the puzzle of the elevating conveyer. My ankle had still not fully healed and it was quite painful so, when making adjustments to the conveyer, I started to lie down on the walkway next to it to rest my leg. From this angle I suddenly realised the ends of the guide rollers were pressing on the undersides of the buckets on the conveyer. Thinking I had over adjusted, I walked round to the other side of the belt and the same thing was happening there. Engineering drawings were looked at and in consultation with PEMREF it was agreed to shut down the conveyer to measure the length of the spindles on the guide rollers. The conclusion was that each spindle was about one inch longer than it should be and in those circumstances the belt would never be able to centre correctly on the drive rollers. One advantage of the refinery being situated in the middle of a desert was that if the Sulpel unit had to be shut down for an extended period any surplus liquid sulphur could be piped directly into the desert and operation of the refinery need not be disrupted.

A planned shutdown was organised. Chyoda provided a gang of Korean construction workers to remove groups of the guide rollers, cut and re-weld the spindles to the desired length and reassemble the corrected items. It was all done very efficiently and within a few hours it was a great relief to restart the conveyor and see the belt centre itself and run as smooth as could be! A question that had puzzled me was answered during this exercise as well. For some weeks I had seen a long haired very languid young man drifting about the work site who seemed to be on very friendly terms with some of his colleagues but I had never seen him actually do any work. I was beginning to wonder what he was there for, companionship perhaps, when who should emerge from under the welders mask but the very same young man; mystery solved.

It was just after this I was in trouble again. My ankle was still very painful and when I told the area foreman about it he said, 'boot and sock off'. The next minute I was in the works infirmary being pumped full of penicillin. The area round the wound marks had started to ulcerate and red lines were emanating from the wound up my leg. I still have a scar on my ankle but fortunately, thanks to some proper medical treatment, nothing more serious developed and I was soon feeling fit again. I did get a note from PEMREF saying, as it was not a work-related injury, they may send me a bill but nothing ever came of it and I decided, reluctantly, to give up going on any more snorkelling trips, for the time being at least.

Following a period of relatively stable operation the unit throughput had been increased until it was producing sulphur pellets at more or less design capacity when the next major equipment fault occurred. The dewatering screen developed an internal rattle which increased until I could no longer ignore it and had to shutdown once again. The location of a conveyer relative to the dewatering screen meant the sections of wedge wire screen mesh could not be withdrawn from the end of the screen, in accordance with the directions in the vendor's manual, thus preventing access to see why it was rattling. At this point I decided I needed some help from a proper engineer. Tony Blenkinsop arrived on site three days later and, after some modifications were made, the screen meshes were removed to reveal that pieces of stainless steel gusset-plate supporting the screen mesh had fractured and broken away and were rattling around inside the body of the screen. Tony prepared some drawings to replace and improve the strength of the supporting gusset-plates, which were faxed to the screen vendor asking for approval to make some urgent temporary repairs while they supplied some properly engineered drawings for a permanent repair. The modifications were quickly done to good effect and we were soon back on line. What really annoyed me was, after a couple of weeks satisfactory operation, the vendor's drawings arrived showing modifications that were almost identical to Tony's sketches. We had all the cost and hassle and the vendor got some free design ideas. I just hope Tony got a good lunch if he decided to purchase the same screens on the next job.

As a consequence of Tony's visit I had a strange experience of mind over matter. After a couple of long hard days we were refreshing the parts with some cans of particularly malty non-alcoholic beer and as each one slipped down I swear I was getting more and more drunk. I started to get quite worried about the walk back to camp in case I got stopped by the religious police!

A few weeks later after a period of steady uninterrupted operation the unit was operating at 102% of design capacity (300 tonnes/day), which was very pleasing as I was given to understand, on my return to England, that none of the other Sulpel plants the company had built had ever achieved design rate. As a consequence, after a further period of familiarisation and training of PEMREF operations staff I was given permission to leave Saudi Arabia. However, that was not to be my final visit because two years later in 1986, I was asked to go back to run some trials to see whether the moisture content of the product pellets could be reduced from around 4.0% to the design value of 3.0% or less.

A number of obvious variables were changed, such as reducing the temperature of the molten sulphur at the prill heads to see if, when prilling a more viscous product, the average pellet size would be increased and less fines produced, thus reducing the moisture carrying surface area and the tendency to clog the screens. The frequency of vibration of the dewatering screen was adjusted to see if that made any difference and a new front section of the dewatering screen, with a larger aperture size, was installed. Nothing gave any long lasting improvement and finally several methods were used to check the true throughput of the plant. The conclusion was that the plant was operating at some 16% above design capacity and at this level it was unlikely that the moisture content could be reduced to the required 3% level. At this point, although there were a few more changes to be tried, PEMREF decided they could continue on their own and packed me off back to England to write up my final report, which I thought would be the end of my involvement with this particular plant and, not too reluctantly, Saudi Arabia.

Some twenty years later I was happily retired when I got a telephone call from some of my old colleagues in the process department questioning whether I could remember anything about a Sulpel plant in Saudi Arabia. Apparently, PEMREF, who still owned and operated the refinery had made contact to see if the capacity of the Sulpel unit, which was still in operation, could be increased to cope with increased throughput from the refinery. I may have said before, that because of the long periods of time I spent out of the office and the frequent relocations of my work base, office and desk, I had got into the habit, at the end of an assignment, of storing my copies of key documents, drawings, operating manuals, reports, etc. at home (much to Dawn's annoyance) rather than taking them back to the company office. So, even after a big clear out when I retired, I still had most of the key documents associated with the Saudi Sulpel unit in a storage box, how sad is that? As it turned out, this was considerably more than the company had because, after head office relocations from London Victoria, to East Croydon and finally to Reading, the master files from many previous jobs had been lost in a fire at the archive warehouse where they were being stored.

As I had not seen many of my old colleagues for quite some time I happily agreed to take the documents that I had up to the process group's offices, located in London, where they could be copied and, in exchange for a good lunch, I could be questioned about the possibilities of increasing the capacity of the existing Sulpel plant. When I heard it was already being run at around 130% of design rate I thought there was very little chance that much could be achieved with the existing unit and when Frank Brown (head of process group) asked if I would like to be paid a nice big consultancy fee to go back to Saudi to review the situation it did not take me long to decline his offer. Had it been Singapore, where another of the units had been built, I might have been tempted but not for long as I was more than happy to be retired and did not want to further complicate my tax affairs.

Apart from updating the company's archives the good thing that came from the visit was meeting a number of friends from my early days with H&G and being added to a list to receive a newsletter about H&G and its employees' activities, both past and present, as well as an invitation to attend a thrice yearly lunch date with a group of my old colleagues. The only problem is that at 75 I am now one of the youngest to attend and each year our numbers decrease.

4.10 Gas and oil production platforms

In the late 1970s early 1980s, with a decline in the number of contracts for plants using H&G's proven reforming technology and the growing importance of work to extract and process North Sea oil and gas, H&G expanded its interest in this area by creating an offshore division. They also formed a consortium with Sir Robert McAlpine & Sons Ltd., BICC and Rolls Royce to study the possibilities of building deep sea production systems for future offshore development. This was an interesting concept and was to be my introduction to the offshore world, when I was asked to review the design for ease of access for maintenance functions.

The idea was to build large sausage shaped concrete structures to house wellhead and primary separation equipment for location on the seabed, in deepwater gas or oil fields. These structures would be linked to a floating or semi-submersible separation/storage platform or ship at the surface, connected by umbilical(s) for transfer of power, air and Remote Telemetry Unit

(RTU), Supervisory Control & Data Acquisition (SCADA) signals to or from the structure and gas/oil products to the surface. Although not normally manned, the structure would also have a docking station for a midget submarine for transfer of personnel for maintenance purposes. A bit like a space station in reverse.

As a first introduction to offshore systems one of the things that really surprised me was to learn of the extremely high pressures and subsequently high temperatures that had to be dealt with. For example in 90 metres of water the sub-sea High Integrity Pressure Systems (HIPPS) including Wellhead X-mass Trees and Emergency Shut Down (ESD) valves are rated for 15,000 psi pressure (~ 1000 bar) and 200 °C temperature, that is a pressure nearly 1000 times greater than atmospheric pressure at the Earth's surface. A consequence of these high pressures was that large and powerful actuators, some two metres long and weighing up to two tonnes, were required to operate the valves. From a maintenance point of view this meant spares had to be located on the structure with lay-down areas, runway beams and mobile cranes included with sufficient access, in a confined space, to exchange critical items as required. Before the introduction of Computer Aided Design (CAD) systems not such an easy thing to ascertain.

Another aspect of a sub-sea environment was providing sufficient reserves of air in the structure to keep visiting maintenance crew alive long enough to make a rescue possible if the supply via the umbilical from the surface was lost. Inhaled air contains approximately 20.84% oxygen (necessary to sustain life) and about 0.04% carbon dioxide (CO_2), while exhaled air contains approximately 13.6 to 16.0% oxygen and 4 to 5.3% carbon dioxide. Additionally, the limit of CO_2 in breathable air that is considered to be immediately dangerous to life is 4.0% by volume, i.e. about the same as that in exhaled air. Therefore, knowing the free volume within the structure and that a single breath, on average, is 0.5 litres per person, it was possible to calculate, if the air supply was lost, how quickly the atmosphere in the structure, for a given number of crew members, would become contaminated to a dangerous level. I can remember it was difficult to arrive at an estimate of the free volume in the structure but it was concluded the number of cylinders of air that had been proposed was nowhere near adequate and that considerable additional storage space would have to be found somewhere for the additional capacity; not an easy thing to do.

Looking at these figures made me ponder the significance of the latest round of talks by the world's leaders to reduce the amount of so-called greenhouse gases in the atmosphere and therefore limit the temperature rise that is effecting climate change around Planet Earth. The world population currently stands at around 7.3 billion people and is increasing almost exponentially year on year. I have just calculated the amount of exhaled CO_2 by 7.3 billion people is approximately 1.8×10^9 tonnes/year which is slightly more than the total amount of CO_2 emitted by all of the coal fired power stations in the USA, one of the biggest polluters on the planet in 2011. Add to that all the CO_2 exhaled by all the livestock raised to feed an expanding population, coupled with the CO_2 and methane (CH_4) expelled in human and animal flatulence, which would probably be more than equivalent to all the greenhouse gases expelled by coal fired power stations in China, the biggest polluter on the planet, then it seems to me that any attempt to limit greenhouse gases must include a means of limiting human population growth. It is not surprising that politicians do not want to raise such a controversial subject, especially after China's attempt to limit families to one child led to a gender imbalance after apparently more boys (wanted) than girls (expendable) were born. However, if we do not do something, it is possible The Earth (Gaia principle?) will do it for us; 3rd World War; antibiotic resistant super-bug spread rapidly around the planet or, in the case of Britain, in a couple of years' time, after we have shut down our coal fired power stations, insufficient power to keep the country functioning over a harsh winter. I did think it was almost criminal negligence by successive governments but now my cynical self has kicked in and I wonder if it may be a deliberate policy to kill off an unwanted aging population.

The situation is, of course, made much worse by the rapid deforestation that is taking place, thus reducing the planet's capability to remove CO_2 from the atmosphere by photosynthesis. It does seem a pity that man, so far, has not developed a tree with highly nutritious, edible leaves, which could both remove CO_2 and feed mankind at the same time.

My next encounter with offshore work was a brief visit to Newcastle to provide commissioning experience to a proposal bid for the design and build of an offshore platform. The only thing that has stayed in my memory was a visit to an excellent Chinese restaurant with a revolving table constantly restocked with different dishes, followed by the project manager's attempts to drag us into a "grab a granny nightclub" which I am glad to say I resisted.

This was followed by a secondment from the onshore to the offshore division of the company to prepare commissioning procedures for a "not normally manned" gas platform to be built and located in the North Morecambe Bay area of the Irish Sea. The whole team were housed in Stag Place, near Victoria Station, on something like the 10th floor of a high-rise office block, giving good views over London but a real test of fitness when an emergency evacuation practice was initiated, with all lifts shut down.

The pre-commissioning and commissioning procedures for the various disciplines were all to be prepared to an approved template, agreed with the client (owner) of the platform, to comply with their own standards and acceptance procedures. The biggest difference to working on an onshore contract was that two sets of documents were required; one to complete the maximum amount of pre-commissioning work possible while the platform was still located at the fabrication yard onshore and a second set to identify all additional equipment necessary to complete hook-up and subsequent testing and pre-commissioning of the platform once transferred to its offshore location. The costs involved for working offshore are considerably greater than working onshore but are increased still further for a "not normally manned" platform, where an accommodation support vessel is required, until commissioning is complete and the platform is fully operational.

Most of the guys I was working with had been involved in the offshore industry for many years so I tried to understand the jargon and glean as much information as I could without appearing too ignorant. Much of the work, such as breaking the job down into clearly identified but readily managed systems for flushing, cleaning, leak testing and equipment checks, was similar to an onshore project with the need to identify, for example, the additional quantities of diesel required for power generation until the platform was hooked-up offshore and gas fired power generation could commence. Towards the end I was involved in writing first drafts of some procedures for the communications systems, which was a totally new field but was achieved without too much "breakdown" as I recall. I should perhaps point out that, at this time, all the procedures were hand written (no computers available) and were then typed up, so a considerable time was spent proofreading and correcting first drafts.

At an early stage in the project I was escorted to Blackpool for a stopover and flying (helicopter) visit to an existing, operating, platform in Morecambe Bay, to give me an idea of what was involved, which was very useful and put things into perspective more readily than merely looking at drawings. Also, a real bonus, once all the onshore pre-commissioning/commissioning had been completed, the company invited staff involved in the project with their wives/husbands/partners to the fabrication yard for an escorted visit round the finished platform, just before it was loaded onto a barge for transportation to Morecambe Bay. It was a super day, which for us, involved driving from Essex to Lowestoft in time for an included lunch at a local restaurant, followed by a guided tour of the platform, all clean and tidy and freshly painted, before witnessing the load out onto the barge. A fascinating experience to watch as this huge platform was manoeuvred, so gently, on computer controlled rollers off the dock onto a ballasted computer-controlled barge, with ballast being expelled to exactly counteract the weight of the platform as it was inched onto the barge. Such a worthwhile experience for the design team to see the finished article as something other than a set of drawings and data sheets and their partners, perhaps, to see what they had been working on for the past year.

After this period with the "oily boys" I returned to my normal duties within the commissioning group and during this period I was quite surprised when, on a visit to the salaries department, one of the women said, 'oh by the way, congratulations, Alan.' On asking what for I was pleased to find out I had been "promoted" to deputy manager of the commissioning department, however, it was a surprise as I had heard nothing about it and had certainly heard nothing about an increase in salary to go with it. With no children to afford and Dawn, by now, earning a good salary, money was not something I was too bothered about but a consequence of working on oil and gas projects, where salaries, at the time, were at a premium, did make me feel I was being underpaid. Therefore, some six months later, when I was asked to move to another offshore project I suggested an increase in salary was appropriate, even if only for the duration of the secondment. Let us think about it was the response.

This new project was massive, probably the biggest the company had ever undertaken or been a part of. It was for the design and procurement of materials to build the topside facilities collectively known as the BP Miller Platform and included the preparation of both onshore and offshore pre-commissioning and commissioning procedures, which is where I came in. It was, in fact, for a central production platform surrounded by and linked to six satellite platforms, which, as will be explained later, complicated the writing of the procedures no end. Our group consisted of an experienced offshore commissioning manager together with a group of nine or ten interdisciplinary commissioning engineers, of whom, I think with one exception, I was the only permanent staff member.

An additional problem on this project was the possibility of sour crude being extracted, that is crude oil containing sufficient sulphur for hydrogen sulphide (H_2S) to be released with the resultant danger to life. This resulted in the need for "double block and bleed" valve systems to provide sufficient isolation on numerous sections of the plant. This not only increased the weight on the platform(s), always a problem, it also complicated the writing of procedures because of the additional number of valves that had to be identified when describing a sequence of events that had to be undertaken.

This also increased my workload considerably, as the first draft of all the procedures were handwritten and then passed to the typing pool to produce a readable version, which in a lot of cases I would proofread. It soon became obvious that, in the first instance, the word "valve" was frequently being typed as "value", all of which had to be identified and corrected.

As with all jobs, the first task was to mark up drawings (P&IDs), to break down the plant into identifiable and manageable systems about which the pre-commissioning and commissioning procedures would be written. These had to be agreed with the client and proved to be a logistical nightmare because of parts of the overall structure being built on seven different inter-connected platforms. This was particularly true when considering the work to be done onshore as, if memory serves me correctly, the platforms were to be built at five different fabrication yards, spread throughout the United Kingdom. This could result in a system such as the fire water pumps and distribution system being split over all six platforms with perhaps only a single pipeline with associated valves on one of the platforms. However, a document would still be required to confirm this single piece of pipeline had been installed correctly and it was clean and clear of any obstructions while onshore. In addition, any temporary blanking pieces, blinds or valves that might be required had to be identified for procurement or fabrication at each separate location as well as identifying all linking or hook-up items that would be required to make the system whole once all the platforms were located offshore. These hook-up items had to be fabricated and bagged up with a system and location identifier on them for shipment with the platform on float-out. Separate data sheets were also produced to keep tabs on the status of all such items.

Another typical difficulty with having the systems split up on different onshore facilities was identifying the temporary, additional utilities and services that would be required at each fabrication yard. For example, compressors of sufficient capacity and pressure rating to supply oil-free air to the pneumatically operated instruments: a particular requirement, for safety reasons, on-plant where flammable gases are present and electrically operated equipment is kept to the minimum to reduce the risk of sparks. Also, all control valves are designated to operate to a failsafe condition, i.e. if for any reason the instrument air supply is lost, the valve will fail open or closed. For example, all wellhead ESD valves should fail closed to shut off the supply of oil or gas to the platform and thus prevent another Piper Alpha situation. Therefore, a good supply of instrument air was required at each fabrication yard, not only to confirm the correct operation of the majority of the control system but also to simply open or close valves to allow other pre-commissioning/commissioning operations to be carried out.

Although all the guys in the team had much more experience of offshore operations than me I realised, after the first batch of draft procedures were produced, that some were very much better at expressing that knowledge in the written form than others. As a consequence I spent more of my time proofreading and suggesting "subtle" changes to content and wording than I expected but it did give me a good insight to some other discipline functions and the myriad difficulties of extracting oil and gas from the North Sea and preparing it for transfer by pipeline to an onshore terminal. I also realised, as we got to know each other, that we had some very different characters in the team. I heard one of the mechanical engineers who sat just behind me on the phone one day enquiring about the cost of buying a second hand battle tank. I could never make up my mind if he was simply a Walter Mitty character or had a second occupation as an armourer for some African or Middle East conflict. He was certainly a bit of a loner and rarely joined us in the Friday lunchtime sessions in the pub!

Another incident that showed the hidden depths of one of my colleagues was at lunchtime when one of the guys got something stuck in his throat and started choking to the point where he was turning blue. Mr Walls, an ex-submariner, who was generally known as Max (for reasons best known to the older readers), leapt up and, demonstrating that his first aid courses had not been wasted, performed the Heimlich manoeuvre, which I had never heard of. The obstruction shot out of the chaps throat and to our great relief he started breathing again. Although he ended up with a broken rib or two I think Max probably saved his life because calling for an ambulance would have taken much too long.

A few months before being seconded to the BP Miller project, feeling a little unsettled with all the recent changes and after twenty-odd years with the same company, I decided I should apply for another job, if for no other reason, than to gain some experience in finding work should the need arise. One daunting interview for a position with the Environment Agency showed me how ill-prepared I was for the task. This was followed by an application and interview for a position as a project manager for work on Foulness Island, a thirty minute drive from my home, for the Ministry of Defence. I thought the interview went quite well and was told I should expect some delay before hearing the result, while security checks were made and my employment records verified. I had almost forgotten about this application when some three months into the BP Miller project I was called into the manager's office to see whether I was unhappy and was there a particular reason why I wished to leave. My employment reference and verification requests had just been received. The outcome was I was offered an immediate, permanent, 12% increase in salary, backdated to my secondment to the offshore division if I stayed. As I was now thoroughly immersed in and enjoying the project and to leave now would mean a cut in salary, I was happy to stay.

Some four months later I was again offered alternative employment.

Throughout my time based in the London office(s) I had kept in touch with some of my erstwhile colleagues (close friends) from the Billericay laboratory days. The laboratory had been closed a few years after I left and Dr Peter Lemin and David Evans had moved to become associate directors of an environmental test laboratory located on the outskirts of Chelmsford, about twenty minutes drive from my home in Essex. I had always let it be known that if the right opportunity arose I would be interested in getting away from the rat race of commuting across London or spending months away from home in some remote region of the planet. Anyway, I got a phone call from David to say the position of laboratory manager was available if I was interested. I pointed out that I had not worked in a laboratory for nearly ten years but also realised that, at the age of forty seven, if I was going to make a move I should do it sooner rather than later. I gathered from the conversation with David that one of the main functions of the manager would be to "smooth" the allocation of staff between the three section leaders and coordinate the overall operation of the laboratory. Following an interview with Hugh Berridge, the founder of the company and chief executive, together with the other associate directors, I was formally offered the position, which, after some further thought, I decided to accept, so handed in my notice to H&G. This resulted in my being offered another 10% increase in salary to stay, as well as the possibility of creating a new position for me, of commissioning manager of the offshore division, with associated perks.

This offer obviously gave me pause for thought, as I would already be taking a small cut in salary to leave but it also made me angry in that I felt I had been undervalued for some years. Because of that, coupled with the feeling that, having never worked offshore, I did not really have the experience to fill the new position, which in any case was likely to prove very stressful, I declined and prepared to leave H&G after twenty four years' employment. The lads on the project gave me a good send-off, which involved a young police woman (stripper) coming into the office to apprehend me. I am not sure who was most embarrassed, must find the photographs, that might give me a clue! Also, the onshore division presented me with a cheque – I later purchased a lovely cut glass bowl, etched with a dolphin design, as a reminder of the good years – along with many cards wishing me well for the future, which made it even harder to leave.

PART 5
Return to a Laboratory

Berridge Environmental Laboratories was, as the name implies, a contract testing laboratory collecting, analysing and reporting on samples taken from land, air or water, together with an advisory service for the routine monitoring or elimination of contaminants from a site. The laboratory employed a nicely balanced mix of twenty to thirty male and female staff, some young and relatively inexperienced who were employed on a day-release basis while studying for ONC/HNCs, together with more mature, well-qualified, chemists, environmental scientists and biologists.

The workload was roughly split between those collecting and analysing water and earth samples. The biologists were checking for microbial contamination, including routine monitoring for Legionnaires' disease, a form of pneumonia spread by breathable water droplets (aerosols), containing a species of gram-negative aerobic bacteria (Legionella) escaping into the atmosphere, which had been identified as the cause of a spate of deaths in the 1980s. A typical source would be from poorly maintained cooling towers and showers in hotels which were not used regularly and/or the hot water system was not operating at a minimum 60 °C. I was quite surprised to learn that we found Legionella in samples from at least one prestigious hotel in London, which I am not going to name for obvious reasons and which, as far as I know, did not suffer any fatalities. A third group was monitoring for contamination in the atmosphere, whether it be hazardous vapours, poisonous gases, dust or particulates or simply traffic pollution in a busy high street. Finally, a fourth group was dedicated to and specializing in the identification and removal of asbestos, particularly from council owned properties in tower blocks south of the River Thames, where asbestos had been used as a building material in earlier years, before the dangers were recognised. Back in the laboratory we had two women with particular experience in the microscopic identification of the more deadly blue asbestos particles in the samples brought back. For me it was a completely new subject that, at the least, required a rapid introduction to the very strict health and safety regulations involved with asbestos identification, removal and disposal.

The majority of our work was from locations within approximately one hundred miles of the laboratory. This was for practical reasons as certain samples had to be back in the laboratory for preparation and analysis within a limited time period or they would deteriorate. Or for cost reasons where travel time and expenses could not be factored into the unit charge for a piece of work. Having said that we did have one job in the Highlands of Scotland that proved to be quite popular. It was to set up a programme to routinely monitor a source of water for a new whisky distillery!

Just after I arrived I experienced one of those very strange coincidences that sometimes occur in life when I asked if there was anywhere local that I could get some food at lunchtime. I was told there were a couple of decent pubs in the nearby village of Writtle or, just up the road in the local factory estate, a mobile burger van. When I transferred to working in the London office and started travelling on the trains regularly, I got into the habit, I suspect like a lot of commuters, of standing on more or less the same spot on the platform every day both on the mainline train to Liverpool Street and the Central Line platform on the Underground. As a consequence I got to know and became friendly with two or three of my fellow commuters who followed the same route to work. One of these was Dennis, a sales manager for *Cosmopolitan* magazine, who was always immaculate in appearance and very sociable who could not help chatting to people nearby, particularly to any women, so that over the years our convivial group grew larger and larger.

After a number of years and following one of my periodic assignments working away from the London office I was once again on the platform at Wickford station commuting up to London when I spotted Dennis's niece and realised I had not seen him recently. I was really surprised when she told me that Dennis, fed up with the rat race, had resigned from his job with *Cosmopolitan* and now had a mobile burger van. Perhaps you can guess where this story is heading; on my first visit to the burger van near my new job, once I got to the head of the queue, there was Dennis, still immaculate in a crisp, clean blue and white striped apron and still chatting to all his customers, particularly the women, which most seemed to enjoy, even if it doubled the serving time! When I had time to talk to him he said it was the best thing he had ever done; he now worked from about 8am to 2pm which was enough to pay the bills and meant he could also enjoy some free time with his new wife and young son.

I spent the first couple of weeks in my new job getting to know the staff and familiarising myself with the laboratory's workload before deciding it was my responsibility to ensure a number of routine safety drills were put in place. The first of these, as we carried quite a large stock of solvents within the building, was to test the fire alarm system and the evacuation procedure. I informed everybody a test was about to take place and made sure they knew where the designated assembly points were before activating the manual alarm. Nothing happened! I was quite shocked, when opening the case of the fairly antiquated alarm system, to find the battery was completely corroded up and obviously had not been tested in years. Following this I called in the local Fire Brigade to inspect the premises and make any recommendations they thought necessary. This did not go down too well with senior management as the addition of fire doors to the upper floor and the need for an external solvent store all cost money. However, I think everybody appreciated it was necessary and I found favour with the rest of the staff, who thought I was looking after their interests, particularly the women, who assured me that a regular visit by some "hunky" firemen was a real bonus.

The company had one, quite prestigious, contract that required the coordination and complete cooperation of all the staff to fulfil its obligations. That was, on a monthly basis, to check the quality of the potable (drinking) water from designated sample points, being supplied to each of the London boroughs, whether that be water sourced from boreholes or treated water from rivers or reservoirs. The water collected from each location had to be tested for some forty-plus different parameters, including individual elements, anions, cations, pesticides, solvents, and microbiological quality, all to comply to specific regulatory limits. Since most of the parameters were present in very small quantities it meant relatively large volumes of water had to be collected to allow concentration techniques to be applied to bring the result within the detection limit of the analytical methods being used. This contract occupied the majority of the laboratory staff for the best part of a week every month. Before sampling, all the glassware to be used had to be chromic acid cleaned, thoroughly rinsed using distilled water and then dried, to ensure no contamination remained from previous samples. At each sample location, a test pack containing a minimum of six Winchester (2.5 litres) size bottles was required, together with a number of smaller vessels for specific tests and agar plates for biological samples, and all had to be prepared and packed, resulting in an intensive work load. The prepared test packs had to be loaded into a designated company vehicle, of which there were four, in readiness for a very early start the next morning. The lads from the asbestos group usually did the driving as they were familiar with routes around London to the pre-ordained sample locations and it needed a bit of muscle to move the sample boxes around once they were full of water. It was always a great relief if all the vans and drivers were in working order and there were no major hold-ups or delays that prevented the samples being back in the laboratory in time for any sensitive items to be put into a refrigerator or incubator, whichever was necessary.

The following days kept everybody busy analysing the samples, beginning with our rhino expert (a qualified nose) smelling the samples for their odour. A new experience for me which I tried to emulate out of interest but could never master with any certainty. Finally, all the results had to be checked and once ratified reports written for issue to the various borough authorities. Any results that were outside the current acceptance criteria had to be immediately reported and usually required further samples to be taken for a retest. It was only after some months in my new job that I began to suspect that this ongoing contract had been won at a very competitive price and for all the hard work that went into it very little real profit was made. It also became apparent that the company had some serious cash flow problems.

One of my duties as laboratory manager was ordering new equipment and ensuring stocks of essential items were maintained. This became increasingly difficult and embarrassing when, on the phone to a regular supplier, I was told that they were sorry but until their outstanding invoices were paid they could no longer supply us. Over the next few months this situation got worse, to the extent that I had to consult with our financial advisor before making even modest purchases as it was becoming a juggling match whether to pay bills or salaries. It was a great shame because, in the main, everybody got on well, worked hard and were a lovely bunch of people to be with. I think one of the big problems was, although we had plenty of work, most of our analytical procedures were still relatively labour intensive as, in the past few years, little money had been spent on updating equipment. This was exacerbated by some of the big water companies, with recourse to all the latest automated techniques, coming into the market to contract out their analytical services at prices we found it very hard to compete with. The outcome of all this was one year and four months into my new job I was made redundant. I was not altogether surprised because of the more senior members of staff, three were associate directors, who were unlikely to make themselves redundant and after a few juniors had been laid off the principal of last in first out meant I was an obvious choice to go next but it was still a shock after being gainfully employed for twenty five years. Sadly my departure did not solve the problem and within a year the company closed for good and all the staff were made redundant.

PART 6
Return to Commissioning

I can remember the rather strange experience of signing on for the dole and the woman interviewing me asking how far I would be prepared to travel to find new work. Now for somebody who had spent the past twenty-odd years working all over the world this was a question I did not really know how to answer. She said most people say fifteen miles, will that do. It was as good as anything else but after a couple of weeks investigating the possibilities of becoming a teacher or a probation officer amongst other things I decided I was stupid not to phone some of my old colleagues in H&G to let them know I was out of work. David Osborne, who had started in the H&G Laboratory at about the same time as me and was now the company's water treatment expert, said there had been talk of starting an environmental section and if I was interested he would organise a time for me to discuss possibilities with the head of process department. A few days later I was back in the head office, which by now had been moved to Croydon, talking to old colleagues as though I had never left and had just returned from another field trip. Halfway through the day the commissioning department manager found me and said, 'Alan, the site manager on an activated carbon regeneration plant we are commissioning in Cambridgeshire has just resigned, do you want a job and can you start tomorrow or the day after?' It seemed foolish not to say yes but I baulked at tomorrow as I had no contract, had no idea what salary was being offered or the pension plan, etc. etc. Four days later, on 24th May 1991, I was officially re-employed by H&G as a principal engineer, after only eleven days to enjoy my time on the dole and was heading up the motor way towards Grafham Water.

6.1 Grafham Water – Cambridgeshire – activated carbon regeneration

To meet the latest EC Directives on the removal of pesticides from potable (drinking) water supplies and also to improve the quality of supply, with regard to taste and odour, Anglian Water had, in collaboration with H&G, been installing Granular Activated Carbon (GAC) adsorption systems into the region's potable water treatment plants. The very large internal surface area of GAC and its resultant excellent adsorption properties meant it was very effective at removing many different types of organic compounds down to limits that were acceptable in drinking water supplies. However, over time , the pores of the GAC become full of the absorbed "rubbish" and the spent GAC has to be replaced. Commercial companies, such as Chemviron, offered a replacement and regeneration service but as the cost of regeneration is typically only 40-60% of the cost of a new inventory, Anglian Water had decided to acquire their own regeneration plant to service the needs of the region.

In accordance with a pre-arranged schedule, spent carbon from the region's water treatment works would be transported in specially designed tankers to the Grafham regeneration plant where it would be transferred to a series of spent carbon storage vessels (pits) of concrete construction with protective spray painted linings. From these wet carbon would be transferred, via a dewatering screw, to the heart of the process, a furnace where the volatiles were driven off and adsorbed organic compounds are burnt off at temperatures up to 1000°C in a controlled atmosphere of steam and air, to restore the active surfaces within the GAC to their original condition. The regenerated carbon travelled down through a series of trays in the furnace to a quench tank, where it was cooled before transfer to a series of clean carbon storage vessels, also of concrete construction, before being transported back to the water treatment works from which it came. The flue gases from the furnace passed through an afterburner to a waste heat boiler and then to a wet scrubber before transfer to the vent stack. Incidentally the flue gas clean-up was the first to comply to the latest requirements of Her Majesty's Inspectorate of Pollution (HMIP) in the UK and required routine monitoring to confirm compliance.

When I arrived on site to take over as the H&G commissioning manager all the preliminary pre-commissioning and commissioning work had been done and the plant was essentially fully operational. I inherited four H&G

staff, three process/commissioning engineers, one of whom had worked on the original design out of the company's Stockport office and Ken Titley, a very experienced site instrument engineer who was a great asset as he had probably forgotten more about the many aspects of site work than I was ever likely to learn. In addition we were assisted by three men and a site fore-man, pipe fitters and general labourers, who had been retained from the con-struction company sub-contracted to build the plant and finally a Belgian commissioning engineer from the company (Calgon, maybe), who were the licensees of the regeneration process. I also inherited a room in a house in St Neots, about six miles from Grafham Water, which the H&G team were renting.

After being introduced to Anglian Water's relatively young plant manager and his deputy, who would take over the operation of the plant once the guarantee tests were completed, and a couple of weeks to familiarise myself with the layout and how everything was meant to operate, I began to appre-ciate where the major problem lay. The plant was designed to regenerate 3000 tonnes per annum of GAC and although apparently working well, analysis of the regenerated carbon showed the regeneration was only 80 to 90% com-plete, which was unacceptable and meant the GAC could not be returned to the waterworks from which it came without further processing. This caused problems on a number of fronts. First, the once-regenerated carbon had to be moved using an eductor from the clean carbon storage vessels back to the fouled carbon storage vessels in order to be passed through the process once more, a labour intensive and fairly mucky business because carbon black water seemed to spread itself about very readily. Second, to improve the regeneration efficiency the furnace was operated at higher temperatures with more air or even oxygen being injected. However, this increased the losses as more carbon was burnt off as CO or CO_2 which in turn meant the capacity guarantees could not be met. It also caused a backlog in the GACs waiting to be regenerated from the different waterworks and although they had not accepted the plant, Anglian Water already had a schedule in place to run it as a commercial venture.

It was fortunate that one of our young commissioning engineers was willing to work more or less permanent night shifts, which left the rest of our small crew to work on resolving the problems during the day and leave him a relatively stable plant to monitor overnight using the automated con-trol system. This was a tough regime to follow because we were all working twelve- to thirteen-hour days with little chance of a break and were on more or less permanent call because if the plant tripped and shut down overnight it needed more than one person on site to get it up and running again, assuming the fault that caused the shutdown could be found and corrected. One of the strangest incidents was an apparent low level in the water tank supplying water to the wet scrubber tripping the plant down. However, on investigation, the water tank was found to be full and Ken (Titley), after checking and recalibrating the level instrument, could find no fault with it. This was most strange because it happened on three separate occasions at around 10pm, which meant we got called back into the plant just after, if we were lucky, we had finished our evening meal and were about to crawl into bed. Eventually, Ken, who felt quite aggrieved that anyone could doubt his instruments, found that once a month at about 10pm Anglian Water operations transmitted, via a radio link, data records to their headquarters. The radio frequency that was used interfered with the frequency used by the level instruments transmitter and caused a bogus trip condition. Problem solved, after changing some frequency settings, but a damn good piece of detective work I would say!

Another very bizarre incident, that also occurred more than once during the night, was the whole control panel losing power and causing a crash shutdown of the plant – not a good thing to happen. It is hard to believe but we eventually realised that power to the control panel was via a single plug and socket on the control room wall. Once a month, during the night, when there were fewer people about, a cleaning company came in and on occasions, without realising what they were doing, unplugged the control panel to plug in their floor cleaners. How stupid was that? – and it certainly warranted a strongly worded problem report to head office with regard to secure power supplies, especially after spending all night on site to restart the plant.

Following three months of striving with limited success in solving the major problem of incomplete regeneration of the GAC ,the project manager from the Stockport office was sent to the site to show the company's concern at the lack of progress. This proved to be very much a political gesture because he was a civil engineer by profession and after a few weeks' monitoring our work ethic he freely admitted he had no real idea what we were doing or how to resolve the technical problems and spent most of his day sitting in a deck chair in the sunshine outside our site hut. What really annoyed me was that at the regular progress meetings with the client, it became obvious he had not even fully read or understood the contract documents and was of little use fending off increasingly snide comments from their contracts manager. By now I was also starting to feel somewhat annoyed at working our "butts" off, with little or no support from anywhere. Most of the problems that arose we resolved ourselves; our Belgian commissioning engineer, although a very nice guy and trying his hardest had no new ideas to offer and we were operating the plant and regenerating carbon for Anglian Water, albeit not as swiftly and efficiently as they would like. At this juncture I pointed out that the contract stated the guarantee runs were to be carried out on carbon from a specific water treatment works and unless carbon from that works was made available I would shut the plant down until it was. Now, I did not know if I would be allowed to do that and I knew the carbon from this works had already been processed before I arrived on site, so was not ready for regeneration for at least a year, but from the sharp intake of breath from their contracts manager I had made a telling point as far as attitudes and our position was concerned.

All this time we had been processing carbon from the Wing water treatment works, with which I was to become very familiar in three or four years' time and despite my threat to shut down, we would have to keep processing until a logical and controlled finish point was reached. It was at this juncture that my starting life as a chemist proved to be a turning point. During the day we had support from Anglian Water who were providing a chemist to carry out the analysis required to determine the efficiency of the GAC regeneration but at all other times I had been taking samples down to the laboratory and doing the analysis myself. The method involved the absorption of an iodine solution into a weighed quantity of the dried regenerated GAC. The iodine could then be titrated with sodium thiosulphate to determine how much had been absorbed and thereby quantify the efficiency of regeneration. However, to stop any sulphur compounds that might be present in the GAC interfering with the titration, the sample of GAC was acid-washed before addition of the iodine. On adding the acid I noticed that a rapid stream of bubbles was being emitted from the GAC, which continued for some time. It suddenly occurred to me that the bubbles could stop the iodine solution penetrating into the pores of the GAC, so performed the analysis several times without adding the acid. Eureka! The efficiency leapt from 80 or 85% to nearer 99%.

The next morning, urgent phone calls to David Osborne (our water treatment expert) resulted in a search revealing a number of papers that indicated the use of lime on water treatment works could interfere with the analytical method being used for determining GAC regeneration efficiency (acid on lime gives off CO_2, hence the bubbles). Armed with this information I went to see the plant manager and explained my findings that my belief was that the regeneration plant was operating perfectly correctly and that it was the analytical procedure that was causing all the apparent problems. I also suggested that they should send some samples away to their own research laboratories for ratification and if still not convinced bring in some carbon for regeneration from another of their treatment plants, which unlike Wing, did not include lime in the treatment process. It did not take the plant manager long to be convinced that he did, after all, have a perfectly good GAC regeneration plant to work with, which was ready for acceptance and it was just bad luck that for the past two or three months the carbon scheduled for regeneration was from Wing. I do not suppose H&G ever recovered any of the cost of all the extra time and effort that had been put in and I like to flatter myself that if I had not been there an answer to the problem may never have been found.

One incident, nothing to do with work, that caused a few raised eyebrows occurred a few weeks after I arrived on site, a police car pulled up to the gate and asked for me. Before rejoining H&G I had been playing in a summer hockey league in Essex where our umpire (Alan) had been head butted by one of the opposition players, breaking Alan's glasses and cutting his nose. Alan, who was not prepared to let the matter drop, had informed the police and asked anyone who had seen the incident clearly to be a witness. The outcome was, after finding out where I was working, a policeman being sent to take a witness statement from me and to determine that I would be available to attend court if there was sufficient evidence to prosecute. Some three months later I was summoned to attend court in Chelmsford, my first ever such experience. Quite a large group of people: solicitors, barristers, witnesses, judge and jury stood about for three or four hours only to be told the trial would have to be postponed as one of the accused's witnesses, who we were told had just started a new job in Aberdeen, after being out of work for some time, had not turned up – a costly absence. A month later we were all assembled once more and this time the trial went ahead. Despite the defence barrister trying to persuade me his client's head had accidently brushed into Alan when he bent forward to hear what he was saying, the accused was eventually found guilty. What I could not understand, after hearing most of the evidence, was why he had pleaded not guilty in the first place. It transpired that he had been offered the opportunity of a very lucrative position in America and knew if he ended up with a criminal record the opportunity would be lost forever.

Once the adjustment to the analytical procedure had been reviewed and accepted by Anglian Water we were able to reduce the operating conditions sufficiently to demonstrate that an acceptable level of regeneration could be achieved without excessive loss of carbon, and Ken had resolved an outstanding problem with the automated control system, we were ready apart from a few Butt List items for handover, which was duly accepted.

Before leaving I decided we all deserved a good night out because all the lads had worked extremely hard, sometimes in a very unpleasant environment, without ever complaining or demanding extra money for completing tasks outside their job description, but where to go? In the end we settled on a pub in the middle of the housing estate close to where most of our sub-contractors were staying, which had a karaoke night on a Thursday. Not my thing but I was only there to pay for the food and the ale. The strange thing was, when we arrived, mine host, who was announcing some karaoke performers, looked very familiar... ex-television actor perhaps, but I just could not place him. I do not recall any of our group getting up to perform but plenty of beer was drunk and the evening was swinging along nicely when under the influence of a few pints I suddenly remembered where I had seen mine host before. For a short period he had been the landlord of The Swan, my local in Wickford, where the hockey team used to repair for sandwiches and beers after a match. Then I made an error of judgement as it was nearly closing time before I had a chance to chat to him and recall some old faces and places. It turned out, when his marriage broke up the brewery moved him on, eventually to his present location. The problem arose when some of the lads, on finding I was "friends" with the landlord, had high hopes the doors would be closed with us still inside and the evening would continue unchecked. I think I just about managed to extract myself without upsetting too many people and after all we were supposed to be at work the next day.

About a month after we had packed our bags and returned to the office, or some other site, I was told they had a big opening ceremony with John Major as the guest of honour (Huntingdon was his constituency) to which we were not invited, so I felt it was a good call spending some of the company's money giving the lads a good night out before I left.

6.2 Potable water treatment systems

Five years of research and development between Anglian Water and H&G resulted in the development of a range of unique GAC adsorber designs for installation on potable water treatment sites. The new technology provided a clean and efficient method of handling the GAC required for removing pesticides, herbicides and other organic pollutants from the drinking water supply. The development resulted in two basic designs:

1) Prefabricated steel pressure vessels that could be mounted in series with capacities ranging from 6 to 50m³ of GAC per vessel.

2) Concrete adsorber(s) totalling up to 500m³ capacity, resembling swimming pools in appearance but with each adsorber divided into two cells of 20m³ or 40m³ capacity, thus allowing tankers designed to transport the GAC (typically of 20m³ capacity), to replace and remove the contents of an absorber one cell at a time.

Over the next four years, interspersed with periods back in head office, I was responsible, as lead commissioning engineer, for the start-up and acceptance of four of these newly developed GAC adsorber systems. The first, located at Stoke Ferry in Norfolk, was of the steel pressure vessel type, which proved to be a very efficient and reliable design which did not present us with too many problems during the initial pre-commissioning and commissioning phases. I say us, referring to a relatively small team, consisting of me, Ravi Velai, a very competent and likable mechanical engineer of Sri Lankan parentage, who I was meeting for the first time and three instrument technicians who set up, operated and seemed to understand the logic of what seemed to me to be a fairly complex control system, for a relatively small plant. One thing that struck me, after a few weeks' sharing the cabin during lunch break with these undoubtedly very bright lads, was their limited vocabulary. A joint effort at doing the "quick" crossword in the *Daily Mail* quite often ended with them asking me for an alternative for a word they had never come across before, which fortunately I could usually supply, even if I was not sure of the spelling. I guess growing up in an era of computer games and perhaps only reading technical manuals and a newspaper has its limitations in comparison to a good book.

A major part of the job was making sure we had everything ready and in place for when a tanker-load of new or regenerated GAC was due to be delivered to the site, so that there was minimal delay in the transfer of the tankers load to a designated vessel. Also, if the plant had been in operation for some time, the reverse transfer of a load of used GAC back into the now empty tanker for return to the regeneration plant. A key feature of the new adsorber design was the minimal use of water required during the transfer and an improved backwash system in the vessels so that the carbon fines, always present in the pores of the newly generated granular carbon, could be flushed out without generating an excessive amount of "black water", thus greatly reducing the waste water holding (settling) facilities required on the site.

It took just five weeks to complete the commissioning and hand-over of the Stoke Ferry plant, which in some ways was a shame as it took under an hour to drive to the site from our cottage in Hoxne, which meant I got the chance to spend some time with my wife during the week, which by then was most unusual. I expect Dawn felt five weeks was more than enough. As it turned out I could repeat the experience about a year later when a very similar plant was ready for commissioning at the Norwich water treatment works, which was also a reasonable driving distance from our Suffolk cottage. Here again I was teamed up with Ravi Velai and some of the same instrument technicians from the Stoke Ferry job so once we established a good understanding with our counterparts responsible for the water works the job moved along very steadily.

Three aspects of working on this site have stuck in my memory. The first was being taken by the Anglian Water staff into an underground reservoir, which they had emptied for cleaning and maintenance purposes. It was a revelation inside, red Victorian brickwork columns supporting a vaulted roof, not unlike being in a magnificent cathedral, such a surprise! The second was diverting from the daily journey along the A140 to Norwich to investigate a sign pointing to Caistor St Edmund as a place of historic importance.

It was a pleasant diversion along minor roads into the valley of the River Tay, where after a little searching the ruins of *Venta Icenorum* presented themselves and proved to be well worth a visit. The Roman Empire's capital of the region around present day Norwich and one of very few greenfield sites not to be succeeded by Medieval or modern towns. The walled settlement includes a street grid system, the remains of a forum and two temples and evidence of glass-working furnaces. It is believed that it was originally the capital of the local tribe, the Iceni, and was developed by the Romans some time after they managed to reverse a heavy defeat inflicted on them by Queen Boudicca, leader of the Iceni. When her husband Prasutagus died, she refused to hand over the rights to her lands to the Romans, which resulted in her being flogged and her daughters raped. A warrior Queen, in the subsequent battles she sacked *Camulodunum* (Colchester), *Londinium* (London) and *Verulamium* (St Albans) and was responsible for the possible deaths of seventy thousand Romans and their associates before being subdued.

The third and least pleasant experience was suddenly developing a severe and debilitating back pain which made driving difficult let alone leading an active existence on site. In the end two or three visits to be contorted by a chiropractor seemed to relieve the immediate problem which was a great relief and well worth the money spent. In retrospect I think years of carrying a heavy briefcase on the journey to the office in London and being jerked and thrown about on the trains and underground was a possible cause but who can tell, all I do know was that it was very painful.

My experience of commissioning the concrete adsorbers was not quite as smooth and trouble free. The first, in 1993, was located in Maidenhead and was a single cell about the size of a badminton court housed inside a protective building. The water works were squashed inside a housing estate with one border separated by a fence from a cutting, through which ran the main railway line from London to the west. I was a little concerned that any inadvertent escape of water on the site could very easily pour into the cutting and flood the railway. Fortunately it never happened while I was there. The cell was shaped a bit like some swimming pools with a shallow end leading down to a deep end and a key feature was that the base of the adsorber was covered in a grid system of plastic pipework fitted with a series of specially designed perforated nozzles. The hole-size of the perforations was less than the minimum carbon granule size which, in theory, would allow water to be pumped upwards to fluidise and backwash the GAC bed without loss of carbon.

The problem at Maidenhead, which I did not fully appreciate until later, was because of limited space, the capacity of the black water discharge sump. After filling the adsorber with a batch of new GAC the necessary backwash to remove the contained carbon fines could only be continued for ten to fifteen minutes before the black water sump was full and the backwash had to be stopped to allow the fines in the sump to settle before it could be emptied. The time was not sufficient for all the fines in the GAC to be removed in one go, so the process had to repeated again and again. Unfortunately, each time the backwash was stopped the fines in the adsorber would settle down again and in addition, because of the differing depth of carbon, the flow through the bed was uneven and tended to roll the carbon over and leave the surface of the bed uneven, which exacerbated the problem. This left us no choice but to drain water out of the adsorber until we could get in and rake the surface even again. Eventually a minimal amount of black water was being discharged and we could set up the adsorber to demonstrate its true function. A few days of steady and uninterrupted operation was sufficient for Thames Water to accept the plant but I left feeling there was something not quite right.

The next concrete adsorber plant to be commissioned was at Wing, in Rutland, where a very large new treatment plant had been erected next to Rutland Water. This was a very different "beast" from Maidenhead comprising, if memory serves me correctly, ten separate but interconnected $40m^3$ GAC adsorbers, together with underground storage reservoirs, connecting concrete pipes and large pumps for distributing the final potable water product. Wing itself was a small picturesque village with little more than the Church of St Peter and St Paul, a pub and a post office and a medieval turf maze, some 40 feet in diameter, to attract tourists or outside interest. Actually, one of the most enjoyable parts of my type of work and lifestyle was visiting some lovely parts of Britain that otherwise would have completely passed me by. This whole area of rolling hills and rural villages of cream coloured stone-built houses making up Middle England, hidden away between the A1 and M1 was a revelation which lost none of its charm the longer I stayed there.

For the first few weeks I stayed on a B&B basis in a pub located on the main square of Uppingham, a fine historic town, dominated by the presence of Uppingham School, founded in the 16th century and "one of the most prestigious seats of learning to rival Eton or Harrow". I soon realised that the size of the project meant I could be there months rather than weeks so I started a search for more affordable accommodation, which lead me to taking a lease on a converted sheep barn in the garden of a grand house near Stamford. The owners, I subsequently found out, were the managers of The George in Stamford, a splendid old coaching inn, to which Dawn and her mother came to stay some time later when I got tickets for a performance of *The Merchant of Venice* at a local open air theatre of some repute. Stamford itself is also well worth a visit and was the "living" set for the television series

Middlemarch broadcast in the 1990s. Following my move, the drive to Wing also took me past the Burghley Estate, famed for its annual horse trials as well as the majestic house, grounds and deer park. On the other side of the road there was the very different aspect of the Castle Cement Works but then beauty on one side can often be highlighted by a necessary eyesore on the other.

The earliest part of the work at Wing was a thorough cleaning and disinfecting of the potable water storage reservoir and interconnecting and transfer pipework that would be used to hold and distribute the water after passage through the GAC absorbers. A somewhat unpleasant aspect was, after obtaining the required confined space entry permits and hazardous gas detectors, taking a crouching walk through the five foot diameter concrete pipes to check they were clean and clear – quite claustrophobic, particularly so when the detector alarm sounded when well-inside the pipes. It was also another time when my training as a chemist came in handy as I was able to calculate the quantities of hypochlorite chemicals needed to dissolve in the water to fill the reservoir and flush through the pipes and then use a test kit to confirm a residual free-chlorine content. It may have been at Wing where we hired in some specialist contractors, suitably booted and suited with breathing apparatus to paddle round the covered reservoir in a rubber dingy to spray the ceiling and exposed walls with disinfecting solution but perhaps it was some other job?

One big problem arose when we test ran the rather large distribution pumps for the first time. After completing all the preliminary checks pressing the start button resulted in the motor tripping out after a few seconds' operation and this was the same for all three pumps. I had vague memories from my first year mathematics course at college of Fourier analysis methods showing that a surge current will occur when a motor first starts before it settles into a steady state operation but whether that was the reason or not I could not tell. After calling in one of our senior electrical engineers and the pump manufacturers, and listening to incomprehensible conversations about "star" and "delta" starters, a solution was found and after some modifications were made all was well.

A major part of the work was preparing the adsorbers for the arrival of the GAC tankers and coordinating the unloading and filling procedures, which, after a few setbacks, soon settled into a well worked system and the adsorbers were filled with the required quantity of GAC. Problems started to arise during the initial backwashing to remove carbon fines from the GAC beds. As with the Thames Water plant at Maidenhead, the black Water holding tank did not have sufficient capacity to complete the backwash procedure in one go so backwashing had to be stopped to give the fines time to settle in the holding tank before the clear water could be discharged. The only problem was the fines brought to the surface in the GAC adsorber settled down as well and then had to be relifted using even more backwash water. The real problem arose when a sharp crack was heard followed by a rush of bubbles and increased water flow through the bed at its deepest point. It was at first assumed that a joint had failed on the lattice of pipework and nozzles on the base of the adsorber but nothing could be done until all the carbon was emptied out into a spare adsorber. On completion, an inspection showed one of the nozzles had indeed blown out of its holder, which, after clean up was re-glued into place and left to harden, assuming a poor quality joint in the first place.

So as not to waste time, while this was happening, another adsorber was prepared and backwashing was started, only for a similar failure to occur. The main problem now was there was no spare adsorber to empty the carbon into, so before coming to any conclusions about the quality of the joints and pipework a third adsorber was selected for backwashing, unfortunately with the same result. This resulted in a top-end meeting of both H&G and Anglian Water staff to come up with an action plan. Our project manager, whose nickname was "pit bull", believing actions speak louder than words, proposed that all the joints on the UPVC pipework in the failed and now empty adsorber should be cut out and remade with full inspection for quality of the rework being done. Although there was no real evidence the original work was faulty, this suggestion, in the absence of any other ideas, was adopted. At the same time temporary storage vessels of sufficient capacity to take the GAC from the other failed adsorber were to be sourced and brought to the site so that it could be emptied and restoration work started where it was deemed necessary.

Another problem that caused me some embarrassment during the initial start-up was due to some of the large diaphragm valves sticking on first being opened or closed. A discussion with the valve manufacturers assured me that once thoroughly wetted they would be fine but the application of a water soluble lubricant to the rubber seat would assist the initial operation. As a consequence I drove into Oakham late on a Friday afternoon, went into the chemists and bought all, bar one, tubes of KY Jelly that they had for sale. I left one tube because I thought it was a bit mean on the residents of Oakham to take all the lubricant available off the shelves before the weekend and was a little embarrassed taking all the tubes up to the young woman behind the till to pay for them, but she did not seem to find anything strange in the purchase even when I asked for a receipt so I could reclaim the cost on my expenses. This was reminiscent of the time one of our site managers, working in the Far East, put in a sizable claim for "palm oil" payments to cover the cost of "sweeteners", I hesitate to say bribes, he was paying to local dignitaries to keep things moving.

While I had access to an empty adsorber I climbed inside to see if I could see any reason for the failure and on unscrewing some of the spray nozzles found the nozzles at the deepest point were completely plugged with a grey/black material with the constituency of putty, while the nozzles at the shallow end were about half-full of the same material. Thinking this must be significant I took some of the material into the laboratory and oven dried it, only to find it was a mass of very fine carbon particles small enough to pass through the slits in the spray nozzles. Before jumping to any conclusions I went in search of David Osborne, a long time colleague and our water treatment expert, who had been very much involved in the design concept, to talk things over. Actually he was easy to spot as he was affectionately known as "Agent Orange" for the bright orange boiler suit he always wore on site. My belief was that not being able to complete the initial backwash in one go was resulting in the spray nozzles becoming plugged with carbon fines until the backwash water pressure blew something apart but not easy to prove or resolve.

The arrival of the temporary storage vessels started a period of hard physical work for me in cold, wet, unpleasant conditions. Although I had some labourers to help me I found it easier to work with them rather than direct operations from afar. The first job was to connect and drag fire hoses across the site to connect the adsorber to be emptied to the temporary vessel to be filled and more hoses to take waste water from the vessel during filling to the black water holding tank. Also, once the GAC had been transferred a backwash regime had to be established to prevent the carbon becoming anaerobic and stagnating.

Whether it was the physical activity or the stress of the situation I was suddenly incapacitated by a recurrence of terrible back pain. After spending two or three hours stretched out on the floor of the site hut and the affect of two or three pain killers kicked in I just about managed to get to my car and drive to my lodgings. The guys gave me one of the first ever mobile phones (about the size of a house brick) to take with me in case I needed help or we needed to communicate about work while I was away. A phone call to Dawn brought her, accompanied by her mother, to my assistance to stock the lodgings with food and other essentials such as more pain killers, which allowed me to spend a very miserable week or more, mostly flat on my back on the bed, before the pain eased enough for me to get to a local chiropractor for some treatment. He put me on a rack and stretched me and tried other forms of torture before his manipulations over three or four sessions reduced the pain to bearable levels, either that or I just got better. Anyway he also gave me a set of exercises to do, which I still do to this day, as a preventative measure and although I have not been totally free of back pain since I do believe they help to minimise the severity of an attack.

While I was away no real resolution to the problem had been reached, so I was sent home to fully recover with a return to the "tranquillity" of life in head office, while Anglian Water and H&G put their heads together to come up with a solution. I believe the problem arose because each subsequent plant that was built was scaled up from the original pilot plant design without sufficiently scaling up the infrastructure to account for the ever larger quantities of GAC in the adsorbers. Whatever the cause, by the time a resolution was found I was no longer working in the commissioning group but, due to a severe slow down in the company's traditional business sectors, had on the 18th March 1995, been transferred to the validation department, a relatively new group that was being established within the company organisation and for me, another major change in career path.

PART 7
A Migration to Validation

Jacobs Engineering, the large American chemical engineering company that now owned and had integrated H&G into its worldwide organisation had recognised that the design and construction of new pharmaceutical plants was one of the few growing market opportunities both in Europe and indeed around the world. To safeguard the public and satisfy the regulations imposed by the Food and Drugs Administration (FDA) in the USA or the equivalent Medicines Control Agency (MCA) in Europe, before any pharmaceutical products from a new plant can be sold the whole process including the design concept, the producing structure and process, including individual equipment items within it has to be checked and tested to very exacting standards written into approved protocols. This became known as "validation" and to satisfy these requirements a new department, under the supervision of an experienced validation manager, was being set up to produce all the necessary standards, protocols and procedures that would be required on future projects.

A brief history may be of use to better understand the need for validation. The Thalidomide tragedy of the early 1960s focussed attention on the lack of a comprehensive medicines legislation and resulted in the passing of the British Medicines Act in 1968. This included the need to obtain product licences to manufacture both "old" and new medicinal products together with manufacturer's licences covering the sites and facilities where those products were manufactured. This in turn led to the issue of guides to Good Manufacturing Practice (GMP) for pharmaceutical products in the 1970s, usually known as the "Orange Guide" in Britain, simply because of the colour of the cover of the first issue, and widely used by the Medicines Inspectorate when reviewing facilities to confirm compliance with the law and the principles of GMP, before a manufacturer's licence is issued.

Changes to the law and new regulations meant that before a product licence was issued, a manufacturer would have to produce trial batches in a pilot plant for testing in a laboratory, usually using animals to test for harmful side effects. Although required by law, this practice was much hated by the 'animal rights' activists and was the bane of my wife's existence in the 1990s when she worked for a company providing such test facilities. It is very worrying to be given a pamphlet by the police about how to inspect the underside of your car with a mirror, before driving off, to confirm whether or not a bomb has been attached. Fortunately not – but some of her colleagues had their cars torched on their driveways and the company's MD was beaten with baseball bats outside his home!

Assuming the trials on animals showed no ill effects this would usually be followed by clinical trials on human volunteers, which became increasingly necessary as the fight against cancer introduced ever more invasive drugs to the market. Rolling forward some forty years I have just read that the latest requirements by the EU's Clinical Trials Directive has effectively increased the cost of experiments to find new cancer drugs more than ten-fold and it is difficult to know where to draw the line between increased safety and the increased costs stopping a potentially new "wonder" drug being produced.

Following other occasions where contamination within the final product had lead to the death of patients it was realised that, if for example 20,000 vials of vaccine are produced from a single production batch over a period of four or five days, testing a small percentage of the final product for compliance would not guarantee the whole batch was fit for purpose. This lead to the concept that testing, to confirm that individual elements throughout the manufacturing process were working to their design specifications, would provide a greater guarantee that the final product would be fit for purpose, with particular need to manufacture in a clean, contamination free and where necessary sterile environment.

In summary a medicinal product is fit for purpose when it is:

- The right product, manufactured as specified to the right design.
- The right strength.
- Free from contamination.
- Free from deterioration when used within a specified period.
- In the right container.
- Correctly labelled.
- Properly sealed within its container and protected against damage, contamination or deterioration.

I was transferred to the validation department in the early stages of its existence with, as far as I can remember, just four other permanent staff within the group plus a delightful, enthusiastic American woman seconded from Jacobs validation group in the USA to help establish the necessary standards and departmental procedures. Most of my new colleagues were relatively young and came from a biological, medicinal or pharmaceutical manufacturing background rather than the chemical engineering design and construction business, so while trying to absorb and understand the fundamentals of my latest reincarnation I could help them integrate into the company structure and better understand its methods of working from design stage through to construction completion.

7.1 Glasgow & Irvine – Scotland

After just over a month working in the London office my illusion that, once transferred to the validation group, I would spend more time at home was shattered when I was asked to transfer to the Glasgow office. The company, operating out of its Glasgow office, had been awarded a contract by Smith Kline Beecham (SKB) to design and build a new production stream for their facilities at Irvine in Scotland. My task was to augment the newly established validation group in writing the Installation Qualification (IQ) and Operational Qualification (OQ) documents that would, after execution and approval, be required to provide the documented evidence that a specific process will consistently result in a product that, with a high degree of assurance, meet its predetermined specifications and quality attributes.

The validation process starts with the production of a Design Qualification (DQ), that is documented verification that the design will fulfil the user requirement to produce a new product.

I think it is fair to say that the exact formulation of any new drug was a fairly closely guarded secret and that the engineering company contracted to design and build a new facility would be required to scale up an already existing pilot plant, built to a DQ approved design, without knowing, perhaps with a few sworn-to-secrecy exceptions, exactly what would be processed to make the final product. This information was not really required to write IQs, and OQs could be written using acceptable placebos – frequently water – while the Performance Qualification (PQ) documents, using the correct ingredients were usually written and executed by the pharmaceutical company themselves.

The initial preparation for producing these documents was very similar to the procedures used for writing pre-commissioning and commissioning documents, with which I was already familiar. Once an acceptable process design had been completed the resulting Process and Instrument Diagrams (P&IDs) or Engineering and Utilities Diagrams (ELDs and ULDs) would be marked up to divide the whole plant into smaller, manageable identifiable systems. Put simply the Installation Qualification is the documented verification that what you have got will meet the design specification. IQ documents are required for each system that will itemise the component parts on a discipline by discipline basis, i.e. pipelines and component parts, instrument items, mechanical equipment items, electrical items, vessels, etc. A document package has to be collated together for each system containing approved specification and data sheets for all the component parts and, once purchased, the corresponding vendors operating and maintenance manuals. Depending on the type of plant, drawings, specification and data sheets defining the civil structure are also required, with particular emphasis in "clean rooms" on the surface finish of walls, floors, ceilings, door types, etc. including the differential pressure ratings between the rooms to minimise contamination into the designated clean areas. In addition, documents defining the layout and component parts of the Heating, Ventilation and Air Conditioning (HVAC) system, with particular emphasis on filter types, for example HEPA (High-efficiency Particulate Arresting or Air) filters and ratings that are necessary to maintain the biological and particulate limits to control the environment within a specified enclosed space are required.

Each IQ document is written with a tick box and "initials" space against each item required so that during execution confirmation of the required documentation's existence in the system hand-over package can be recorded. In addition, the bottom of each page has signature and date spaces for completion by both the person executing the IQ document and for final approval by the client's QA/QC department. Prior to an IQ document being released for execution, draft versions are checked by senior members of the validation group and are then forwarded to the client for final approval and sign-off as acceptable for execution. Quite important, as once approved and issued for execution, any mistakes or omissions require regulatory approval for corrections to be made. During the IQ execution a physical examination of the plant will result in a written confirmation being made that for each system all the component parts have been installed in accordance with the approved design drawings and specifications, that the correct materials have been used, items are correctly tagged and where required are correctly calibrated with appropriate, in date, test certificates. Not quite as easy as it may sound. I remember one occasion where tagged relief valves were installed in their correct locations, according to the P&IDs, close inspection showed that the relief pressure stamped on the body of each valve was incorrect for four out of five valves with the same flange size. They had been installed without reference to their pressure rating and tagged once in place, so looked correct but were potentially a disaster waiting to happen if not spotted.

Put simply the Operational Qualification (OQ) is the documented verification that what you have got operates to the design specification and OQs were written in a similar format to IQs on a system by system basis. A test procedure would be included for each item of equipment to confirm that it was operating to or within its design specification. For example, pump flow rates would be verified by either pumping water through a flow meter or by timing the drop in level from a supply vessel or, if neither of these options was available, by strapping on a temporary external flow-meter to a suitable length of pipework. The test would be repeated to confirm consistent results and all the measuring equipment used, either permanent or temporary, would need to have a valid calibration certificate for inclusion in the document package.

At that time the Glasgow office was situated in Park Circus Place in Glasgow's West End, which is a relatively select area and contains some fine buildings built by Glasgow's rich merchants as the city prospered in the eighteenth and nineteenth centuries. The office overlooked an oval of elegant, mainly two storey, buildings from the same period, which provided a fine aspect, somewhat spoiled by the rows of sweaty trainers placed on window sills or balconies by the students from the University of Glasgow, who now occupied the apartments that some of the buildings had been converted into. But, hey, it added a certain piquancy and gave the area a feeling of energy and living in modern times. I had managed to find lodgings in a B&B in a similar grand building on the Great West Road, a short walk from the Botanical Gardens, which, when it was not raining, provided a very pleasant twenty minute walk to and from work. My route took me through Kelvin Grove Park, exiting through Park Gate into Park Circus Place and it always gave me a feeling of wellbeing to pause and watch members of the Chinese community practicing Tai Chi at the park entrance each morning.

Another advantage of lodging where I did was a friendly pub just down the road which was good for a pint of heavy (I was starting to learn the language) after a hard day at work and which ran a quiz on a Thursday evening. After a few weeks of suggesting an answer or two to a group of students sitting next to me – there are some categories when being old has its advantages – they invited me to join them which gave me a new group to socialise with. However, the biggest advantage was that crossing the Great West Road from my lodgings led into a thoroughfare that was within easy walking distance of the University of Glasgow, so that the whole area including a maze of side streets was student land. This meant there were plenty of fast food outlets, mini supermarkets that stayed open until past midnight, plenty of pubs and descent little bistros that meant eating alone was not a problem in what was generally a friendly and agreeable atmosphere. One bistro in particular became a firm favourite because around ten o'clock most nights a young woman came in to meet her boyfriend who was the manager. It was only a small place with limited seating so she would often end up sitting at my table while she waited and once we got talking there was no stopping us. I think it fair to say she enjoyed our conversations and my company as much as I did hers and that you can sometimes meet somebody in unlikely circumstances that you have a real affinity with. The funny thing is I cannot remember her first name, I know her surname was Rafferty and her first name wasn't Jerry, but that is about the best I can do.

I have probably given the impression the area was a bit downbeat but in fact there were some high class restaurants to be found; the Ubiquitous Chip in Ashton Lane being one such, a very posh brasserie that needed to be booked if you wanted to eat in the main restaurant where a mix of Glasgow's movers and shakers could usually be found. I treated myself a couple of times to get a feel for the ambience before taking Dawn there when she came up for a long weekend. Another advantage of the location was being close to Hillside station, a stop on the underground which meant I could take the "clock-work orange" – the carriages were coloured a particularly bright orange – into Glasgow if I wanted to meet some of my work colleagues for a night out or a meal in one of the myriad Indian restaurants scattered across the city. There were so many to choose from I decided Glasgow is probably the curry capital of the world.

After some three months working in the Glasgow office, preparations were made to transfer to Irvine for closer liaison with our counterparts in the

SKB organisation in order to complete document preparation and initiate the execution of the IQs. For this phase, after flying to Glasgow, I would pick up a hire car at Glasgow Airport and drive to the SKB site at Irvine where, once the execution work started, we operated a rather peculiar shift system. Four twelve-hour days before a day off leading into four twelve-hour nights, followed by a four-day break. In the four-day break it was possible and permitted for any that wanted to do so to fly home, travelling time included in the four days but not paid for. After finishing the last night shift, driving to Glasgow Airport for an early morning flight to London required a lot of concentration, and I usually had no trouble dozing for most of the flight and onward train journey to Essex. With luck and no delays I could arrive home by late afternoon and then found it was best to go to bed for a couple of hours so that I was not a complete zombie when Dawn got home from work.

These changes also made it necessary to find new lodgings and I ended up in the Laurie Land Hotel, located in a small hamlet midway between Kilmarnock and Irvine. Mrs Hill, the landlady, was very good and once she understood my strange working patterns tried to put me in a room as far away from the noise and bustle as she could, so that I could sleep during the day when on the night shifts. She was also happy to cook me a good "breakfast" at around 19.00 hours before I left for work. As this was my first opportunity to see anything of Scotland (being a southerner I had not ventured too far past Watford Gap before) I decided not to waste the change-over day between day and night shifts but to explore as much of Scotland as I could within seven to eight hours' driving distance.

I started with a few local castles and then drove to the coast to take a look, as a very occasional but hoping to improve golfer, at Royal Troon, not that I expected or wanted to play there, and then on further down the coast to Turnberry. Before reaching Turnberry I came upon the dramatic view of Culzean (pronounced "Cullane") Castle. Standing on the cliff tops, overlooking the Isle of Arran, it was an arresting sight and one that could not be passed by so I spent the rest of the day exploring the castle and beautifully laid out grounds. Started as a fortified tower castle it was converted by Robert Adam between 1777 and 1792 into what is probably the finest Georgian castle in Scotland with a splendid circular saloon and oval staircase acknowledged to be Adam's final masterpiece. In 1945 the 5th Marquis of Ailsa gave the castle to the National Trust but with a request that the top floor be converted into a self-contained apartment to be offered, as a life-time tenancy, to Dwight D. Eisenhower as a means of thanking him for his part in the Second World War. Eisenhower and his family visited on a number of occasions, including once during his term as president of the USA when Culzean Castle became an extension of the White House.

On another day I continued my exploration down the A719 and A77 and with the good fortune of it being a fine, sunny day was treated to some truly magnificent scenic views, that coupled with diversions to some picturesque coastal villages and harbours, I believe makes that stretch of Scotland one of the finest coast roads in the world. Perhaps not quite as dramatic or scary as Italy's Amalfi coast but the absence of other traffic means you can just relax and enjoy a wonderful drive.

Other memorable trips were along the A82 around the west side of Loch Lomond before crossing over to Loch Fyne and Inveraray, where I resisted the temptation to buy some of their famous kippers, before continuing round Loch Awe to reach Oban and a quick stop off at a salmon fishery before another wonderfully scenic drive on a fine day back down the A816 before heading for what had now become home. A long day but I got back in time to have a couple of hours' sleep before going into work to start the night shift.

Another trip that I am glad I made was into the Highlands as far as Glen Coe which, with dark lowering clouds hanging over the hillsides, had a strange forbidding atmosphere about it. Having never skied in Scotland I was interested to take the chair lift, which, although not winter, was still operating up to the visitors' centre to see what was on offer. There were still some pockets of icy snow in some of the gullies and I decided on a bleak windy winter's day with limited runs available it would not be a place for southern softies, although the views were magnificent, so I expect we will continue to hop across the channel on EasyJet from Southend-on-Sea to Geneva for a week or two in the Porte du Soleil region of France. That is if my injured knee and enlarged spleen (non-Hodgkin's lymphoma) allow me to ski again. It would be a shame to give up now that I can get a seniors' lift pass at reduced rates!

One other event that sticks in my memory was going to the pictures in Kilmarnock to see *Brave Heart* which had just been released. After the particularly gruesome ending of Willy Wallace I slunk out of the cinema hoping that nobody would recognise they had a Sassenach in their presence. The best part about it was, on returning to the Laurie Land Hotel, a real live Willy Wallace was sitting on his stool in the corner of the bar with a few of the other regulars and I could recount something of what I had just seen without fear of getting lynched.

As my first experience of on-site validation the type of plant we were validating for SKB was quite similar to other chemical plants I had worked on with none of the complexities of clean rooms and sterile areas that I was to encounter later on and after four months on site most of the work had been completed and I was sent back to the London office, so ending my first foray into Scotland.

There followed a period that was pretty much the norm for working in the validation department: becoming part of a team put together to prepare IQs and OQs for the next contract we had been awarded and then travelling to site to execute the protocols once they had been approved and the site construction or modification work had been completed. Planning for these events to be mutually compatible with regard to time spent on each phase was never easy and one of the most difficult tasks to get right if man-hours and/or human resources were not to be wasted.

As part of this regime in 1996, I spent five weeks, I think on my own, executing protocols at Haverhill in Suffolk, about mid-way between our homes in Wickford and Hoxne but still too far to travel every day so staying on a B&B basis in one of the Country Inn chains. This can always be a bit of a danger when, after an evening meal, there is a convenient bar available to relax and find some company in. I believe I only went over the edge once and that was when I found a nice cold cider was a pleasant alternative to my usual bitter and did not notice just how easily they were slipping down.

The next assignment was to a Pfizer site at Sandwich on the Kent coast – a very large and expanding establishment, particularly after the discovery of the somewhat surprising side effects of a certain little blue pill they were manufacturing. Our job was to validate an existing production stream, nothing to do with Viagra, that had been extensively modified for a new product line. The big change for me was that I had been put in charge of the small site team allocated to complete the work. As far as I can remember, apart from me, the team consisted of two of our reasonably experienced validation engineers, a young woman, Layla, fairly recently graduated who, as far as I know, had never been on site before and a senior process engineer from our Indian office who had been sent to England for training and to gain experience in the validation process. The job was not without its problems, finding relief valves correctly tagged but with the wrong pressure rating, as previously mentioned, was but one of them and by the time we started work on the OQs we were getting behind on the planned programme. To some extent my relative inexperience meant that I did not call for extra help soon enough but like most programmes in our industry they seem to be drawn up with no contingency for delay or rework. In the end Pfizer stepped in and included some of their own validation process engineers to speed things up and we completed the work in four to five months, so everybody was reasonably happy.

One of the good things about the job was it took you to places, for an extended period, that otherwise you would probably have never been to or would just pass through without time to explore. That area of the Kent coast and the surrounding countryside was well worth a visit and the nearby Cinque Ports offered much with quaint, picturesque streets and buildings and a fascinating history. I did have one painful memory of my time in Kent. I was in the middle of my evening meal in the coaching inn I was staying in when an exquisite pain struck in my lower back. I thought I had a kidney stone and more or less crawled up to my bed where I spent an agonising night. In the morning I phoned the landlord who organised for a local doctor to come and see me and contacted my colleague Layla, who was also in the same B&B, to let her know I was in trouble and that she would have to make her own way into work. The doctor could find no definite reason for the pain so agreed to give me a pain killing injection which, once it took effect, allowed me to drive back to Essex where I could see my own doctor and at least suffer in my own home. The outcome was not a kidney stone but a recurrence of my lower back pain and after a few days' rest and sessions with a chiropractor it went its way but left me with a reminder to keep doing the regular preventative exercises that I had been given after the first episode. It is another one of those things that when working long hours away from home can easily get neglected.

7.2 Speke – England

My next assignment starting in January 1997 was to be a very different experience. I was asked to go to the Evans Medical Pharmaceutical Complex located at Speke, near Liverpool, to assist them in the validation of a number of their existing autoclaves. Since my previous experience of an autoclave was seeing one standing in the corner of a laboratory it was just as well I was being used as an extra pair of hands in their validation group during their autoclave revalidation programme. After being introduced to their validation group I was given an autoclave Standing Operating Procedure (SOP) and an autoclave validation protocol to read before being paired with one of their experienced staff to assist him while being taken through the complete validation process.

Evans Medical, to a large extent, had specialised in egg-based vaccine production and at that time were responsible for producing a high proportion of Britain's flu vaccine amongst a number of other product lines. Vast numbers of specially hatched eggs were used each week in the production process and after seeding and incubating, the part of the egg containing the vaccine had to be extracted in sterile conditions in specially constructed clean rooms. All equipment going into these clean areas was passed through an autoclave where it was steam sterilised and all used equipment and waste material leaving the clean areas was passed through another autoclave where a steam sterilisation cycle was run to kill off any contaminants.

Each autoclave was the size of a small room with a sealable door at each end, one opening from the "dirty" area and the other into the "clean" area, with a control sequence that would not allow this to happen at the same time. Two or three layer stainless steel trolleys could be loaded with specified equipment items required for a new production batch before being wheeled into the autoclave for sterilisation prior to entry into the clean area.

The essence of the validation procedure that I was assisting with was to confirm that all locations within the autoclave and its load, during the steam (moist-heat) sterilisation cycle, consistently attained a temperature of not less than 121.5 °C for at least 15 minutes. Under these conditions saturated steam transfers heat energy to materials very rapidly on contact and can therefore destroy any microorganisms, even highly resistant spore forms of bacteria in a relatively short time and thus achieve the sterility required during the production process.

Problems that could affect the achievement of sterility are:

- Incomplete air removal from within the load or chamber thus reducing the effectiveness of the steam contact.
- Steam quality (saturation, purity or supply).
- Equipment malfunction or personnel error.

Most of the above would be checked during regular validation of the autoclave itself but our prime concern was proving that all points within the load, e.g. inside tubing or heavy stainless steel equipment items could be penetrated by the steam sufficiently to attain sterility. To this end thermocouples, independent of the autoclave, would be placed in specified locations within the load and the autoclave itself to monitor and record the temperatures achieved during the sterilisation cycle. For clarification a thermocouple is formed by joining together two dissimilar metals, e.g. copper and constantan, where the resistance at the junction of the two when a current is passed through them varies very precisely with the temperature at the junction. In my young days in the laboratory the thermocouple would be connected to a device known as a Wheatstone Bridge so that values monitored could be compared on a chart to give precise temperature readings.

Progress had been made since my young days and I was introduced to Kaye Instruments Validator 2000, a very compact self-contained piece of kit that had been developed to simplify and improve thermal validation procedures. At this time I had very little to do with setting up or programming the validator and was simply shown how to use it, but it was a good introduction for later jobs where its use was to play a major part in the work being done. Among many other features, up to twelve tagged sensors (thermocouples or pressure transducers) could be pre-wired into a SIM (plug-in Sensor Module) which, once plugged in to the validator, allowed easy transfer of data during a programmable cycle run. Collected data could be viewed *in situ* and was stored in the validator's internal memory for connection to a parallel printer for online printout of raw data, or transfer to a floppy disk, or direct connection to a PC. Many other features were available, for example report writing or an alarm indication if the detected temperature on a particular sensor dropped below a pre-determined set point. The validator could accommodate three SIMs of up to 12 sensors each, and with additional kit the sensors could be calibration-checked and each SIM had a built in memory to store calibration offsets. Importantly for validation purposes only authorized access was possible via a user ID and password and result files could not be tampered with. Any failure to reach the required parameter values could not be simply written out and would require suitable explanation when submitting a protocol for review. For example a thermocouple may have been damaged, which would require replacement and the whole procedure and operational cycle to be repeated.

The validator could not, of course, be placed inside the autoclave, so thermocouples of sufficient length had to be connected and fed through a special sealable port, capable of taking 12 thermocouples, into the autoclave's interior where each (tagged) thermocouple tip would be placed in a predetermined position in the autoclave's interior or against a specific "load" item. One thermocouple always had to be placed in the autoclave's drain (coldest spot) next to its built-in temperature sensor for comparison purposes during a porous load sterilisation cycle. Therefore, if a full load consisted of 36 items, at least three runs would be necessary to monitor the temperature at each item plus free space around the trolley/autoclave and the drain. The tricky thing was selecting items so that each load would be relatively well balanced with regard to heat capacity (large stainless steel items take longer to heat up), difficulty of penetration of the steam (small bore tubing) and position on the trolley for consistent results during replicate cycles.

As well as the thermocouples, chemical indicators were included which changed colour as a result of the presence of moisture, sterilising temperature and minimum time. Most of the load items would come packaged with a chemical patch on the package and thermocouples would be held in place using autoclave tape containing a chemical indicator stripe. This was not absolute proof of lethality but a good indication that sterilizing conditions had not been met at a particular location, if the stripe had not changed colour. I cannot remember if Biological Indicators (BI) – usually a strip of hard to kill *Bacillus stearothermophilus* spores – were included in these validation cycles as they were on future jobs, I do not think so, as I cannot remember sending them to a biology laboratory, after the cycle, for proof of complete lethality.

One thing I soon learned was not to be tempted to try to enter the chamber too quickly after the completion of a cycle to disconnect the thermocouples and remove the used load in preparation for the next run. Lots of hot stainless steel in a confined space was a recipe for picking up burn blisters, especially if rushing to complete another cycle before the end of the day.

After a couple of weeks of close liaison I was given an autoclave of my own to work on but always in close cooperation with Evans Medical staff as I was still not fully conversant with how the autoclaves worked or Evans somewhat novel procedures. After six weeks, the backlog of work had been completed and I returned to the London office but hardly had time to unload my briefcase before being sent back to Scotland to prepare more IQs and OQs for a new phase of work for SKB on their Irvine Site. This assignment lasted for about six months before I returned home and took the opportunity to fit some holidays in, not always easy as Dawn was also in full-time employment. Fortunately, not too many people want to holiday from September to December, but for us, with no children to consider, it was almost a preferred time. In the end we managed a tour of Italy and then, after renewing our visas, a return to Southern India, where we spent a delightful relaxing Christmas period at Kovalam Beach and on a converted rice barge on the Kerala backwaters.

With hardly time to unpack my bags it was a repack for colder climes and a return to Speke and another assignment at Evans Medical. That usually meant an early start on a Monday morning to catch a train to Liverpool Street then underground to Euston and a main line train to Runcorn where I could pick up a taxi into work. On the previous assignment, as I didn't think I would be there long enough to warrant finding lodgings, I had been staying in the reasonably priced Gateacre Hall Hotel on a B&B basis, so at the end of the day, this is where I returned, a short taxi ride away from the Evans Medical Works, to see some familiar faces and renew acquaintances with some of the regulars in the bar. Normally, unless I knew I was going to be on a long-term assignment, I would resist attempts to push me into finding lodgings where contracts had to be signed and deposits paid as well as all the problems of self-catering – laundry, etc. When working long hours there is a lot to be said for staying in a hotel and being looked after even if the same menu is repeated week after week.

On the new assignment I joined a team of Jacobs' employees, mainly contractors, who had been put together to complete the validation of a new product line that had been installed for an American company (Aviron) within the Evans Medical Site. I think it fortunate that one, Chris Driver, was our on-site team leader as he had a wealth of knowledge of vaccine production as well as clean-room technology and was capable of keeping us on the right path, as I certainly had a lot to learn and I got the impression so did some others, including the project manager. Chris was an interesting character and had recently returned from several years in Brazil where he had a good position helping to set up a burgeoning pharmaceutical industry. Unfortunately, he had to return to look after his mother who had dementia but I got the impression Brazil had attractions to offer that Liverpool lacked and, you never know, he may have returned to tackle the Zika virus and prepare the country for the Olympics. I believe Chris was the only smoker in our group and it amused me that his frequent visits to the smoking hut in the middle of the site provided more up-to-date information about what was going on all over the works than all the bulletin boards put together.

My recent experience came into good use because there was validation required on autoclaves leading into and out of the vaccine production clean areas. By the time I joined the team trial batches of vaccine were already being produced, which involved large numbers of eggs being processed. This made our job more difficult as we had to fit our validation procedures into the process without disrupting progress too much and required good cooperation with the production staff. All went well until an intermittent fault caused the decontamination autoclave, at the outlet to the facility, to tripout midway through its cycle, which meant the whole procedure had to be started again. The knock-on effect was a build up of used eggs within the facility and the real problem came when the operators overloaded the autoclave with used eggs to try and get rid of them, rather than reducing the intake. After one successful cycle I opened the discharge door of the autoclave to find the whole floor covered in semi-cooked egg. It smelt revolting and was enough to put you off omelettes for life! That was the limit of my cooperation, I simply closed the door and called for Evans staff to come and clear it up and do a thorough clean.

It was only later I realised how difficult it would be to delay the intake of the eggs once the vaccine production process was underway, and that was when I was moved to validation of the incubators used just after the start of the process. Not being from a biological or pharmaceutical background I had little understanding of the complexity or critical timings required during the vaccine production process so started to ask questions and seek advice. As far as I can gather and I apologise for any howlers in the following, the process started with pathogen-free embryonated chicken eggs being flown in from controlled hatcheries, in this case, I believe in America. Once received, the eggs could be held in the Egg Virus Unit (EVU) cold store for up to seven days before being passed through an egg sanitizer to clean and remove bio-burden from the eggs' surface before incubation to develop the embryo within the eggs.

The primary incubator was a large room with a central walkway that had stacks of tagged trays containing the eggs stretching from floor to ceiling on each side of the walkway. The incubator was designed to give a carefully controlled uniform environment, usually within a temperature range of 37.5 ±1 °C and a relative humidity of 50 to 55%. The forced air incubator had internal fans to circulate the air uniformly around the eggs and an automatic mechanism that turned the eggs periodically during the incubation period. My job in all this was, in accordance with an approved protocol, to locate thermocouples throughout the incubator and a batch-load of eggs to confirm the set temperature could be uniformly and consistently maintained throughout the incubation period of 11 days, and the equilibrium state could be re-established within ten minutes after a typical door opening for access or when the incubator was loaded with a new trolley-load of eggs. It was quite an arduous task to position the thermocouples in the first place as it was hot and humid in the incubator and you were soon soaked in sweat. I seem to remember working in a paper boiler suit so I could have a wash and change of clothes when I came out. It was also necessary to enter the incubator each day to confirm everything was still in place and nothing had been moved or added to the load being monitored. This could sometimes be a problem because, although cooperation was generally good and entry and exit periods into the incubator had to be logged, the operations staff were a bit of a law unto themselves and could go in and reorganise things a little if they decided they needed more space.

The tricky thing for the operations staff was to keep a log of how long each tray of eggs had been incubating – time enough for the embryo to develop (11 to 12 days) but not more than 20 to 21 days when the chicks would start to hatch. Nobody wants to chase fluffy yellow chicks round an incubator and then have to put them to death and incinerate them once they have been caught. It has happened!

After primary incubation the eggs were transported back to the Aviron Viral Unit (AVU) to be seeded by inoculation with a live virus culture within the confines of a laminar flow cabinet. Once seeded, each batch of eggs was moved to the virus growth incubator where the eggs were maintained at a temperature of 32 to 34 °C for two to three days. During incubation, the virus replicates in the chorioallantoic membrane or the allantoic cavity (white of the egg).

Once the incubation period was complete the eggs were transferred to the egg chiller room to be cooled to 5±3 °C, within a period of four hours, before the virus in allantoic fluid was harvested by specially trained operations staff pipetting the fluid out of the eggs, approximately 10 ml per egg, within the confines of laminar air flow cabinets. Once harvested the product was pooled into containers before being centrifuged at a controlled temperature of 5±3 °C for final purification. Hence, once in progress, timing is critical and, without considerable waste, difficult to hold up for whatever reason.

As all of the processes being carried out at controlled temperatures had associated IQ/OQ/PQ protocols to be completed that involved temperature mapping, there was plenty of work to do. Also, for me something new, I was introduced to the stringent requirements for testing and approving the operation of laminar air flow cabinets, which, as they are designed to prevent the escape of pathogens and protect operators' lives, is no bad thing.

As an aside, hard as I may try, I cannot now remember the name of the incubator manufacturers but some years later on one of our wonderful holidays in South Africa we were visiting an ostrich farm in Oudtshoorn when I spotted the same name on the incubators they were using to hatch ostrich eggs. By the way did you know an ostrich's eye is bigger than its brain?

In the end, from what I thought was going to be a relatively short assignment, I spent about nine months working on the Aviron Caiv process and as it was coming to a close I was moved onto yet another design and build project Jacobs were responsible for on the Evans Medical site. To start with I became part of an ever-expanding validation group, most of whom I had not met before, who were in the final stages of writing the IQ/OQ protocols that would be required to validate the process once construction of the new facilities was complete.

All of this time I had been staying in the Gateacre Hall Hotel, mostly on my own, but now with some company as new members of the team arrived and stayed for a week or two while searching for alternative accommodation. Some would get together and rent a house but I still resisted suggestions that I should find somewhere cheaper to stay. Gateacre (pronounced "gat-acca") was a small village, conveniently located not too far from Speke (Evans Medical site) or Liverpool city centre. It became a conservation area in 1969 to preserve mainly the Grade II listed, black and white mock Tudor houses, built to house rich city merchants and had little else of note other than a church and the Black Bull pub, which I frequented, mainly on quiz nights as I had managed to inveigle my way into one of the local teams. Like always in a new area I asked some of the taxi drivers for any recommendations for a change of scene, and apart from warning me off a couple of pubs on the way to Speak (boarded up windows didn't make them look very appealing) they suggested Woolton village as worth a visit. A three quarter mile walk from Gateacre it was quite upmarket, with streets of terraced houses that had been renovated to make them both attractive and appealing, if you could afford them; a good high street, a couple of decent pubs, a Chinese restaurant and a wonderful old fashioned single screen Picture House which was still in operation.

It was an interesting area to explore if, like me, you grew seeing The Beatles rocket to mass adoration and worldwide fame in the 1960s. Penny Lane was not far away and I would pass the house John Lennon grew up in on the way into Liverpool. One of the regulars in the bar at Gateacre Hall told me that the grave of "Eleanor Rigby" (title of song on Beatles 1966 album *Revolver* and a successful 45rpm single) could be found in St Peters Churchyard in Woolton village, so one evening I took myself off to find it. I found a whole group of "Rigby" graves but no Eleanor, although there was an Eleanor with another surname very close to them, so I imagined them hanging out in the churchyard and putting together a combination of names that suited the music. As it happens there was a group of youths sitting around the church porch, so I asked them if they knew were Eleanor Rigby was buried. I was quite surprised when they said 'never heard of her'; fame is fleeting; but they told me Bob Paisley, one of Liverpool Football Club's legendary managers was buried down the bottom of the church yard if I wanted to go and visit him. So I never found the grave, but as Paul McCartney and John Lennon first met at a garden fete in Woolton village in 1957 I suspect there must be a strong connection.

It was about this time a very strange coincidence took place. Most mornings I would go down to breakfast, put my newspaper on an empty table and collect fruit juice and cereal from the buffet. When I got back there was a lady sitting opposite that I did not recognise. After a polite good morning I thought from her accent she was probably an Essex girl and further conversation confirmed we were near neighbours as Patricia lived in Billericay. I had just found out she was on an assignment working at Liverpool Airport when her work colleague arrived and sat down next to me. I turned to look at her and realised it was Audrey, who had been my mixed doubles badminton partner at Battlesbridge Badminton Club for about ten years until I got too old or was away too much to continue playing. Both Audrey and Patricia worked for a freight handling company based at Southend Airport and were on assignment to train staff and establish a new business at Liverpool Airport.

So developed another friendship which has passed the test of time. Audrey only stayed for about a week to help Patricia settle in, so it was Patricia I would see most days, either in the morning or in the evening, where would share a table for an evening meal and then a drink in the bar. My estimation of the chef went up when I found out Patricia was a vegan and had brought her own recipes with her to pass to the kitchen in the hope of getting some variety in the meals she could eat.

I had already made some evening excursions into Liverpool, skirting Toxteth, famed for the riots of the 1980s on the way in and passing the relatively new Roman Catholic cathedral or "Paddies Wigwam" as it was affectionately known, to do a walking tour of the city. A visit to The Cavern, where The Beatles started on their road to fame and fortune was a must as was the imaginatively reconstructed dockside area with a boat museum, good views of the iconic Liver Birds sitting atop the twin towers of the Royal Liver Assurance building and trendy boutique shops and café/restaurant society which gave the whole area a good vibe. Having Patricia for company made the whole experience more enjoyable, especially when visiting China Town, which we thought was our best chance of finding somewhere to eat a vegetarian meal, or going to the theatre for a taste of culture. Remembering the pleasure of seeing Giselle, while in Russia, before Patricia arrived, I had gone on my own to see another ballet in Liverpool and remember being somewhat embarrassed at the interval to find I was a lone male sitting amongst an audience of mothers with their young daughters.

Back to work where the team were starting to execute the now approved IQ protocols; initially confirming that all the specified documentation for each system was available and liaising with our document group in the head office to chase anything that was missing, then walking the newly constructed plant to confirm everything was installed and tagged correctly, using the specified materials and in accordance with the specified drawings. I can remember that confirming all the piping lines were installed with the correct slopes was particularly difficult but important to ensure there were no loops or low points where liquid could accumulate and bacteria start to grow. Something not fully appreciated by most of our construction group where, like me, working on pharmaceutical projects was a relatively new experience.

It was during this time that I received a phone call to tell me my much-loved mother had died. Although she was 99 years and 2 months old and I knew she could not live forever it still came as a complete shock as I was convinced she would be with us long enough to receive her telegram from the Queen. It was a sad journey home and another aspect of working away so much is that you are often not around when most needed. At least I was in the UK and not halfway round the world somewhere. Sitting here sixteen years later I am having difficulty seeing to write this!

It was also during this period that I met another work colleague, Niamh O'Dwyer, who was to become a close friend. Our friendship started to develop when we were paired up to execute some of the OQ protocols, where collaborating for five or six hours a day in the close confines of a clean room environment soon tells you whether you can put up with each other's little idiosyncrasies and enjoy working together. The remarkable thing was when the project at Evans Medical was completed we both returned to the London office and started work on the preparation of protocols for the Genentech project in Spain. Some two and a half years later having completed the job in Spain we were still kept together working on a large new development for Wyeth located in the Republic of Ireland, Niamh's home country, more of which later. Altogether, we worked closely together for more than seven years, longer than a lot of marriages, and in that time I saw her, I suspect, break a few hearts but a few years after leaving her in Ireland I was very pleased to receive an invitation for Dawn and me to be guests at her wedding. Quite a gathering and celebrated in true Irish fashion.

When the work at Evans Medical came to an end I decided that I could not leave the Gateacre Hall Hotel, which had been my base overall for nearly three years, without throwing a party which the hotel staff were happy to organise so long as I paid for it. It was a good evening with an eclectic mix of guests; a good number of the hotel staff, some of the regulars from the evening sessions at the bar, most of my work colleagues and a selection from Evans Medical staff that I had worked most closely with. I still have a musical leaving card that I was given, it opens to Tina Turner singing Simply The Best. I felt a pang of nostalgia when I looked on Google to find the Gateacre Hall Hotel was no more; it had been knocked down some years later to make way for the Woodsome Park Housing Development. Perhaps just as well I was never asked to return, I think I would have felt most put out!

7.3 Porrino – Spain

On returning from Speke to the head office in Croydon I, along with most of the permanent staff, was included in the team required to prepare the IQ and OQ protocols for the revamp of an existing plant owned by Genentech, an American company but located in Porrino in Galicia, North West Spain. So it was back to the daily grind of driving an hour and a half each way round the M25 into Croydon which I cannot say I ever really enjoyed even when there were no holdups and I could switch my brain to "auto" and listen to *The Archers* on the way home. I soon found that the traffic was slightly less horrendous if I did not arrive into the office until after 9.30 and did not leave until after 18.00 hours but it made for a long day with limited prospects of any social life in the evenings.

The fact that an existing plant was being modified to produce a new product made the task of writing the protocols more difficult and time-consuming than it should have been. A lot of the existing equipment, large vessels, etc. was to be reused but the required changes to the interconnecting pipework and instruments had not been fully thought out before we started writing. This required constant reviews to be made and resulting modifications to the protocols as the drawings were updated. Also, access to design drawings, data sheets, specifications and operating manuals for the existing equipment was not always readily available. To avoid falling behind the planned programme some of our standard protocols for a piece of equipment would be used as a first draft. Unfortunately when an operating manual became available, unless it was read very carefully for any peculiarities and the first draft read sensibly, it could pass through the system for approval without the necessary changes being made.

After nearly a year working on the project in the Croydon office man-hours allocated for this phase of the work began to run out and with no other large project to occupy the group's time it was decided to move most of us to Spain to start on the next phase. From what I had heard of progress in Spain this seemed much too early and a few phone calls to some old contacts in the construction department confirmed my belief that this was probably some six months too soon. However, money talks and arrangements were made to continue the transfer to Spain. Aged 59 and with the prospect of drawing a reasonable pension I had been debating for some time whether I should start on another, what was looking like, lengthy project away from home.

However, this was Spain and not Libya or Saudi Arabia, so Dawn said, 'try it and if you do not like it simply resign', so it was I set off for what proved to be a very enjoyable two years in Galicia. In fact when I returned I almost needed counselling to readjust to an English timetable and normal way of life.

As it turned out, time away from home was not continuous as we were allowed to fly home once a fortnight for a long weekend provided we worked a minimum of forty hours per week, excluding travelling time, while in Spain. This was achievable by taking an early train to Gatwick on a Monday morning for a flight that arrived in Porto, in Portugal around midday. A pre-arranged hire car was then collected for the one and a half hour drive north into Spain, on brand new EU-paid-for highways, to arrive on site, barring hold ups, around mid-afternoon. Working nine-hour days with an occasional Saturday morning if required allowed us to leave mid-afternoon on Thursday week for the drive back to Porto and a flight back to England. Since Dawn was still working at that time and located in Suffolk it meant I got the chance to play a round of golf every other Friday with some of my retired or semi-retired self-employed mates, which made a nice change.

To start with I stayed in the Zenit Hotel, located on Gran Via 1, in the centre of the busy port town of Vigo and the most difficult part of my journey was finding a route through the labyrinth-like street system, with no satnav or navigator, to the hotel without getting lost. I must admit that once found I rarely ventured off the route I knew and the same applied to the route out of town to Porrino to get to and from work and this was probably the most dangerous part of my daily journey. Although mostly duel carriageway it was a magnet for accidents and on dark mornings with the rain sweeping in off the Atlantic, crazy Spanish drivers still going flat out, it was a nightmare. Still I survived without any major trauma, other than to my nerves, and the first thing needed most mornings when I got to work was a strong cup of coffee.

The hotel was ideally situated in the centre of some of the smartest shopping venues in Vigo and about five minutes walk to Corte Ingles a superior department store that rivalled Harrods and sold almost anything that one could wish to buy. I particularly liked visiting the food halls around Christmas time to view the display of wonders to tempt every palate. Surprisingly, or perhaps because, Vigo was one of the biggest and busiest fishing ports in the world, fish was by far the most expensive and sought-after fare to serve over the festive season. I remember being invited to a Christmas meal by the client and when the main course turned out to be a choice of salmon, salt cod, octopus (Galician style) or various shellfish a few of the lads slipped away for a burger before the evening's serious drinking started. About ten minutes walk in the opposite direction brought you to the vast dock area, probably not an area to visit late at night but just inland took you into the narrow cobbled streets of the old town which had great charm and was mostly given over to restaurants and bars inter-mixed with souvenir shops to cater for the cruise ships that now regularly docked in Vigo.

At work, the refurbishment and changes being made to the existing plant were still ongoing and, as I feared, far from complete. One reason, I believe, was because Jacobs, in their bid for world domination had bought a local Spanish company who were essentially civil contractors but had been given the job of supervising the design changes being created in England for an American company. One thing that made a nice change was the validation team sent out from England was augmented by some Spanish validation engineers which made it much easier to interface with the local staff and also a great help when trying to find suitable apartments to rent and generally to integrate into a Spanish way of life. We were also offered the chance to take Spanish lessons, which most accepted, and some became quite proficient. Unfortunately, despite our teacher – the lovely Gloria's best efforts, I never got much past ordering some food or drink.

After three or four months we had more or less completed the writing of all the protocols and were starting to eat into the man-hours for the execution phase when Genentech's American arm decided they wanted the protocols written to a different format. At first I was really annoyed as it felt as though we had just wasted six months of effort but in retrospect realised that it kept us all busy while the construction work was being completed and probably saved Jacobs a lot of money as a claim could be made for additional costs and man-hours.

As far as the validation team were concerned it was indeed a saviour because the construction phase was turning into a complete disaster to the extent that piping supervisors and draughtsmen were brought over from England and the required changes were more or less done in situ, with drawings being revised as they went along. As someone who had worked on a project as large and complex as the BP Miller Platforms I could not believe we had made such a mess of a relatively small, simple job but then identifying and making changes to an existing plant is probably more difficult than starting from scratch with a new design. In the end, as construction neared completion, we were under pressure to get all the revised protocols completed and approved for the execution phase to start. I can remember one very busy Sunday where John, our manager, and I operated like a mini conveyer belt system. I would make all the small changes identified as necessary in the draft protocols before passing a revised version on to John for a final proof-read and an approval signature in readiness for hand over to the client for sign-off as acceptable for the execution phase to begin. It was very intense, I think we worked for nearly ten hours with hardly any break and without any interruption, it being a Sunday, and thoroughly deserved the beers we went for at the end of the day.

Over this period I was still staying in the Zenit hotel in the centre of Vigo but was becoming increasingly isolated as most of my colleagues had succumbed to the pressure to find cheaper rented accommodation. I did have some social life as, once a week, I would meet some of our American colleagues in a café on the waterfront to spend the evening playing bridge. The café owner did not mind so long as we put in a regular order for drinks and snacks and I found it quite stimulating trying to remember all the bidding techniques after quite a long period since I last played.

Most nights I would eat alone, either in the hotel restaurant, which became increasingly boring as the menu did not change very much week to week, or in one of the many café bars scattered around the hotel. My favourite was situated almost directly underneath the hotel and I became such a regular that when I walked in and sat down a beer and a plate of olives would arrive at the table with a menu without a word being said, other than perhaps a Spanish "good evening and how are you". On the weekends when I was not going home, Saturday night was still a good night out. I would arrange to meet up with some of my work friends in one of the many tapas bars in Vigo for a drink or two before going on to one of the night clubs. The problem was, the Brits had not learned to pace themselves in the same way as the Spanish, usually starting earlier and drinking faster so by five o'clock on a Sunday morning when the club tipped out there could be some sad cases to be seen. Actually it always surprised me how relatively civilised it usually was with hardly ever a fight and few people being sick or collapsing on the street, and they were usually the Brits I am ashamed to say.

After some weeks of searching for the right venue another Sunday activity that I really started to look forward to, that is if I could get up in time without too much of a hangover, was playing a round of golf. I found a lovely course at Mondariz Balneario, about twenty-five miles inland from Vigo, where I could hire clubs and pay and play without necessarily making a booking. It was in a lovely setting in the foothills of the nearby mountain range and bordering the Chabrina river. At first I played on my own and it was a real pleasure just walking round in the fresh, clean air, not that it was always bright and sunny; on the occasions when the rain was sweeping in from the Atlantic it could be quite daunting and only the foolhardy stayed out on the course. After some time I was joined by some of my work colleagues who enjoyed a game or I got invited to join in with some of the locals who regularly played on a Sunday.

One of my favourite anecdotes relates to an attractive young women who was often to be seen in the clubhouse, apparently on her own, after I had finished playing. My limited Spanish and her limited English established that her name was Begonia, that she was having lessons and had never actually played more than a few holes on the course, so I asked her if she would like to play a round with me the following Sunday after her lesson. All went reasonably well until I realised, once on the green, she did not always putt out even when quite a distance from the hole, simply picked up and walked off. Intrigued, I managed to ask her why and she said her tutor had told her, 'you should never more than three putt', so she took him at his word and never did. For somebody who is a crap putter I think it is a sound policy. Still an undoubted pleasure after the game was sitting on the clubhouse balcony in the evening sunshine with a cold beer or glass of white wine and plate of nibbles and gazing down the third fairway into the distance of surrounding hills.

The golf course was associated with a relatively new hotel complex and spa, the Meliá Balneario Mondariz, which Dawn made the most of when she came out for a visit to see how life was treating me. Just opposite the new hotel was the burnt out remains of what was once a grand hotel where I could imagine, in an earlier age, the rich and famous came to take the waters from the medicinal hot springs and cure their ills. At one point I toyed with the idea of moving into the new hotel but decided against it as I would be even more isolated and, apart from the golf club, there was little else of interest in the area.

After about five months and with the job not looking as though it was going to end any time soon I decided it was time to move out of the hotel in Vigo, so began the search for an apartment. Some of my colleagues were already staying in Baiona, to the south of Vigo, near to the border with Portugal and using their local knowledge this is where I ended up; in a two bedroom apartment with a combined lounge and kitchen area plus two balconies. Quite a change for me as I had to come to terms with the idiosyncrasies of a Spanish cooker and, more importantly, washing machine, so that I could do my own laundry and having two balconies came in very handy with sheets and towels to hang out to dry. On the plus side, after settling in, I really began to appreciate having a place I could call my own where I could leave all my stuff without packing and moving, albeit to a different room in the same hotel, once every two weeks. Also, it made a pleasant change to cook for myself and it improved my Spanish and made me feel much more at home having to go regularly to the supermarket and shops to stock up with food and other essentials.

The apartment was on the sixth floor of a fairly ugly concrete block on the edge of the town and was surrounded by a parking lot, bordered on one side by the coast road which separated it from a shingle beach and the Atlantic Ocean. However, it possessed one aspect that made it very special. One of the balconies looked out across the sea to the Cíes Islands with a view to the right of the Castelo de Monterreal sited at the head of the bay and now housing one of Spain's paradors, a chain of upper-class hotels located in historic buildings across the country. Arriving home on a summer's evening, after a hard day at work, it made it all worthwhile to pour a glass of cold white wine and sit on the balcony, as the sun went down, looking out across the ocean to the Cíes Islands in the distance with time to meditate on the beauties of nature. Actually it was the Cíes Islands that shielded and saved Baiona's main beaches and oyster beds from a disastrous oil spillage when the oil tanker MV Prestige got into trouble in a storm and eventually sank on November 13th 2002, after neither the Spanish, French nor Portuguese governments would agree to let it dock. I can remember being totally impressed, when driving along the coast a few days after the event, to see all the local people working flat out to clean up the mess that had been deposited on the shore and save as much of the contaminated fauna and flora as they possibly could.

Before the summer ended another benefit of my new location was, after getting back from work, taking a book and a towel and having an hour on the beach, or rather in a lovely little cove with a shell beach just across the road from the apartment. I was usually surrounded by mothers and children; the mothers playing lotto and the children doing what children do, so not exactly peaceful but still a lovely way to spend an hour at the end of the day. One incident really amused me. Some of the older children got really excited when they found and dragged an octopus from under the rocks at the shore's edge but then did not seem to know what to do with it. After some shrieking and poking a grandmother got up, waddled down the beach, pushed the kids out of the way, grabbed the octopus and smashed it against a rock and with a look of disdain dumped the body on the sand for the children to collect and take home for the night's supper. Galician octopus cooked with paprika was a dish I learnt to enjoy during my time in Spain, as was squid in its own ink; I really surprised myself on some occasions.

Baiona was a town with a lot of character. A mediaeval walled historical centre of narrow cobbled streets overhung with typical Galician terraced houses behind a more modern sea front area; a tourist destination with a marina and popular beach to augment the older fishing and shellfish production industry. Its real claim to fame was that, in March 1493, the Pinta, one of Christopher Columbus's fleet of ships returned to Baiona, making the town the first to receive news of the discovery of the New World (America). An event celebrated every year by a massive street party with people dressed in medieval costume being entertained by tumblers, jugglers and musicians and enjoying food stalls selling all manner of goodies, both old and new. There is a full sized replica of the Pinta moored in the bay and the festivities start with men rowing ashore to declare the finding of the New World.

One thing I never really got used to was the Spanish habit of not eating an evening meal until around ten o'clock at night and that included young children. On evenings when I did not feel like cooking for myself, if I walked into a restaurant before nine thirty it would be almost empty which is not very appealing, so by the time I finished my meal and moved on to my local, the Castelo (Castle), for a quick beer it was turned ten o'clock. Mine host spoke a little English but by the time some of the regulars arrived, who also spoke some English, it was turned eleven o'clock, which made it hard leaving the apartment to drive to work at seven thirty in the morning!

For most of the year the drive to and from work was an enjoyable experience and I was always amazed at the wonderful panorama that opened up as one drove down out of the surrounding hills to see Baiona, the coast and the offshore islands come into view. However, in late July and the month of August the tourist swarms arrived to enjoy the beaches and locally caught shellfish and the population grew from around 11,000 to nearer 45,000. This could add a good thirty minutes to my normal journey time and meant there was nowhere to park on the land around the apartment block. Fortunately I had a parking slot underneath the building but hated using it as there was a serious risk of scraping the hire car at every turn. I doubt modern four by fours would have managed it without adding their paint to that already deposited on the walls and pillars that supported the building.

At work sufficient progress had been made for us to start some practical work and execution of the OQs was underway, mainly in the laboratories and buildings surrounding the main production area where last minute *in situ* changes were still being made. It was during this period that it became apparent just how important it was to fully understand how a piece of equipment was designed to work before writing the protocols. The test procedure for a number of large industrial refrigerators required thermocouples to be placed throughout the storage space to confirm that, over a twenty-four-hour period, a set temperature of $5\pm 0.5\,^{\circ}C$ could be consistently maintained. Unfortunately when the test was run it was found the refrigerators were designed to include a once in twenty-four-hour built-in defrost cycle to prevent ice build up. This caused a spike in the temperatures being recorded above the acceptance criteria and so a failure was reported. In the end I believe it was agreed that it would be acceptable to rewrite the protocols to place the thermocouples inside small vials of water or glycerol to confirm the temperature of any product being stored in the refrigerators would remain within the acceptable range despite the short defrost cycle. As it turned out it was a valuable lesson learnt because on the next assignment the very same refrigerators had been installed and a similar error was avoided during the writing of the protocols.

During the summer I was persuaded to take up another activity from my past. One of our American colleagues, Irina, Russian by birth but married and living in America for many years, was keen to get together a group to play tennis before her son arrived from America during his college vacation. Actually, I believe she only took the job because she was very keen to get her son out of America for the first time in his life to see something of the outside world. I think it was about 35 years since I had hit a tennis ball but it made for some very enjoyable evenings after Irena got together a mix of Americans, Brits and Spanish to hire some court time and test our skills. I found it strange because my brain was soon back in playing mode but my timing and coordination did not live up to its expectations, so I was never quite sure where the ball was going to end up. Still great fun and when Irena's son arrived I believe he enjoyed himself and after a few weeks I suspect friendship with a young senorita broadened his outlook on life.

Once winter arrived another activity from my past which was reprised in Spain was playing badminton. One of the new boys in our team was keen to play and asked around to see if anybody else was interested. When I said yes he used his reasonable Spanish to find a venue and came up with a sports hall on the outskirts of Baiona where, a couple of nights a week, we could go along and pay and play. There were two courts being used by a group of local men, which we were happy to join, as it made for some variety for both them and us. Singles seemed to be the game of choice and as I was still reasonably fit in my sixties, once I had brought my old wooden racket (never could get on with the modern steel or fibre glass frames) out from England my years of experience playing at a fairly high level (Essex League at one time) made me something of a challenge for the better players in the group and I ended up with the rather fine nickname of "the maestro". I just had to be careful not to get drawn into too many games or I would end the evening absolutely shattered. After a few weeks, at the end of the evening, we were invited to join some of the guys at their local for a much needed beer or two. It came as a bit of a surprise when we were offered the chance to partake of some of their home grown "grass" from a big bag that was being passed round. We politely declined but it made me realise growing their own was probably a local pastime and why, if you walked down one of the streets in the town late at night, you could get high just inhaling the atmosphere!

Another event which I think is worth recording was the celebration of my 60th birthday. Niamh and some of my other long-term work mates suggested I could not let my 60th pass without some happening to mark the occasion. It became a little complicated because I was taking a few days leave to fly home to England where Dawn had booked us into a "mysterious" but very posh hotel for a couple of nights and then we were both returning to Spain where Dawn would take a fortnight's holiday to see something of Galicia. Before I left I drew up a list of twenty or so British, Spanish and American friends to invite and left it with Niamh to find a suitable restaurant to hold the party, which I was quite happy to pay for. A few emails later let me know a suitable venue had been found and was booked for 20.00 hours on the day of our return. We duly arrived back at the apartment with two or three hours to spare, settled in and got ready for the evening. When I turned the door handle to leave the apartment the knob came off in my hand. I could not fix it back on and we could not open the door without it. Shouting from the sixth floor balcony only resulted in a few turned heads and a wave but my Spanish was not up to asking for help. So there we were stuck! There was no telephone in the apartment but fortunately for some time I had been feeling somewhat vulnerable driving around the countryside without any means of calling for help if I had a breakdown or accident so, with Dawn coming to join me, I had elicited the help of a Spanish-speaking colleague to go into town and buy a mobile phone the week before leaving for England. I phoned Niamh, no reply; two other colleagues, no reply and then the restaurant. I got a reply but could not get anybody who spoke English to talk to and my Spanish was not good enough to get them to pass me on to one of the party who by now should be gathering. In the end I managed to contact my land-lord, who did speak English, and lived in the penthouse on the top floor of the apartment block. Five minutes later his wife came down with a spare key and opened the door from the outside. Saved! We arrived at the restaurant to a room full of expectant faces only about thirty minutes late for my own party and much in need of a glass of wine. Two old ladies locked in a lavatory kept coming into my head.

By April/May of the next year good progress had been made with the validation of the plant to the extent that it was available for some trial batches of the new product to be processed, with a successful completion in early May. This made for a much more relaxed atmosphere between ourselves and our American counterparts and resulted in them inviting a select group to join them on a chartered yacht for a day sailing up and down the local coast. It was a super day and, with two reasonably experienced sailors to take charge, fairly relaxing apart from at one point when the engine housing belched smoke. I guess the highlight was stopping on the Cíes Islands which was a protected nature reserve and I am glad to say showed little or no signs of the oil spill that had occurred some six months earlier. However, seeing the coast from offshore and sailing into the Ria de Vigo and up close to row after row of the frames growing the mussels the region was famed for was really interesting and a great pleasure.

By early June it was decided my presence was no longer required so preparations were put in place to return to England. However, as the lease on the apartment was paid for until the end of June I decided to fly home, collect Dawn and my car, take some outstanding leave and take a leisurely drive through France and back to Spain in order to clear the apartment of accumulated bits and pieces as well as enjoying a well-earned holiday. Preparations were rushed through to modify the car for driving in Europe as well as getting the necessary insurance cover and booking a tunnel crossing for the outward leg and a ferry crossing from Bilbao to Portsmouth for the return journey. After that we planned a route to take us through central France using a "Special Places to Stay French Bed and Breakfast" guide that would limit most days driving to under two hundred miles and give us time to explore and enjoy some of the unusual and lovely towns or villages we ended up in or passed through en route. Our last stop in France was in Biarritz from where we crossed the remaining edge of the Pyrenees to travel along the north coast of Spain, stopping at some delightful locations, until we reached Galicia where we treated ourselves and stayed one night in the Hotel Reis Católicos, thought to be the oldest hotel in the world, the Old Royal Hospital and now the impressive parador of Santiago de Compostela, a refuge at the end of the pilgrimage routes across Europe to the magnificent cathedral built to house a bone of Saint James.

It was a lovely way to finish a long assignment because once back in Baiona we still had time to explore the relatively deserted but beautiful Galician coastal region as well as the impressive cities of Tui, with its once walled old quarter surrounding the castle/cathedral, built in the 12th century during the reign of King Ferdinand, and Valenca do Minho surrounding the huge Fortress of Fortaleza, guarding the border across the River Minho between Spain and Portugal. It was also a chance for Dawn to once again meet the likes of Niamh and John, and the remainder of the team who were finalising the work to complete the project, during a farewell party at John's villa and under less stressful circumstances than on my 60th birthday when I thought I was never going to get to my own party.

After ten days of a very enjoyable holiday it only remained to cram the car full of the accumulated contents purchased during my stay in the apartment and depart back across the north of Spain to Bilbao and the ferry back to England and my proper home (it did take a little while to readjust). This time we took a route inland from the coastal region but still full of interest, including a stop at another parador, the original buildings of which had been another staging post on the pilgrimage route to Santiago de Compostela. One aspect of the journey that has stayed in my memory was passing through rows of massive wind turbines. It was strange and quite disturbing, I felt as though I was being threatened for invading this giants abode and was quite glad to emerge unscathed.

From a starting point of debating whether or not I should go to Spain at all or resign and hang up my hard hat for good, in the end, after nearly two years away from home, I was sad to leave a rather beautiful and relatively unspoilt region of Europe which I would probably never have visited if it were not for work. Once back in the Croydon office the proposed move to Reading was getting ever closer, which meant my redundancy was getting ever closer as I had already decided I would not stay with the company once it had moved its base to somewhere across London and diametrically opposite my home in Essex. Typically I had only been back in the office for four days when my manager asked if I could go to Ireland for a few months. 'Will it affect my redundancy if the move to Reading takes place whilst I am away?' 'No not at all.' So it was that I was packing my bags once more for a short assignment to a large pharmaceutical plant being built for Wyeth Biopharma, another American company making the most of the tax breaks, at Grange Castle just outside Dublin.

7.4 Grange Castle – Ireland

Like most assignments it usually starts with finding the best way to get there and accommodation once there. In this case an EasyJet flight from Stanstead to Dublin seemed to be the best option because, after the initial journey to transfer the bulk of my luggage, I could repeat the journey with only a carry-on bag, thus saving both money and time. Also it was an eight minute walk to Wickford Station to catch an early morning fast train to Liverpool Street followed by a short walk to change platforms to catch a train on the frequent service into Stanstead Airport. Once at Dublin Airport I could pick up a pre-arranged rental car for a twenty minute drive to the Grange Castle Business Park where the Wyeth plant was located. Door to door a five to six hour journey, all being well. The first choice of accommodation was the Citywest Hotel and Conference Centre located off the N7 Dublin to Naas road and conveniently only about five miles from the business park. It was a huge complex standing in parkland with space for 4,100 guests and surrounded by two golf courses, although this had nothing to do with the decision to stay there. One of them was a championship course designed by

Christy O'Connor Junior and a bit too much for me to take on more than a couple of times for the experience.

Initially, while we were writing the IQ and OQ protocols, we were working a five day week and were allowed a flight home every weekend, which in any case cost less than staying in the hotel over the weekend. It was a very big job with a large team, comprising Wyeth permanent staff, H&G permanent staff and contractors all mixed in together which made for good variety and a lot of new friendships and fortunately very little aggravation. It is also good that each job develops its own characteristics and although we were all speaking the same language there was a definite Irish flavour about this one

We were split into different groups to cover different areas of the plant, and to start with I was covering the rooms surrounding the main production areas. These rooms contained equipment required for intermediary product storage as well as laboratory testing and analytical services and had to be in place with validation completed before the main production facilities were fully operational. It was perhaps fortunate that I was working on this section as I recognised that a number of large industrial refrigerators were the same model and made by the same manufacturer that we had encountered in Spain and I was, therefore, able to ensure an acceptable protocol was written that avoided the problem caused by ignoring the fact that the refrigerators had a built-in defrost cycle. This phase of the work, moving from writing to execution of the protocols, which, in my case, once again included a considerable amount of temperature mapping and use of a Kaye Validator 2000 lasted for five to six months, a little longer than I was led to believe back in the office in June but not exceptional. So, it came as a bit of a surprise, as the work came to an end, that I was asked to stay on and move to another section covering the validation of one of the main production areas. Since, for the most part, I was enjoying my time in Ireland I agreed and in retrospect it was a good choice as it meant I ended my career on a relatively high note.

In contrast to the job in Spain, this was a well-run project with most of the construction work being completed according to plan which meant much of the IQ work had already been completed. To start with, to familiarise myself with the area and to better understand what was required and the processes involved I was given some OQs to write before being asked to proofread documents written by other members of the team and ensure any corrections that had been identified were included before the documents were passed to management for final approval and signature. Being me, I had to check any calculations that were being included and verify, both against approved drawings and by going into the area that, for instance, thermocouples could be physically located into the position designated without in any way disrupting the process being monitored.

There were a lot of new aspects to this project that made it both interesting and sometimes aggravating. The main process area contained some large stainless steel vessels housed on two floors; the top of the vessel and all associated pipework on the upper floor and the bottom of the vessel protruding through the upper floor to the lower level, so it took a while to establish where everything was. Also the whole process was contained in a designated clean area and could only be accessed through a double air lock. At an early stage in the validation process Wyeth decided that to enter the area people should go through the required training to become fully familiar with clean entry requirements. This involved removing lab coats or outer area protective clothing, passing through the first airlock into a dressing room where a pair of disposable latex gloves would be put on before handling and donning a paper overall (boiler suit), overshoes, mask, a disposable mobcap and a beard snood (if required); finally putting on a second pair of disposable latex gloves and spraying the gloved hands with a methanol spray before passing through the second airlock into the clean production area.

The aggravation came about if you did not have all the required equipment, drawings, protocols, notebook, pen, etc. with you because that meant leaving the area through the outlet airlocks on the opposite side of the building, removing and discarding all the protective clothing before collecting what you had forgotten, returning to the inlet side of the area and repeating all the robing procedures before entry. It certainly encouraged you to prepare in advance and was a good reason for getting everybody familiar with the correct procedures before the area was made "live" although it must have cost a fortune in disposable protective clothing.

Virtually all of the stainless steel pipework, stainless steel vessels and associated equipment would be steam sterilised before use and in between different batches during the production process. Verification that the required *in situ* temperatures could be reached to achieve sterilisation was a major part of the validation process as well as the inclusion of biological indicators (*Bacillus stearothermophilus* spore strips) on a scale that was quite new to me. To monitor the temperature within a vessel during the steam sterilisation process, thermocouples had to be distributed at prescribed points throughout the vessel. This was not as easy as it may sound because dangling thermo-couples of different lengths through an entry port at the top of the vessel meant they would all hang in the centre of the vessel and not reach to the outer edges as required. To overcome this problem we had to make up rigid frames; weld rod was the material of choice, to which the thermocouples and biological indicators could be attached with autoclave tape before being suspended in the vessel. This required fairly accurate measurements to be made so that thermocouples of suitable length could be made up to reach from a Validator 2000 located on a platform somewhere outside the vessel being tested to the monitoring point inside the vessel. One aspect of the work I really enjoyed was actually making up the required thermocouples. Back in the office block we had reels of different thermocouple wire which would be run out down a corridor until the right length was reached for a particular location. Lengths would be cut off, the ends twined together and fixed with a bead of solder before an identity tag for the vessel and location point to be monitored was added. Further calibration checks and integrity tests would be made in association with and connection to the Validator 2000 before taking the complete kit back into the process area for the validation qualification to be run. Of course, to save time and money, once the testing of one vessel had been completed frames and thermocouples could be utilised to test the next vessel of similar size and so on.

It was during this period that I rather foolishly damaged the cartilage in my knee. To save time, rather than calling in the fitters I tried hauling on the clamping bolts to open one of the vessel ports myself. Of course I did not save time and as it was very painful, I was assigned to office duties as limping about in and out of the production areas was not really an option. So I was back to proofreading and vetting the OQs that were being completed by other members of the team before final sign off and transfer to Wyeth QC/QA department for ratification and approval.

As stated earlier I started my short stay in Ireland in the Citywest Hotel along with a couple of my more senior colleagues, Mike Radley and John Jackson, once his role in Spain had been completed. Although the hotel had a couple of fine restaurants, eating in-house every night soon began to pall so at least one night a week we would venture into Dublin or the surrounding countryside to see what was on offer. Dublin, with Grafton Street and other areas obviously had a lot of attractions but unless we were making a night of it for perhaps somebody's birthday not exactly relaxing after travelling in and out, finding somewhere to park and somewhere to eat that was not too crowded. Consequently, a favourite place to go was a pub in the heart of the countryside, about thirty minutes' drive from the hotel, which had a good wholesome menu and certain nights of the week live music of the Irish traditional variety – a really great atmosphere with a good pint to go with it. What really surprised me was, when the smoking ban was introduced, even the good old boys in the public bar obeyed the new rule and took their pipes or rollies outside for a puff!

When it became obvious my stay in Ireland was going to be extended I started the search for alternative accommodation but in the end, after trying a couple of B&B's, settled for moving from the main hotel at Citywest into a self-contained apartment in one of the large blocks surrounding the main building. This had a number of advantages; it was cheaper but with a bedroom and en-suite bathroom, together with a lounge and combined small kitchen area, it gave me the freedom to live a more normal life as well as still getting cleaning and laundry services provided by the hotel. I could not retain the same apartment when travelling home, so still had to pack a bag with my personal items to be deposited in Left Luggage, which was a little inconvenient but not a problem so long as I could easily retrieve it on my return after picking up the key to my new apartment. However, I soon learnt to make sure I knew exactly where in each block the apartment was before lugging my bag around the site looking for it, especially late at night and in the rain, a not infrequent occurrence on the Emerald Isle.

Once established in an apartment it was more convenient for Dawn to fly over for a visit. On her first day, while I was at work, she caught a bus into Dublin to go sightseeing. When I got home and asked how her day had been she said, 'great, I have been to the Guinness factory'. On the second day following a similar enquiry she said, 'great, I have been to the Jameson factory'. I think you can see a pattern emerging here? At the weekend I thought the healthy option was to drive out to the Wicklow mountains for some fresh air and exercise.

Another venture into the Wicklow Mountains which lives in my memory was an excursion with a large group from work to an evening performance of traditional Irish dance, not Michael Flatley but very professional and full of energy and charisma. I made a point of not sitting in the front row but was very impressed by Niamh's skills when she was encouraged to take part. All those years of dance lessons at school were not entirely wasted.

The Wicklow Mountains would also play a part in the slightly bizarre experience of becoming a member of the Ski Club of Ireland. At that time, and before I injured my knee at work, as the year end approached I would start to think about preparing for our annual ski trip, usually to somewhere in Europe. After making enquiries I found there was a floodlit dry ski slope in the aforementioned Wicklow Mountains, which meant I could fit in some practice after work. It took a bit of finding in the dark and on roads that were not too well signposted but once there I found I could hire boots and skis for an hour session, having first paid a very reasonable membership fee. There were only two slopes, one for beginners and another graded intermediate and advanced depending whether you got of the drag lift halfway up or at the top of the slope. Not exactly testing if you were reasonably experienced but on a cold starlit evening standing at the top of the slope with a super view across open countryside to the twinkling lights of Dublin and the coastal towns bordering St George's Channel, with a little imagination you could be poised at the top of a fearsome black run somewhere in the Alps. Not to worry that five turns later it was back on the drag lift to go back up the slope but there was a good atmosphere and it made early season training a pleasure. What a surprise after leaving the Emerald Isle to receive a Christmas card from the Ski Club of Ireland, which until then I did not really know existed.

Another moment in time that has stayed with me was being told not to miss *Veronica Guerin* a recently released biographical crime film starring Cate Blanchett as the Irish journalist intent on exposing a local drugs baron. I went on my own to the nearest cinema to my lodgings, which happened to be in Naas high street. It was a gripping and horrifying story of how Veronica Guerin was gunned down by a contract killer who followed her as she drove home after she attended Naas Crown Court on a speeding charge. It was not until I came out of the cinema I realised the crown court was right opposite me and as I drove home I had to stop at the very same lights where she was murdered. It gave me a very cold feeling and I never stopped looking in my mirrors the whole time I was sitting there.

At work the execution phases were progressing steadily without too many mistakes or failures being recorded and as the OQs got signed off the large team of mainly contract staff started to be reduced as more of the plant was handed over to Wyeth for PQ execution to take place. One of the nice things about this type of work is meeting and getting to know a lot of new faces, especially when they are from a whole range of different nationalities and cultures. Also, because of the specialised nature of the work, there was every chance of renewing an acquaintanceship made on some previous job, as the grapevine, especially amongst the contractors, kept each other informed of any new projects in the offing. Of course tensions could arise, especially when shift work and/or overtime was required to be worked. Most permanent staff accepted that their hourly rate would be considerably less than contract staff for doing the same work, to offset the benefits of a pension scheme, paid holidays, etc. However, to still be paid a lower rate for shift work and overtime was aggravating if it went on for months rather than days and the company was not renowned for volunteering to make any bonus payments despite making a handsome profit on their labour charges. I do not think I endeared myself to senior management back in London by pressing the point that it was an injustice that should be rectified and in the end some recompense was made, although later than it should have been.

In July 2004, I took advantage of being on the permanent staff to use my BUPA membership to get some rapid treatment for the knee that I had damaged at work. I was booked into the private Nuffield Hospital in Brentwood for keyhole surgery to remove/repair the cartilage and was quite impressed by the facilities and attention that I received, that is until the afternoon of the day after the operation, with my knee still swathed in cotton wool and bandages, I was seen by the consultant and told I was fit to go. Having already ordered a nice supper with a half bottle of wine I was quite affronted to be told I should leave, especially as Dawn was in Suffolk and I had to arrange for my mother-in-law to come and pick me up and make sure that there was a crust of bread in the house so that I did not starve.

As with all jobs away from home or in a new country it was always more enjoyable once you got to know somebody from the local community. In the case of the Republic of Ireland it was Niamh's home country, not that I spent that much time with her other than at work in the first few months, as she was staying with her parents on their farm in the Port Laois area; a good drive down the N7 from our place of work, and the social life mainly centred around Dublin. Later, I think she felt it was time to put down some roots of her own and bought an apartment in Naas, which was much closer to the centre of things as far as any work-related social events were concerned. However, the one invitation that I most appreciated was being taken to Croke Park, Dublin's sports stadium, to see Laois play Dublin in the semi-final of the Leinster Senior Football (Gaelic version) Championships and the final of the Minors Championship. This was the equivalent of being at Wembley to see Manchester United play Manchester City in the FA Cup Final; terrific atmosphere and a completely new experience for me. Niamh's father and brothers were heavily involved in both playing and the management of the Laois team, so I suspect we may have had complimentary tickets but nevertheless I went kitted out in all the blue and white clothing I had with me so as to fit in with my honorary status as a Laois supporter. I am not sure I fully understood the rules or the scoring system but happily roared on Laois to a winning score in the Seniors' game and a draw in the Minors' game. The incident that most intrigued me though was the arrival of Bertie Ahern, the Taoiseach, in the interval between the two games. He was all on his own and sat down in an empty seat just across an alleyway from us. I did not realise who it was until a couple of the lads in the row in front of us turned around and said, 'hallo there Bertie, how are you doing son?' To which he just nodded and smiled. Can you imagine Tony Blair, our prime minister at the time, arriving at Wembley without a cavalcade of security men and just taking a seat in the stands. Such a difference in perception of status and importance! The two or three hours spent in the pub with Niamh's brothers and father and other Laois supporters after the game was quite an experience as well, from what I can remember of it.

A couple of weeks later Niamh asked me if I would like to go to the replay of the Minors' game, which was at a stadium close to her parents home. Now, feeling part of the Laois community, I concurred and after being given precise directions duly arrived at her parents' farm to pick her up. There I met her mother and granny and other assorted family members, which was a real pleasure but it was only on such occasions that I felt my age; realising that I was older than Niamh's parents did give me pause for thought. An added bonus was that Laois Minors won the replay to take the championship, a good season to be in Ireland.

Actually, it was about this time that I did start to feel my age, or it would be more true to say, emotionally I was less able to deal with things going wrong or minor situations that aggravated me. Not that at work there was a great deal going wrong, in fact more and more of the OQ protocols were being completed to schedule and signed off for sections of the plant to be handed over to Wyeth for process qualification to begin – to the extent that at the beginning of December I was informed that my services would no longer be required after the Christmas break, so my two or three month assignment that lasted for eighteen months was coming to an end.

A telephone conversation with my manager back in London indicated that further work at the Pfizer site at Sandwich in Kent was in the offing. However, following one or two telephone conversations with an old friend, Linda, in Jacobs' human resources it seemed unlikely that the redundancy offer, resulting from the company's move to Reading, would still be available if I took another assignment so, with some apprehension I decided it was time for retirement. Initially, I believe the whole process of severing my association with a company I had worked with for the best part of thirty-eight years was conducted by phone calls and emails. However, because of my break in service, I was only entitled to twelve years' redundancy pay and even that the company managed to calculate incorrectly, an error which I managed to get corrected in the few hectic weeks before the Christmas shutdown.

Once the decision was made I had a few weeks of flights home to clear my apartment at City West of the bulk of my accumulated personal possessions and my desk of any work-related items that travelled with me from job to job that I felt it essential to keep, at least in the short term; especially my work diary with all the contact details of the company and colleagues from present and previous contracts as well as expenses to be claimed and holiday entitlement – something else that becomes confusing once shift work is involved and the full working year is cut short. Fortunately, based on past experience of being away from home around Christmas time, I had booked, well in advance, a return flight for the evening of the 23rd December which gave me Friday the 24th December at home as my last day of work to finalise any correspondence that had to be sent to head office.

Because of the nature of my work and arriving home at the last minute, assuming there were no serious travel delays, it was not unusual for Dawn to bear the brunt of the preparations for Christmas and whether we would be celebrating in Wickford or at the cottage in Suffolk, would depend, to some extent, on the health and wellbeing of my mother (in her later years) or more recently Dawn's mother. In any event if we spent Christmas at Wickford we would frequently try to de-camp to the cottage in Suffolk for New Year's Eve as most invitations to parties and social gatherings came from friends in and around the village. So it was not until well into the new year that it hit me that my working life for a company that I had been with for the best part of thirty-eight years had come to an end via a couple of emails and telephone conversations. I cannot say that I was too sorry about not being required to travel to Reading, where the head office was now located, as most of my long-term colleagues and friends in the process and validation departments were now based in an office in Central London but it still left a sour taste in my mouth. I think it was perhaps an illustration of how Humphreys and Glasgow being taken over by Jacobs, a large global oriented American company, changed the ethos from an almost family-based attitude to management to an aggressive corporate policy toward business and staff. Having said that, it kept the company from going broke, which kept me in work, which for the most part I thoroughly enjoyed and the pension fund is in a healthy state, so I have many reasons to be grateful!

PART 8
Retirement

Starting my retirement over Christmas and New Year did help to reduce the feeling that I should be getting up early with my bags packed to catch an early morning flight to somewhere in the world or, less exotic, into the car for the joy of driving round the M25 into Croydon, or to Reading. In fact it took very little time for me to adjust my daily schedule so that getting up before nine o'clock seemed quite irrational and I still cannot understand why most of the veterans at the golf club deem it desirable to meet at 7.30 in the morning to organise the twice-weekly games; we are all retired for goodness sake!

One of the first things I had to do after retiring was buy a half-decent computer so that I could keep in touch with the world. I did still have, in its original packing, a Sinclair ZX Spectrum – wonder how much it would be worth on eBay? – but apart from trying to learn some basic programming it was hardly ever used. I had become reasonably familiar with using computers at work as a tool for preparing documents, emails, etc. but had had minimal instruction as to how they really worked and how to make the most of some of the other programs available such as preparing spreadsheets, which had always seemed a useful function to master. Like most things what little has been learnt can soon be forgotten if it is not used regularly over a sustained period, so I was quite pleased having bought a desk top computer, printer, screen, etc. to get all the bits out of their boxes and, after some swearing and cursing, to connect them all together and after plugging them in to find they actually worked, without recourse to the tech guys you could call on at work, in such circumstances. Of course it was still mostly a mystery to me, so without children (or more likely grandchildren) to fall back on I decided one of the first things I needed to do was find some lessons to go to.

Fortunately, as part of a Training for the Millennium initiative a "learn direct" course in the use of computers for beginners was being run in Wickford, which I was able to join. It was a very mixed bunch, some young but plenty of grey heads in evidence and a friendly helpful attitude by both the tutors and the other attendees, so quite an enjoyable experience for two one-hour sessions each week. By April I had completed the "Surf Direct" module which gave a basic history and introduction in the use of computers and the World Wide Web and then found, if I was prepared to pay the appropriate fee, that I could take further units towards a City and Guilds Level 1 Certificate for IT users E-Quals. This was a little more serious as, if you wanted to qualify, you had to take an examination at the end of each module but still enjoyable and by June 2006 I had acquired a Distinction in "Spreadsheets, Databases and Desktop Publishing". I would happily have taken some of the other units on offer but unfortunately the Wickford Centre became a victim of economies and was closed down, and as I did not feel like travelling to other available centres at Laindon or Southend my learning programme came to an end.

I did put some of the training to good use by preparing spreadsheets to compare and contrast the options available to me before taking my pensions, mainly whether to take all or part of the 25% tax-free lump sum that was then possible to self-invest or spend and how that would change my income in the long term. I still remembered enough to repeat the exercise for Dawn when it was time for her to start drawing a pension but am afraid I would need to take some serious refresher courses if I needed to use the same skills these days.

After a few months being at home and, as the weather improved, one of my first approaches to improving my social life was to join a local golf club, selected for convenience and because I already knew two of the women members who had also been members of the Wickford mixed hockey team that I had played for and captained for many years in my younger days. I was not altogether sure I had done the right thing when, on the very first round I played, I was partnered with three chaps who apologised if they were a little slow because two of them were recovering after heart attacks... nothing like fresh air and exercise to keep you fit and well! Actually it was a very good move because it was a very welcoming club to play at and soon introduced me to a whole new group of friends and acquaintances. The Three Rivers Golf and Country Club had two courses; a full sized par 72 "Kings" course and a smaller par 64 "Jubilee" course, and although when I joined I intended to play both courses, for the first two or three years I played nearly all my games with the Jubilee Veterans on the smaller course. This proved to be a mistake because although very friendly and sociable I ended up with, at one point, a very flattering handicap of 16, now back to 18. The problem is when playing on a full sized course, even when playing well, I have never got close to a score commensurate with an 18 handicap, which can be a little embarrassing sometimes. Still, as people are fond of telling you it is not winning that is important but taking part, which to a large extent is true after an enjoyable game and some good company even if it does mean you end up buying the teas once back in the club house.

Another pastime I took up was as a volunteer with the RSPB at their visitors' centre at the Wat Tyler Country Park, not that I was all that expert at identifying the different birds that visited the park or that could be seen from the hides, particularly the marsh and wetland varieties, but I was not bad at making the tea and coffee and showing the visitors around while trying to encourage new memberships or taking money for the cards, books, soft toys or other promotional items on sale. Promotional days such as those set up at Leigh-on-Sea waterfront with telescopes and binoculars, timed to show the passing public the flocks of Brent geese that had just arrived and other waders in the Thames Estuary, were quite good fun if the weather was kind and if we were very lucky a view of seals out on the mud flats always went down well.

Although I had spent a lot of time away from home during my working life and it was good to have a more stable existence now retired, the wanderlust had not been fully assuaged so the freedom to travel more or less when and where we liked was taken up with enthusiasm. Dawn had ceased full-time employment in 2003, and not having had a family to drain our resources, we could afford to indulge ourselves. Skiing at least once a year, knees, backs and bodies permitting, was still a priority so we tended to avoid arranging anything else in January or February and with two houses and gardens to look after we did not like to be away for more than three or four weeks maximum. More distant highlights have included ten weeks in total on self-drive holidays touring South Africa, Swaziland and Namibia, guided and organised by our ski partners and great friends John[3] and Diane Peake; touring China, Cuba, New Zealand (round the world with stopovers in Hong Kong and Los Angeles), Peru (including Machu Picchu), Ecuador and the Galapagos Islands, the Caribbean, Canada and Alaska.

Closer to home, memorable holidays have included Egypt, Venice, Sicily, Berlin, Barcelona, Morocco, The Azores, Gozo, Iceland and staying with friends in Spain, Budapest and Varna (Bulgaria). More recently we have

---

3   Sadly lost to bowel cancer in 2016 and greatly missed.

succumbed to the blandishments of the cruise industry with trips around Britain, the Norwegian Fjords and to the Baltic Sea (ports of call included Tallinn, Warnemunde, Stockholm, Helsinki and St Petersburg, as well as missing Copenhagen because it was too rough to get there on time) and finally the Douro River in Portugal.

At the end of 2009, just after returning from the Galapagos Islands, an event occurred that was to have a profound effect on my life and retirement activities. After attending the pre-Christmas dinner dance at the golf club I suddenly developed an intense pain in my abdomen. It was so bad I could not lie down in bed and had to sit up in a chair all night. I remembered slipping while dancing and assumed I had pulled a muscle or something similar but was reluctant to go to Basildon Hospital A&E at just past midnight on a Sunday as they had recently had a very bad report of their performance in the local paper. In the morning I managed to get an emergency appointment at my doctor's practice, where I was diagnosed with shingles and given some antivirals to take. The pain had reduced but a few weeks later I still did not feel right and with a ski holiday in the offing returned to the doctor. I saw the same doctor but this time there was a young female doctor – a trainee GP – in attendance who, when she examined me, said, 'I think he has an enlarged spleen'. I saw a look of horror on the doctor's face and thought this does not sound good. I was sent to Basildon Hospital with forms marked "Urgent" to get blood samples taken and got a phone call at home the same afternoon to be at Orsett Hospital the next morning to see the consultant haematologist. Dawn rushed back from Suffolk to be with me when I saw Dr Watts, an English gentleman of the "old school" who managed to make Dawn titter when, from behind the screens, while examining me, he uttered "what a whopper". Apparently my spleen reached almost to my ribs on the right side of my stomach when it should have been tucked safely under my ribs on the left side. The blood tests also showed that I was very anaemic and the conclusion was I had leukaemia. As you can imagine, quite a shock. Dr Watts took the trouble to assure us that, although not completely curable, there were treatments that could reduce the effects of the cancer and hold it at bay for some years to come. Just before leaving, Dawn asked if we should cancel our ski holiday at the end of the month. After a discussion about the merits of The Three Valleys in France – he was also a skier – he said, 'with a spleen the size of yours I think you should go next year not this year'. It was not until I got home I realised what good psychology that was, he was offering us hope for the future!

After further blood and bone marrow tests it was concluded I had non-Hodgkin's lymphoma not leukaemia and from then my feet did not touch the ground. I was given steroids to counteract the anaemia and by the end of the month was starting on a course of chemotherapy. I am glad to say, without too many bad side effects, it worked and by the end of six months my spleen had reduced in size to nearly where it should be and I was no longer anaemic so could get back to living an almost normal life. Not afraid to mix with the germ-laden public once more, playing golf, drinking a moderate amount of alcohol and planning some more holidays. The spleen can provide about 30% of the body's immune system by producing special infection-fighting white blood cells, making red blood cells and platelets as well as removing old red blood cells and recycling iron into one's new red blood cells so, although not essential, it is quite a useful organ to have working properly. Before starting treatment I attended St Bartholomews Hospital in London to be examined by one of the country's leading splenectomy surgeons in case it was decided my spleen should be removed. He seemed quite keen to get such a splendid organ into one of his preserving jars but so far I have managed to avoid his attentions. For the last six years I have been on a "Watch and Wait" programme with a visit to a consultant following a blood test about every six months, without need of any medication or any other treatment, so not too restricting to a normal lifestyle. However, over the past couple of years my spleen has started to increase in size again to the point where it causes some discomfort and needs protection, especially on something like a skiing holiday (with all the padding on I look like Michelin Man) and as my travel insurance does not cover me for anything related to the non-Hodgkin's lymphoma, a little worrying. In fact we have just had to cancel a holiday to Costa Rica and Panama because my consultant deemed it too risky with my haemoglobin count reduced once more to a point where more treatment was required. So, on the January 16th, 2017 it was back to hospital to start another round of six months of chemotherapy, which I am glad to say has just been successfully completed, and that I can once again resume an active and enjoyable retirement.

Another major activity both before and during retirement has been that most English of pastimes, gardening. The plot of our Wickford home is quite large by modern standards and included established fruit trees, hedges, lawns and both flower and vegetable beds plus a greenhouse, while the Hoxne cottage stands on a double plot of a similar nature. Now there always seems to be something that needs digging, planting, weeding or cutting back and as the years go by the effort required seems to increase exponentially. It is good exercise and I often wonder if I should advertise for people to pay me to come and work in my garden instead of going to the gym and they would have the added bonus of fresh air and a robin or a blackbird for company as long as they are turning over something of mutual benefit. In the end, health problems and increasing age persuaded us that we should spend some of our retirement funds in order to get both gardens re-landscaped to reduce the workload, make them more manageable and bring them into the 20th century in both style and visual quality. The ancient outbuildings in the Hoxne garden were virtually falling down so had to be completely replaced with a new garage-come-garden storage building, including a veranda overlooking a small pond and water feature which resulted in a delightful area to sit with a glass of wine and contemplate the beauties of nature.

Similarly, the Wickford garden had two garden sheds that needed replacing and Dawn's biggest challenge, in league with the landscaper contracted to do the work, was persuading me to throw away most of the "treasures" stored for over forty years in the old sheds rather than move it all into the new shed that was replacing them. It was dirty work and unearthed a few surprises but well worthwhile as we can now walk into the lovely new shed and find almost anything we need. Actually, there is a similar challenge in the loft of our Wickford home which also contains forty years worth of accumulated indispensable items. The problem is that the pitch of the roof is so low I do not think I could now get in there even if willing. Goodness knows what might be unearthed; I do know there is a trunk up there which I took to the job in Russia in 1967 and which still contains some of the items I brought back, which have not found a home anywhere else; plus books and cigarette card collections from my childhood; treasures indeed!

PART 9
Epilogue

Looking back I feel fortunate to have had a working life that was always interesting, sometimes challenging and for the most part fulfilling. I never became a captain of industry or made a discovery that would leave my name in the history books but have played a part in keeping the country supplied with gas, either manufactured or natural; extracting and processing oil and gas to provide petroleum products from both onshore and offshore wells; processing and helping to improve the quality of fertilizer products required to improve the production of food supplies around the world and the development, as part of the UK's aid programme, of both existing and new power generation facilities in countries such as Sudan. Closer to home I have been responsible for commissioning and starting up a Granular Activated Carbon (GAC) regeneration plant and a number of GAC treatment plants built to improve the quality of the country's potable water supplies as well as managing an environmental testing laboratory responsible for, amongst other things, checking the quality of London Boroughs' drinking water, air quality testing, asbestos removal, soil sampling for contamination and hazardous material and biological testing for dangerous pathogens. Finally, the validation of a number of new or existing pharmaceutical production facilities that will hopefully supply us with the ever increasing high-quality drugs necessary to keep us alive in an overcrowded world. Ironically, the last but one plant I worked on in Spain was being prepared to produce Rituxan (Rituximab) the monoclonal antibody drug that I am being treated with to combat non-Hodgkin's lymphoma. So, in my working life, I may have gone almost full circle, from working with a whole range of noxious chemicals and in atmospheres that might well have triggered the development of the cancer in the first place to helping to develop a manufacturing facility that can produce a drug that can combat the cancer sufficiently for me to yet enjoy a few more years of happy retirement.

Along the way I have come into contact with many different cultures and made new friends and acquaintances that have certainly enhanced my life and I hope that in some small way I have done the same for them. From starting life in a village with little more than a pub and a post office, together with holidays, I have now set foot on seventy plus countries or autonomous islands (see Appendix 2) which seems quite a lot but the world is a big place so given reasonable health and fitness the future offers much to be explored and, who knows, I may yet try space exploration as a new venture.

One aspect of work that has changed dramatically over the last fifty years is the attitude towards health and safety in the workplace. I do not believe that some of the conditions I worked in during the start of my career would be tolerated now and the wellbeing of their workforce was not high on the agenda of the state-run management of the contracts undertaken in the Eastern Bloc. I am glad to say, in the later years, during my time as a commissioning or site manager I did not have one serious accident or injury to report and only one incident requiring investigation by The Health and Safety Executive; a fibre glass vessel containing water treatment resin got pressurised, split and resin pellets were "fired" across the work place. Fortunately nobody was in the vicinity at the time. All reputable companies will now issue a health and safety handbook to their employees describing good safety practises that should be adhered to and employ safety officers who will come regularly to sites to give advice and a "Tool Box Talk" to new contractors before they start work. However, it is still the site manager's responsibility to see that all are wearing the prescribed protective clothing for the task in hand; the required safety equipment and warning signs are available and deployed correctly; a Permit to Work system is available and being operated correctly; COSHH (Control of Substances Hazardous to Health) assessments for all the chemicals, gases, etc. required on the site have been completed and Material Safety Data Sheets have been issued and all lifting equipment used or brought to the site is correctly certified and the operator properly qualified. Ensuring all equipment on the site that requires routine testing and certification has been completed within its prescribed time scale is quite an onerous task and I have never quite understood why a site manager can be prosecuted and even imprisoned if he fails in his duty of care towards his workforce, while a parole board or psychiatrist can release somebody from prison or a mental hospital only for them to kill or seriously injure a perfect stranger, within days of release, without any real censure under the Health and Safety at Work Act, since they have obviously failed in their duty of care to the general public.

For any reading this that have not yet started out on "A Working Life" I would recommend making the most of any educational opportunities that present themselves in subjects that interest you and that you enjoy rather than in the current top ten best-paid career prospects. I think in the future, especially in the UK, scientists, engineers and experienced technicians will be in greater demand than in recent years. Whether they will be paid commensurately remains to be seen but being able to find work to start a career is no bad thing and rewards will follow – be they in monetary terms or job satisfaction. Be adaptable to the circumstances you find yourself in but retain confidence in your own knowledge and abilities. When problems do arise, gather as much information as you can as to the possible cause and the circumstances linked to the fault. Do not rely totally on the internet to provide a solution because without sufficient knowledge to ask the right questions you will not get the right answers. Hard work and perseverance will often bring a result but a fundamental fault in design can be the hardest to spot as nobody wants to believe or acknowledge it exists. Finally, do not be afraid to seek the help of those around you with greater experience and expertise in a particular field, especially, if like me, you have ended up becoming a Jack of all trades and master of none.

Appendix 1
Site Work

Year	Duration	Destination	Plant Type	Purpose
1967	5 weeks	Swansea – Wales	Towns Gas	Commission iron chelate gas absorption unit
1967–68	6 months	Novopolotsk – USSR	Ethylene	Analytical equipment installation, commissioning and method training
1968	4 weeks	Vratza – Bulgaria	Ammonia	Chemical analysis of Benfield unit
1969	6 weeks	Wigan – England	Textile	Run pilot plant waste treatment unit
1970	2 weeks	Barton-on-Humber	Ammonium Nitrate	Prill additive trial
1970	4 weeks	Arklow – Eire	Ammonium Nitrate	Prill additive trial
1970	6 weeks	Shiraz – Iran	Ammonium Nitrate	Prill additive trial
1972	4 weeks	Rainham – England	Ammonium Nitrate	Prill additive trial
1973–74	13 months	Varna – Bulgaria	Ammonia/Urea/ Ammonium Sulphate	Analytical equipment installation, commissioning and method training
1975	2 weeks	Mangalore – India	Ammonia/Urea	Preparatory survey
1975	3 weeks	Porto Marghera – Italy	Ammonium Nitrate	Prill additive trial
1975	2 weeks	Maastricht – Holland	Urea	Analytical training
1975–76	5 months	Mangalore – India	Ammonia/Urea	Analytical equipment installation, commissioning and method training
1976	5 weeks	Ambergate – Derbyshire	Towns Gas Plant deconstruction	Safety officer
1977	4 weeks	Toulouse – France	Ammonium Nitrate	Prill additive trial
1977	7 weeks	Lome – Togo	Refinery	Shift chemist during guarantee runs
1978–79	8 months	Flotta – Orkneys	Liquid ethane storage facility	Commissioning supervisor
1980	5 months	Corfe – England	Gas/oil Separation	Commissioning supervisor
1981	4 weeks	Khartoum – Sudan	New power station	Nile water treatment trials (flocculation aids)
1982	7 months	Stowmarket – Suffolk	ICI Paints production plant	Commissioning manager

1982	3 weeks	Dharhan – Saudi Arabia	Aramco on & offshore GOSPS	Emergency breathing apparatus study
1982	1 month	Khartoum – Sudan	Old power station	Training & analytical requirements study for ODA funding
1983	2 weeks	The Hague-Holland & Dharhan – Saudi Arabia	Aramco on & offshore GOSPS	Present findings of emergency breathing apparatus study
1983	3 weeks	Libya	AGOCO Oil & Gas facilities	Review plants for maintenance contract
1984	6 weeks	Yanbu – Saudi Arabia	Sulphur pelleting	Construction completion
1984	2 months	Yanbu – Saudi Arabia	Sulphur pelleting	Commissioning
1986	2 months	Yanbu – Saudi Arabia	Sulphur pelleting	Commissioning completion
1988	1 week	Newcastle – England	Offshore platform	Proposal preparation
1991	6 months	Grafham Water – England	Activated Carbon Regeneration	Site commissioning manager
1993	5 weeks	Stoke Ferry – England	Potable water activated carbon treatment	Site commissioning manager
1993	7 weeks	Maidenhead – England	Potable water activated carbon treatment	Site commissioning manager
1994	3 months	Norwich – England	Potable water activated carbon treatment	Site commissioning manager
1994–95	9 months	Wing – England	Potable water activated carbon treatment	Site commissioning manager
1995	7 months	Glasgow & Irvine – Scotland	Pharmaceutical	Validation documentation (IQ & OQ) preparation and execution
1996	5 weeks	Haverhill – England	Pharmaceutical	Validation (IQ & OQ) execution
1996	4 months	Sandwich – England	Pharmaceutical	Validation (IQ & OQ) execution
1997	6 weeks	Speke – England	Pharmaceutical	Validation (IQ & OQ) execution
1997	6 months	Glasgow & Irvine – Scotland	Pharmaceutical	Validation (IQ & OQ) preparation & execution
1998–2000	2 years	Speke – England	Pharmaceutical	Validation (IQ & OQ) preparation & execution
2001–03	2 years	Porrino / Vigo – Spain	Pharmaceutical	Validation (IQ & OQ) preparation & execution
2003–4	18 months	Grange Castle / Dublin – Ireland	Pharmaceutical	Validation (IQ & OQ) preparation & execution

Appendix 2
Countries & Autonomous Islands Visited

Name	For	Name	For	Name	For
Austria	H	Iran	W	San Marino	H
Azores	H	Ireland	W & H	Saudi Arabia	W
Belarus	W	Italy	W & H	Scotland	W & H
Belgium	H	Jordan	H	Sicily	H
Bulgaria	W & H	Jersey	H	Singapore	H
Canada	H	Langkawi (Malaysia)	H	South Africa	H
China	H	Lebanon	T	Spain	W & H
Cote D'Ivoire	W & H	Libya	W	Sri Lanka	W
Croatia	H	Luxembourg	H	Sudan	W
Cuba	H	Majorca	H	Swaziland	H
Czech Republic	H	Maldives	H	Sweden	H
Dubai	T	Malta	H	Switzerland	H
Ecuador	H	Monaco	H	Tenerife	H
Estonia	H	Morocco	H	Thailand	H
Finland	H	Namibia	H	Togo	W
France	W & H	Netherlands	W & H	Tobago	H
Galapagos Islands	H	New Zealand	H	Turkey	H
Germany	H	Niger	T	USA	H
Gozo	H	Norway	H	Vatican City	H
Greece	H	Oman	H	Wales	W & H
Guernsey	H	Orkney Islands	W & H	Zimbabwe	H
Hong Kong	H	Peru	H	Yugoslavia	H
Hungary	H	Portugal	H		
Iceland	H	Russia	W & H		
Isles of Scilly	H	Sardinia	H		
India	W & H	Saint Lucia	H		

H = holiday W = work T = transit

Appendix 3
Pictorial Representation

Photograph	Description
01	My father circa 1940
01a	Author – formative years
01b	Wickford Junior School 1952
01c	Chelmsford Technical School 1958
03.2	Author circa 1968 – working in H&G Laboratory
03.2b	Author circa 1969
03.2c	H&G Laboratory party circa 1971
03.3	Author USSR 1967
03.3b	Letter home USSR 1967
03.3c	Russian stamp 1967
03.4	Iran 1970- Shiraz postcard
03.4a	Iran 1970 – Shiraz Ammonia Plant
03.5a	"My girls" Bulgaria 1974 – Ammonia Plant Laboratory
03.5b	"My girls" Bulgaria 1974 – Ammonium Sulphate Plant
03.5c	Varna Bulgaria 1973 – Apartment block
03.5d	Varna 1973 – Party time Dawn & big Eddy
03.6a	The Gates of India 1975
03.6b	Ullal India 1975 – Our bungalow
03.6c	At home Ullal India 1975
03.6d	Invitation to cocktails – Ullal India 1976
03.6e	MCF India – Ammonia and Urea Plant
03.6f	Mangalore India 1975
03.6g	Taj Mahal India
03.6j	Khajuraho temple India
03.6k	Temple carving India

03.6l	Khajuraho villager India
03.6o	Road to Amber India
03.6p	Amber palace welcome, India
03.6q	Nilgiri blue train India
03.6s	Mangalore India
03.6t	Mangalore India
03.6u	Fishing fleet India
03.6w	Mangalore ammonia-urea plant
03.8a	Snake catcher – Togo 1977
03.8b	Accommodation huts – Togo 1977
03.8c	Lome – Togo 1977
03.8d	Tannery workers – Togo 1977
03.8e	Market day – Togo 1977
03.8f	Refinery acceptance celebration – Togo 1977
03.8g	Togo Oil Refinery.- Opening day 1977
03.9	H&G Laboratory 1978 – Author drying MOPS
03.9a	H&G Laboratory 1978 – Author working
04.1a	Flotta 1978 – Liquid Ethane Storage Vessel
04.1b	Flotta 1978 – Author working
04.1c	Flotta 1979 – Ethane away
04.2a	Climatic Test Chamber at RARDE – Chertsey, Surrey
04.3a	Wytch Farm Dorset 1980
04.3b	Wytch Farm Dorset 1980
04.3c	Wytch Farm Dorset 1980
04.5	Stowmarket ICI Paints 1982
04.7a	Old Nile water intake, Sudan 1982
04.7b	New Nile water intake, Sudan 1982
04.7c	Nile water treatment – Burri Power Station, Sudan 1982
04.9a	Sulpel Plant – Yanbu Saudi Arabia 1986
04.10a	Gas Platform load-out, Lowestoft
04.10c	Gas Platform in position, North Morecombe
04.10d	Gas Platform, North Morecombe
04.10e	Leaving H&G & BP Miller project

06.2a	GAC Water Treatment, Norwich
06.2b	Author at work, Norwich
06.2c	Instrument Technicians, Norwich
07.0	Validation group lunch 1995
07.3a	Bridge evening, Vigo Spain 2002
07.3b	Pinto replica, Baiona Spain
07.3c	Sailing day, Baiona Spain
07.3e	Mussel beds, Ria de Vigo, Spain
07.3f	Sailing day lunch, Spain 2003
07.3g	Inside apartment, Baiona Spain 2002
07.3h	View from apartment balcony, Baiona Spain
07.3i	Baiona Mariner & Parador
07.3j	Hams & cheese restaurant, Baiona 2002
07.3k	Niamh centre, relieved to see us, my 60th birthday party
07.3l	Dawn & myself, 60th party, Baiona Spain 2002
07.3m	Genentech Production of Retuxan, Porrino, Spain 2003
07.4a	Dawn site seeing, Dublin 2004

About the Author

Alan Frederick Lodge was born, the youngest, by some margin, of three brothers, on the 6th September 1942, during World War Two, in the relative safety of the small (one pub and a Post Office) Essex village of South Hanningfield, where his father was the village blacksmith. In 1945 the family moved all of five miles to Wickford which, rather uniquely, has been the location of his main residence ever since. Education moved from Wickford infant and junior schools, after passing the 11 plus examination, to Chelmsford Technical High School. An enjoyable time culminating in becoming Head Boy and Captain of Sport and leaving with sufficient A level GCSE's to start a General Degree course (external London University) in Chemistry, Physics and Mathematics at South West Essex Technical College. Four years later armed with a BSc General Lower Second Class Honours Degree the search for full time employment could begin.

Work experience had been gained during both school and college years with a number of summer and Christmas holiday jobs but the prospect of foreign travel eventually led me to the then Humphreys and Glasgow Ltd. one of the world's foremost process engineering and construction organizations. Over the next 38 years that decision has resulted in work in nineteen different countries around the World as well as numerous locations in Great Britain starting in the companies analytical services and development laboratories in Billericay in Essex, before transferring to the Commissioning Group in the London Offices and finally the Validation group including a move to new offices in Croydon. None of which improved my journey time to work. The assignments varied quite considerably from commissioning equipment and training laboratory staff on an ethylene plant through a Russian winter in the communist era and in the middle of the cold war period; to ammonia and urea plants in Bulgaria and India; to an oil refinery in Togo and a sulphur pelleting plant in Saudi Arabia; to the heat and dust whilst surveying oil and gas facilities in Saudi Arabia and Libya and preparing procedures prior to commissioning oil and gas facilities in both the North and Irish seas; to developing water treatment facilities for a power station in Sudan as well as commissioning a number of potable water purification systems in the UK. Finally preparing procedures and validating pharmaceutical production facilities in England, Scotland, Spain and Ireland.

One of the joys of my working life has been to make new and lasting friendships; meet people and experience cultures and regimes that in some cases have been changed for ever and over a time line where all work procedures were initially written by hand and communication with loved ones, when away from home, was almost exclusively by letter. In addition all reference material, drawings and necessary procedures had to be taken with you or carried in your head. Hard to believe now with the rapid growth of communication devices and internet access to all almost all data providing you know the right questions to ask.

Fortunate to have grown up with a strong constitution and a fit and healthy body and mind, apart from the odd sporting injury and a possible near death experience whilst snorkelling in the Red Sea I was lucky not to have suffered from any really serious illness or injury during my working life and only found out I had Non-Hodgkins Lymphoma after retirement. Naturally a curtailment to some activities, thanks to administrations of a wonderful NHS, it is being kept in check allowing us to lead an almost normal and active retirement. Naturally sporty, fitness levels have been maintained throughout by participating in football, athletics and tennis during the early years, followed by hockey, badminton and skiing up to retirement age and now walking, maybe skiing and golf. The great thing about playing sports, particularly to a reasonable level, is that when on your own and away from home for a long period, it can be a means to participating in an activity that you enjoy whilst joining a new social circle.

Lightning Source UK Ltd.
Milton Keynes UK
UKHW020954070419
340582UK00005B/36/P